The Songs of John Lennon

atles Years

John Stevens

Edited by Susan Gedutis

Berklee Media

Associate Vice President: Dave Kusek
Director of Content: Debbie Cavalier
Marketing Manager: Jennifer Rassler
Senior Designer: David Ehlers

Berklee Press

Senior Writer/Editor: Jonathan Feist
Writer/Editor: Susan Gedutis
Production Manager: Shawn Girsberger
Production Assistant: Louis O'choa

ISBN 0-634-01795-0

1140 Boylston Street
Boston, MA 02215-3693 USA
(617) 747-2146

Visit Berklee Press Online at
www.berkleepress.com

DISTRIBUTED BY

HAL•LEONARD®
CORPORATION
7777 W. BLUEMOUND RD. P.O. BOX 13819
MILWAUKEE, WISCONSIN 53213

Visit Hal Leonard Online at
www.halleonard.com

This book is dedicated to my family,

Mum, Dad, Darryl, Jan,

without whom...

CONTENTS

PREFACE

You could say that this book started back in December 1963, when I first heard a Beatles record at the end-of-the-semester holiday party in my high school library. Susan, the first Beatles fan I ever met, brought in a brand new album. It was called *Meet the Beatles*. She placed it on a turntable, and soon the normally hushed library was transformed into a mini-Beatlefest, complete with singing, dancing, and refreshments. I thought, "These Beatles are great!"

That was my introduction, but I was really sold when I first saw the Beatles on *The Jack Paar Show* one month later in January 1964. That's right, *The Jack Paar Show*. He was actually the first person to introduce the Fab Four to the American public. It was a black-and-white film clip of one of their "live" shows from 1963. Everyone chuckled at all the media attention they seemed to be getting in England and Europe with their "Yeh Yeh" songs and their schoolboy haircuts. At that moment, neither Mr. Paar, nor his audience, nor I was aware of the history-making film that we were viewing.

When the Beatles appeared just a few weeks later—live on *The Ed Sullivan Show* on February 9, 1964—I made sure I had a ring-side seat 'round the ol' telly. Thirty-eight years later I find that, like many, I have followed the Beatles into a career in music.

I first started my "Music of John Lennon" course at Berklee College of Music back in 1981 to celebrate the music Lennon brought to the world. Now twenty years running, the class explores Lennon's Beatles period in the first half of the semester and his solo period during the second half of the semester. Over the many years of teaching this class, Lennon's songs have become like old friends to me. I thought it was finally time to share my explorations of his songs with more than just my classes. So, I have written a book that will serve as a reference tool for my classes while at the same time function as a window on the songs of John Lennon for other readers. I hope that you find this journey through his songs as wondrous and entertaining as I have.

ACKNOWLEDGMENTS

I express sincere thanks to several people who were instrumental in the realization of this book:

Jack Perricone, chairman of the songwriting department at Berklee College of Music, has been extremely supportive in my endeavor to complete this book. He was the first to suggest that I go forward with it. The unique analysis system used in this book is based upon the work of Jack, Pat Pattison, and the entire songwriting department over the last two decades.

Songwriting faculty member Jon Aldrich and Berklee alumnus and former Lennon class member Hunter Holmes get kudos for helping me nail down the incredibly creative chord progressions Lennon used in his songs.

Many thanks also to Dave Kusek, Jonathan Feist, and all those at Berklee Press for their continuous encouragement and support. A special thanks to Debbie Cavalier, who was particularly skillful at securing rights to the printed musical examples. Her thoughtful guidance was helpful throughout the final edit. I want to express a particularly hearty note of gratitude to my editor, Susan Gedutis, who untiringly gave her eyes and ears to the book as we journeyed through the kaleidoscope of Lennon's songs.

I would like to give a nod of thanks to my Beatles band, the Blue Meanies, for their inspiration in keeping Lennon's songs alive and real. Thanks, Rick, Matt, and Steve (and Jason, Ken, and Corin, too!)

Finally, I thank all the students in my John Lennon classes over the years. They have inspired me in my research of Lennon's songs. I hope that I, likewise, have inspired them as they explore the world of music.

INTRODUCTION

There is no shortage of ink devoted to the Beatles and to John Lennon, who was arguably one of the greatest singer/songwriters of the twentieth century. Most of the books have been about the Beatles' personal lives, or details of the tours and the recording sessions, but few have tackled the topic of the songs themselves. It's not surprising; the Beatles themselves admitted they had no idea what really made their songs so special. Lennon was particularly adamant about *not* needing to know all the attendant music theory behind his successful songs. Perhaps he was right. We may not *need* to know. However, twenty years of teaching students about John Lennon's songs has proven to me that there are many of us who *want* to know. This book is for those inquisitive music lovers.

The chapters to come lead you on a guided tour of Lennon's songs from his time with the Beatles, 1964–1969. I examine twenty-five of his songs through the lens of songwriting's three basic elements: melody, harmony, and lyric. I will explore how Lennon integrated each of these to fashion his music. Then, I sharpen the focus to reveal other subtle, below-the-surface song elements, such as form, phrasing, and prosody. While you don't have to be a music theory expert to enjoy this book, a basic understanding of music theory is assumed. If you need a refresher course, you'll find discussions of basic music lingo in chapter 1.

Lennon was a true explorer of song. He would constantly look for new and different ways to express himself in the songwriting idiom. He embraced the prevailing standard forms in songs like "A Hard Day's Night," but would also probe the outer reaches of song form and convention with compositions like "Revolution 9."

Much of Lennon's greatness as a songwriter was in the way he put his own stamp on what was expected or standard. His trademark was in his mastery of subtle—sometimes radical—deviations from the norm. He would delay or divert resolution of chords or melody, and break up traditionally square musical forms in unusual ways (e.g., organizing measures in a 2 + 4 + 4 + 6 pattern, instead of the standard 8 + 8). He regularly offered listeners delightful surprises by using asymmetrical and internal rhyme, and he would present compelling lyrical stories rife with commentary on many sides of complex human issues and emotions.

When it came to creating a hit, Lennon had a gift. He fashioned songs that were at once widely accessible and appealing yet uniquely his own. It is this ability to capture both the familiar and the peculiar that makes his songs timeless, while other hits that were merely conventional ended up as the discarded dregs of a flash in the pan. As we shall see, the unique "twists" are what make his songs unmistakably and eternally Lennon.

About John Lennon

John Lennon was born on October 9, 1940 in Liverpool, England to Alfred and Julia Lennon. His childhood was as delightful as it was terrifying. His father disappeared from the family when John was five years old. Before long, even his mother abandoned him to the care of her sister Mimi and her husband George.

Lennon lived with George and Mimi throughout his teens. Along the way, George taught him how the play the harmonica and how to read the newspaper, both of which would become instrumental in Lennon's music. Mimi bought him his first guitar, as John began to show great interest in the pop and folk music around him in the 1950s.

By the time Lennon reached the age of eighteen, many dramatic changes had occurred in his life. He had met Paul McCartney and George Harrison by 1957. Together, they formed his first band, the Quarrymen, named after Quarry Bank High School, which they all attended. Also, Lennon had met Cynthia, the woman who would become his first wife. And traumatically, he had lost his mother Julia—struck down by a drunk driver as she crossed the street near John's home.

By 1962, just five years later, Lennon, McCartney, and Harrison had paid their dues as a fledgling band in Hamburg, adding first Pete Best, and finally Ringo Starr, on drums. Starr completed the group that would go on to conquer the world of pop music: The Beatles.

Lennon forged a strong link with McCartney, who had also lost his mother. They became fast friends and perfect songwriting companions. Their efforts to write songs together began as early as 1958 and continued throughout their time together as the Beatles. In addition, both songwriters often composed songs on their own as they matured as writers.

Lennon's career as a songwriter can be viewed in three parts: his "early years" from 1957 to 1963, with the formation of the Quarrymen and their evolution into the Beatles; his "Beatles period" from 1964 to 1969; and finally, his "solo period" from 1970 to his death in 1980. This book focuses on the middle period.

How This Book Is Organized

Each chapter of this book discusses a selection of songs from each year of the Beatles, from 1964 to 1969. The year 1964 is actually covered in two chapters, in order to spotlight Lennon's transformation as a songwriter during that momentous year of worldwide Beatlemania. The exploration of each song is divided into four parts:

- **Background** provides a brief history of the song and setting in which it was written.
- **Structure** explains how each song is constructed, including the basic musical and lyrical form, as well as the lyric content.
- **Phrasing** describes the way the chords, the melody, and the lyrics are expressed. Each song section (verse, chorus, bridge) is discussed separately.
- **Prosody** explores the way the melody, harmony, and lyrics interact to give the song its full impact.

The structure, phrasing, and prosody sections each address issues of form, transport, melody, harmony, and lyric, utilizing analysis techniques and concepts developed by and taught in the songwriting department at Berklee College of Music.

This four-part analysis will help you understand just what it is that makes Lennon songs work so well. The musical examples are designed to be understood by musicians and nonmusicians alike, though some musical training will be helpful. Those who could use a review can

1964

February 25
You Can't Do That

February 27
If I Fell

March 1
I Call Your Name

April 16
A Hard Day's Night

August 11
Baby's in Black

August 14
I'm a Loser

September 29
I Don't Want to Spoil the Party

October 18
I Feel Fine

1965

February 15
Ticket to Ride

February 18
You've Got to Hide Your Love Away

October 12
Norwegian Wood

October 16
Day Tripper

October 18
In My Life

1966

April 6
Tomorrow Never Knows

April 14
Rain

June 21
She Said She Said

November 24
Strawberry Fields Forever

check out chapter 1, the music lingo primer, for clear explanations of the music terminology used. Readers who are experienced musicians should also read this chapter, as it will clarify what these terms mean in the context of this book.

At the beginning of each song discussion is a sheet of music, as well as a recommended recording. **Be sure to continually refer to both the written music and the recorded version as you delve into each song analysis.** The more familiar you are with the music and lyrics, the easier it will be to absorb the analysis.

Songs are presented chronologically, by date of recording. Experiencing Lennon's music from beginning to end gives a more thorough understanding of his contribution to popular music and will give you greater insight into his growth as a writer.

This book covers only twenty-five of the eighty-five songs Lennon wrote during this five-year period from 1964–1969. The selection covered here provides an excellent cross-section of Lennon's songwriting from the Beatles period. The timeline below lists the songs covered in this book.

Lennon Timeline

The timeline below shows the dates on which Lennon introduced the songs into the recording studio.

1967

January 19
A Day in the Life

March 1
Lucy in the Sky
with Diamonds

June 14
All You Need Is Love

September 5
I Am the Walrus

1968

May 30
Revolution 9

July 10
Revolution

October 13
Julia

1969

July 21
Come Together

Lennon Songs

Be sure to check out these recordings of the songs in this book.

"I Call Your Name," Lennon/McCartney
Beatles: Past Masters, Volume One
1988 EMD/CAPITOL

"All You Need Is Love," Lennon/McCartney
Yellow Submarine
1969 EMD/CAPITOL

"A Hard Day's Night," Lennon/McCartney
A Hard Day's Night
1964 EMD/CAPITOL

"If I Fell," Lennon/McCartney
A Hard Day's Night
1964 EMD/CAPITOL

"I Feel Fine," Lennon/McCartney
Beatles: Past Masters, Volume One
1988 EMD/CAPITOL

"In My Life," Lennon/McCartney
Rubber Soul
1965 EMD/CAPITOL

"Baby's in Black," Lennon/McCartney
Beatles for Sale
1964 EMD/CAPITOL

"I Don't Want to Spoil the Party,"
Lennon/McCartney
Beatles for Sale
1964 EMD/CAPITOL

"I'm a Loser," Lennon/McCartney
Beatles for Sale
1964 EMD/CAPITOL

"You've Got to Hide Your Love Away,"
Lennon/McCartney
Help!
1965 EMD/CAPITOL

"Norwegian Wood," Lennon/McCartney
Rubber Soul
1965 EMD/CAPITOL

"Julia," Lennon/McCartney
Anthology 3
1996 EMD/CAPITOL

"Rain," Lennon/McCartney
Beatles: Past Masters, Volume Two
1988 EMD/CAPITOL

"Strawberry Fields Forever,"
Lennon/McCartney
Magical Mystery Tour
1967 EMD/CAPITOL

"Lucy in the Sky with Diamonds,"
Lennon/McCartney
Sgt. Pepper's Lonely Hearts Club Band
1967 EMD/CAPITOL

"A Day in the Life," Lennon/McCartney
Sgt. Pepper's Lonely Hearts Club Band
1967 EMD/CAPITOL

"Tomorrow Never Knows,"
Lennon/McCartney
Revolver
1966 EMD/CAPITOL

"I Am the Walrus," Lennon/McCartney
Magical Mystery Tour
1967 EMD/CAPITOL

"Revolution 9," Lennon/McCartney
The Beatles (White Album)
1968 EMD/CAPITOL

"You Can't Do That," Lennon/McCartney
A Hard Day's Night
1964 EMD/CAPITOL

"Ticket to Ride," Lennon/McCartney
Help!
1965 EMD/CAPITOL

"Day Tripper," Lennon/McCartney
Beatles: Past Masters, Volume Two
1988 EMD/CAPITOL

"She Said, She Said," Lennon/McCartney
Revolver
1966 EMD/CAPITOL

"Revolution," Lennon/McCartney
Beatles: Past Masters, Volume Two
1988 EMD/CAPITOL

"Come Together," Lennon/McCartney
Abbey Road
1969 EMD/CAPITOL

CHAPTER 1 — music lingo primer

This chapter is a brief introduction to some of the musical concepts covered in the book. If you are familiar with music lingo, you may choose to skim this chapter to ensure that you understand the terms as I use them in context. If you are new to music lingo or could use a review, dive in! Be sure to check out the summary on page 13.

LEAD SHEET

Before every song in this book is a page of music called a **lead sheet**. The lead sheet emphasizes melody, harmony, and lyrics. These three elements are the nuts and bolts of the song.

- The **melody** is the tune of the song.
- The **harmony** is the chord progression or cadence that supports the melody and lyrics.
- The **lyrics** are the words to the song.
- The lead sheet also includes the **time signature**, the numerical symbol at the start of a lead sheet. Also known as the meter, the time signature indicates the rhythmic feel of the song.

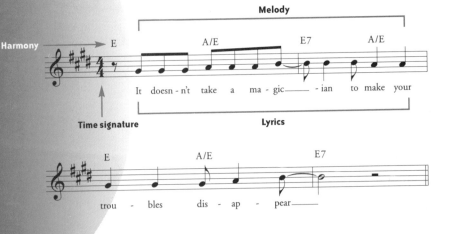

Fig. 1.1. Lead sheet excerpt

The lead sheet provides a road map for the musicians to follow. It does not describe the parts or notes performed by the guitar, piano, bass, drums, background voices, horns, strings, or other instruments. That is called the **arrangement**.

PARTS OF A SONG

Most songs are made up of several parts. The most common parts are the verse, chorus, refrain, and bridge. Songs contain some or all of these parts, in many different combinations.

Songs generally tell a story or communicate a point. Each part of the song plays a particular role in telling the story. Most songs have a beginning to set the stage, a middle, in which the story is developed further, and an end, or conclusion. Somewhere in between, the music and the lyrics build to reach a climax or high point, and that is where we discover the point, punch line, or moral to the story. In Lennon's music, the climax often involves a clever twist to pull the story together for the listener. (For more information, see *Songwriting: Essential Guide to Lyric Form and Structure*, Pat Pattison, 1991: Berklee Press.)

Verse

Lyrically, the **verses** tell the main story. Musically, they build up the melodic tension and release it like water overflowing a dam into the next section, which may be the chorus or bridge.

Refrain

The **refrain** is a part of the verse. Most of the time, the refrain is the line that includes the song title. It is usually found at the end of the verse. For example, in the Lennon song, "Please Please Me," the line "Please please me, oh yeah, like I please you" is the refrain. The refrain is usually the sing-along part of the song.

Chorus

The **chorus** is repeated several times during a song. Usually, it is comprised of a single set of lyrics and contains the song title. (Songs that have choruses usually do not have a refrain.) Often, the chorus is sung after the verse. Its usual lyrical function is to summarize the point of the story told in the verses. The chorus most often contains the high or low point of the melody and often includes the climax of the song's story.

Choruses usually end on the **tonic**, the note that represents the key of the song. The **melodic rhythm**—the speed at which the melody moves—is often slower than the rest of the song. Longer melody notes and the frequent appearance of the tonic within the harmonic progression give the chorus a more static feel.

Musically speaking, each chorus or refrain provides a mini-climax to its respective verse. These mini-climaxes often contain the highest note, the lowest note, the longest note, or an unusual chord or rhythmic pattern to **spotlight** the most important lyrics in the song.

Bridge

A **bridge** is a transitional passage that connects two other, more important song sections. Bridges tend to have a forward-moving feel. They usually end with **open harmonies**. They often do not arrive at the tonic in the melody or harmony. They feel unresolved, giving the listener the sense that something is coming. Often, the bridge does not include the tonic at all.

▶ *Primary Bridge*

The **primary bridge** serves as a sort of "release" from the verses. It most often occurs only once during the song. Like the chorus, the primary bridge has only one set of lyrics. Lyrically, the primary bridge provides a different point of view by contrasting and complementing the verse lyrics. It doesn't summarize like the chorus, but rather connects the end of one verse to the beginning of another. It may also connect the end of the chorus to the beginning of the final verse or back to a repeating chorus.

▶ *Transitional Bridge*

The **transitional bridge** (also known as the climb or the prechorus) is a specific kind of connecting section. The transitional bridge follows every verse. It builds up the energy created in the verse to such a pitch that the listener seeks resolution in a chorus or, less frequently, in a refrain. Commonly, the transitional bridge is found between the verse and the chorus or the verse and the refrain.

FORM

Form refers to the order in which song parts are played. Sometimes letters are assigned to the parts of a song and the form is analyzed in terms of A, B, and C, etc. One of the classic forms is AABA. Lennon used the AABA form often in his songwriting.

A	A	B	B
Verse/Refrain	Verse/Refrain	Primary Bridge	Verse/Refrain

Sometimes, there are more than just two parts of a song and all those letters can get confusing. In these cases, I will refer to song sections by their actual form names rather than as a series of letters.

HARMONY

When notes in a scale are sounded simultaneously, they form a **chord**. The notes below, when sounded together, form a C major chord.

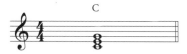

Fig. 1.2. The notes C, E, and G sounded together make up a C major chord.

The series of chords used to support the melody is referred to as the song's **harmony** or **chord progression**. Harmony and melody depend on each other. The connection is so close that many people can remember the lyrics and melody of a song just by hearing the chord progression.

The rate at which chords move is known as **harmonic rhythm**. Songs that have fast harmonic rhythm—fast-moving chords—have a great sense of motion. Songs that have slow harmonic rhythm—one or two chords per section—will have a sense of grounding. They create and build tension, even to the point of annoyance.

For practical purposes, there are three categories of chords: **tonic**, **subdominant**, and **dominant**. Tonic chords are stable, dominant chords are unstable, and subdominant chords are somewhere in between.

Chords built on scale degrees 1, 3, and 6 (symbolized as I, III, and VI in Roman numeral analysis) are tonic chords and are considered stable. Chords built on scale degrees 2 and 4 (II and IV) have a slight sense of forward motion and are called subdominant chords. Chords built on scale degrees 5 and 7 (V and VII) tend to sound unresolved. They create a strong sense of forward motion in a progression. **Chromatic chords** (which contain one or more notes that are not in the key) will be indicated like this: ♭II, V7/V, V7/II, ♭III, ♭VII, etc.

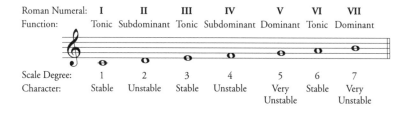

Roman Numeral:	I	II	III	IV	V	VI	VII
Function:	Tonic	Subdominant	Tonic	Subdominant	Dominant	Tonic	Dominant
Scale Degree:	1	2	3	4	5	6	7
Character:	Stable	Unstable	Stable	Unstable	Very Unstable	Stable	Very Unstable

Many musical examples in this book include Roman numeral analysis. You will notice that they often have parentheses around them.

- Parentheses placed around a Roman numeral like this (V7/V), mean that the chord in question did not resolve, or move to its expected resolution. This is referred to as a **deceptive resolution**.
- Parentheses placed around a Roman numeral that is directly above another Roman numeral indicate that the song has moved to another key, or **modulated**. In its own way, this is also a deceptive resolution:

$$(\flat II)$$
$$I$$

This illustration indicates that a chord is first heard as ♭II of the old key, but then becomes the I chord of the new key.

Except for the tonic chord, nearly all chords provide motion forward within the key. Most are in a constant search for arrival at the stable tonic. The tonic will give a stopping point, a period at the end of the sentence.

Open/Closed Structures

A line of music that ends with unstable or unresolved harmony—any chord that is not tonic—is called **open**. Open harmony will impart a sense of forward motion. The line will sound like it wants to "go" somewhere. It's like using the word "and" to end a sentence and. [!] The reader (or listener) wants to know, "And what?" Often, songwriters will combine an incomplete lyric line—such as a phrase that ends with a word like "and"—with a harmonic progression that ends with an unstable chord, so that both lyric and harmony work together to move the song forward to the next line. By contrast, a line of music that ends with the tonic will have a restful feel and will therefore produce a closed (resolved) effect.

Song sections have general harmonic tendencies. Choruses, which tend to function as complete units, usually have a closed feel. Bridges connect sections, and usually have open endings to maintain the song's momentum. Verses, which usually lead into a bridge, chorus, or another verse, have an open feel. (The exception is verses with refrains; refrains have a **closed** ending.)

LYRIC AND PHRASING

The **lyrics** are the words to a song. For a song to connect with many listeners successfully, it must present a universal theme. Whether about love or life or fantasy, the most popular songs resonate with lots of people. The larger the story and the larger the context, the more difficult this becomes. The greatest songwriters can tell big stories with just a few words.

Lyrics are delivered in **phrases**. A lyric phrase is best described as a line of a song. Just as spoken phrases make it easy to understand what a person is saying, phrases help break the music up into bite-sized pieces. The phrase "gently down the stream," from the song "Row, Row, Row Your Boat" is a lyric phrase. It is one part of a complete idea. The melody that goes along with it is called a **melodic phrase**. The harmony that underlies the lyric and melody is called a **harmonic phrase**.

The determining factor in phrase analysis is the lyric. For instance a very long lyric line might be set with a series of short melodic phrases. The ear, however, will tend to hear one long phrase rather than several short phrases:

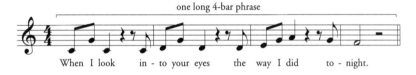

Fig. 1.3. One long melodic phrase

Conversely, several short bursts of lyric set to a long musical line will tend to break the long melodic line into shorter phrases:

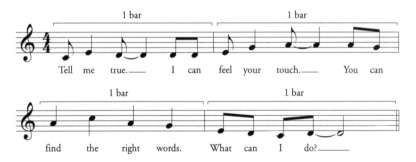

Fig. 1.4. Several short melodic phrases

We will consider two factors in analyzing musical phrases—the length of each phrase (in bars) and the beat that the phrase ends on. Phrases are indicated with lower-case letters such as ⓐ and ⓑ. Phrases end at the last syllable, *not* the last note of the last word, sung. If a syllable starts on the **upbeat**, also referred to as the "and" or "+" of the beat, we consider this an anticipation of the next beat, and so the phrase is analyzed as ending on the next beat. (Sometimes there is more than one rhyme in a line; lyrics of secondary importance will sometimes be in parentheses.) Phrase endings are illustrated in this manner:

Fig. 1.5. Melodic phrases end at the first syllable of the last word sung.

Fig. 1.5 is a condensed and simplified version of fig. 1.3. In this example, the first 4-bar phrase is analyzed as ⓐ, and ends on beat 1 of the fourth bar, with the syllable "night" from the word "tonight." In this particular song section, an ⓐ phrase would be any phrase that is four bars long and that ends on the first beat of its fourth bar.

Within every measure of music, some beats are considered strong, and some are considered weak. In 4/4 time, beats 1 and 3 are considered strong, while beats 2 and 4 are considered weak. When a melody ends on a strong beat, it has a sense of finality. When it ends on a weak beat, it has a sense of forward motion and anticipation. Here's a quick breakdown, utilizing 4/4 meter:

- A melody that ends on beat 1 creates the strongest sense of conclusion.
- A melody that ends on beat 4 creates the greatest sense of forward motion. The effect can be so great that the phrase ending often feels more like an anticipation of the next phrase than a conclusion.
- A melody that ends on beat 3 has some sense of stopping, but not as great as beat 1.
- A melody that ends on beat 2 has some sense of moving forward, but not as great as beat 4.

Taking that discussion one step further, let's look at strong and weak bars. Normally, in standard 8- and 16-bar sections, the odd bars are strong and the even bars are weak. Because the first bar begins the section, it automatically comes with great weight. The emphasis shifts from bar to bar throughout the section. If a song section contains an odd number of bars—seven or nine bars, for instance—then the section will end with a strong bar. This gives the section a bit of forward momentum into the next part of the song. We will explore this more as we progress through Lennon's songs.

MELODIC PHRASING NOTATION

In many of the musical illustrations in this book, melody is stripped out of the phrase to focus attention on the phrase length and ending, where rhyme most often comes into play. Phrases end at the last *syllable* sung, not the last *note* sung. Spotlighting the length and ending helps you recognize the important points at which the song starts, stops, and/or pauses along its journey.

The lyric in this next example creates four 1-bar phrases out of the long melodic line illustrated in fig. 1.4:

Fig. 1.6. Melodic phrasing notation

The three 1-bar phrases that end on beat 3 are analyzed as (a), while the 1-bar phrase that ends on beat 4 is analyzed as (b). The resulting phrases create an *"aaba"* inner phrasing pattern. (Remember, the lower-case *"aaba"* represents inner phrase analysis, while the upper case AABA is used to illustrate song form analysis.)

Phrasing helps to achieve a sense of unity and motion in a song. I will discuss phrasing in terms of **balance**, **imbalance**, **acceleration**, and **deceleration**.

Song sections in the classic 8-bar format are often presented to the listener in balanced units of two or four bars (2 + 2 + 2 + 2 or 4 + 4). Dividing the same 8-bar section into units of three and two (3 + 2 + 3) creates imbalance. Uneven phrase lengths do not endow the song with a strong sense of stability.

Sections of unusual length may also sound balanced. For instance, a 20-bar verse may be divided into four 5-bar phrases. Even though the 5-bar phrase itself is an odd length, its repetition helps to impart a sense of overall balance.

Phrases that have the same length and the same ending will create two effects: static motion in that section, and a good setup for lyric rhymes. Rhymes placed at the end of lyric lines contribute toward creating a sense of stability within a song section. Rhymes within a lyric line, referred to as **internal rhymes**, create momentum and forward motion. For example, listen to the way internal rhyme creates momentum in this lyric line from "A Hard Day's Night": "But when I get home to you, I find the things that you do...."

Phrase length also affects the overall sense of pacing in a song. Moving from long phrases to short phrases creates acceleration, while doing the opposite creates deceleration. Songwriters often use acceleration or deceleration as a tool to emphasize lyric content. As we will see, Lennon used it often to emphasize differences between song sections and to spotlight particular lyric content.

MELODY AND PROSODY

The notes of the melody have an important effect on the feel of the song. They may create many effects—dramatic or comic, static or expansive, swampy and smoky, or bright and uplifting. Great songwriters like Lennon carefully select their notes, whether consciously or subconsciously, to create their desired effect.

The way the music and lyrics support each other to create any given effect is referred to as **prosody**. Prosody includes: how the music fits with the tone of the story; how the rhythmic setting of the lyric fits with the flow of the words themselves; or, how a certain peak or dip in the melody supports a particular word or phrase.

In a major key, there are seven basic notes or scale degrees. C major is illustrated here:

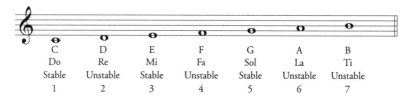

C	D	E	F	G	A	B
Do	Re	Mi	Fa	Sol	La	Ti
Stable	Unstable	Stable	Unstable	Stable	Unstable	Unstable
1	2	3	4	5	6	7

Fig. 1.7. The notes of the major scale and their function

Each tone of a scale, or scale degree, has a function as either **stable** or **unstable**. The three most stable notes in the scale are Do, Mi, and Sol. The tonic Do is considered headquarters or home base. All melody notes except for the tonic note tend to move toward tonic. Mi and Sol also provide some stability, but this stability is temporary—more like a comfort station on the highway than like home. All of the other notes—Re, Fa, La, and Ti—are marked unstable. These notes are very forward moving.

Here are the resolution tendencies of each note in the scale:

> **Do** is the most stable; it is home base.
> **Re** moves to Do.
> **Mi** is stable.

Fa moves to Mi.

Sol is stable.

La moves to Sol.

Ti moves up to Do.

The combination of melody and harmony can create many different effects. For instance, ending a section on Do, over an unstable chord, creates forward motion. This may be described as an open ending.

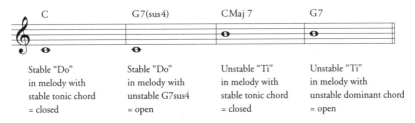

Fig. 1.8. Open and closed melody/harmony configurations

Conversely, if a section ends on the most unstable note of all (the 7th degree, Ti), but then uses the tonic chord as the setting, the motion is stopped by the harmony, or **closed**.

A melody note that is not present in the chord that supports it is called a **nonchord tone**, as in bars 2 and 3 of fig. 1.8. Nonchord tones are very prominent melody notes and are often used to **spotlight** a certain lyric. Whether or not the nonchord tone has a stable or unstable character in the key, it will create great interest for the listener when positioned over a chord that does not contain it.

Songwriters may also use **chromatic** notes—notes that are not in the key of the song. All chromatic notes are considered unstable, no matter what chord supports them. Very often these chromatic notes are indeed present in the chord of the moment, but they stand out because they are not diatonic to the key.

Song sections or phrases that end on stable notes tend to be at rest, or **closed**. Sections or phrases that end on unstable notes tend to be searching for home, or **open**.

Structural Tones

In analyzing melody and harmony relationships, I often will just illustrate the most important melody notes. These are called **structural tones**. The musical examples work like an outline, leaving out the details of the rhythm and lyric, and highlighting just the most important notes using **whole notes**, or open circles, on the musical staff.

Substructural tones, notes of secondary importance, appear as smaller diamond-shaped whole notes. Structural and substructural tones are illustrated like this:

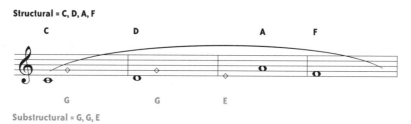

Fig. 1.9. Structural and substructural tones

CONCLUSION

Phew. This is a lot to learn, but don't be overwhelmed. You can still find meaning in the song discussions without being a music theory expert! As we continue now into Lennon's songs, keep in mind that music is a system and follows many "rules." Of course, rules are made to be broken, and Lennon broke them frequently—but in just the right ways. That may be the very reason that his music has been so enduring! Now that we've got our lingo in order, let's go back to 1964 for a closer look.

SUMMARY: PARTS OF A SONG AND THEIR FUNCTION

The chart on the following page provides a very general overview of the parts of a song, with their harmonic, melodic, and lyric tendencies.

	Melody		Harmony		Lyric
	Melodic Rhythm	Melodic Contour	Harmonic Rhythm	Harmonic Ending	Content
Verse	Often faster than rest of song	Builds up, range-wise, to the chorus or refrain	Movement towards tonic, but not usually the tonic itself	• Open (unresolved) • Moves forward to chorus or bridge	• Contains the main story
Chorus	Often slower than rest of song	Contains high or low point of song	Movement towards tonic and includes the tonic itself	• Often closed (resolved) • Ends on tonic • More static feel than rest of song	• Summarizes the point of the story • Clarifies content of verses • Provides an arrival point for verses • May include climax of story
Transitional Bridge	Often faster than the verses	Builds up energy	Contrasting harmony to the verse and chorus	• Open, most forward moving • No tonic arrival	• Continues story of verse, leading to chorus or refrain
Refrain	Often slower than the verses	Often has a sing-along nature	Movement towards tonic and includes the tonic itself	• Often closed • Harmonic arrival point; usually ends on tonic	• Summarizes the point of the story • Clarifies content of verses • Provides an arrival point for verses
Primary Bridge	Provides contrast to other sections: may be slower or faster than other sections	Usually contains a high point of song	Contains unstable harmonies that lead to tonic	• Open • Forward moving	• Provides unique viewpoint, different from verse • May explore deeper than rest of story

CHAPTER 2   1964, part I

The year 1964 was momentous for the Beatles. It was the year of Beatlemania. The band burst onto the American scene with live appearances on *The Ed Sullivan Show* in February 1964, and released two hit albums, *A Hard Day's Night* and *Beatles for Sale*.

Immediately upon returning to England after the Ed Sullivan shows, the Beatles entered the recording studio to reckon Lennon's newly written songs onto tape. Most of the songs recorded at sessions from late February through mid-April wound up on the album *A Hard Day's Night*. Lennon did not return to the studio until the end of the summer, save for a brief two-day session in June. The second major session, from mid-August to late October 1964, resulted in *Beatles for Sale*. Four songs from each of these historic sessions are covered in chapters 2 and 3. The four songs covered in this chapter are:

"You Can't Do That"
"If I Fell"
"I Call Your Name"
"A Hard Day's Night"

The songs from the February/April 1964 sessions reveal a still-budding songwriter working with one song form: AABA. AABA is one of the classic song forms of the twentieth century. It was popularized in the 1920s and 1930s, the heyday of Irving Berlin and Cole Porter. This was the music John's parents listened to, and it is clear from his early songwriting ventures that he was influenced by it. While his songs sound like neither Cole Porter nor Irving Berlin, Lennon chose to work with the AABA form that these composers brought to billions of listeners worldwide.

By the 1950s and 1960s, however, the AABA form had given way to the verse/chorus format in popular music. With the Quarrymen, Lennon performed such verse/chorus songs as Larry Williams' 1958 r&b hit, "Dizzy Miss Lizzie," and the Isley Brothers' 1962 smash, "Twist and Shout." While Lennon the performer was singing verse/chorus songs such as these, Lennon the composer clung to the tried-and-true song forms of a much earlier period. As Lennon grew as a composer, he began to embrace the verse/chorus form in his own writing. (See chapter 3.)

You Can't Do That

Words and Music by John Lennon and Paul McCartney

I got some-thing to say that might cause you pain,— if I catch you talk-ing to that boy a-gain— I'm gon-na let you down— and leave you flat.— Be-cause I've told you be-fore: Oh!— You can't do that.— Well, it's the Ev-'ry-bo-dy's green— 'cause I'm the one who won your love.— But if it's seen— you talk-in' that way, they'd laugh in my face— So

(Refer to following page for verses 2 and 3)

Verse 2

Well, it's the second time I caught you talkin' to him,

Do I have to tell you one more time I think it's a sin.

I think I'll let you down and leave you flat,

Because I've told you before: Oh, you can't do that.

Verse 3

So please listen to me if you wanna stay mine,

I can't help my feelings, I'll go out of my mind.

I'm gonna let you down and leave you flat,

Because I've told you before: Oh, you can't do that.

BACKGROUND

Title	You Can't Do That
Recording Date	February 25, 1964
Meter	4/4
Key	G blues and G major
Song Form	AABA
Phrasing	A = *aabb*
	B = *abacc*
Recording	*A Hard Day's Night*
	1964 EMD/CAPITOL

The Beatles had only been back in England for one day after completing their trio of February *Ed Sullivan Show* appearances when they returned to the studio. The day was February 25, 1964, and it was George Harrison's twenty-first birthday. The group convened at Abbey Road studios to record "You Can't Do That" and two other songs. The song was wrapped up in only nine takes.

John said that he was trying to capture the Wilson Pickett sound in "You Can't Do That." His beautifully coarse vocal, along with Paul's classic Wilson Pickett four-to-the-bar cowbell, capture the smoky, grit-and-grind sound for which Wilson Pickett was so famous. To add to the effect, George Harrison opens the song with a 12-string guitar lick that is a bluesy duel between the 3rd and lowered 3rd of the key (B♮ and B♭). The guitar lick comes off more like a bluesy honky-tonk piano than like the usual 12-string folk sound associated with the period. It sets the gritty tone of this passionate rocker.

"You Can't Do That" was released as the B-side of the "Can't Buy Me Love" single in America on March 16, 1964, and four days later in England. In America, it appeared on *The Beatles' Second Album* released on April 10, 1964. Those in England had to wait for the release of *A Hard Day's Night* album on July 10.

STRUCTURE

Song Form

Lennon used the classic AABA form for the song, or **Verse/Refrain with Primary Bridge**:

A	A	B	A
Verse/Refrain	Verse/Refrain	Primary Bridge	Verse/Refrain
12 bars	12 bars	8 bars	12 bars

Each of the verse/refrain sections is twelve bars long, in the classic 12-bar blues style that had such a big influence on Lennon. But the addition of an 8-bar primary bridge pushes the song into the pop realm and leaves the blues form behind. The result is not a blues song, but a blues-*based* pop song.

Lyric Content

The story conveyed by the lyric is not an unusual one for a fiery blues song: a boy is telling a girl to be true. Ah, jealousy. It makes a good story. The singer spends the verse sections pleading for faithfulness, but the bridge lyric brings the story into a deeper psychological realm. In the bridge, we learn that he fears he will lose face with his friends if she continues to fool around on him.

PHRASING

Verse

▶ *Harmonic Phrasing*

Harmonically, the verses follow the standard 12-bar blues progression, as shown in Fig. 2.1 on the following page.

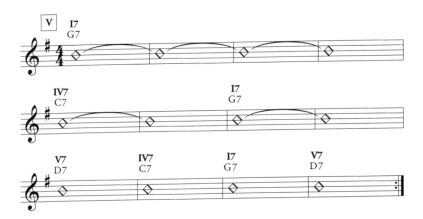

Fig. 2.1. Verse harmonic phrasing

❯ Melodic Phrasing

The melodic phrasing that Lennon chose for the verse is derived from the melodic rhythm and the lyric. The section starts off with a burst of 2-bar phrases, followed by two complementary 4-bar phrases:

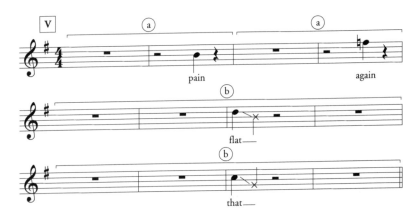

Fig. 2.2. Verse melodic phrasing

    The first two phrases end on the strong third beat of bar 2. This is followed by two 4-bar phrases, which emphasize the lyrics by ending each phrase on beat 1, the strongest beat of the measure. This accentuates the power of the protagonist's message: "flat" is how the singer is going to leave his flirty girlfriend if she does not toe his line. Rhyming it with the lyric "that" is a perfect way to spotlight the commanding title, "You Can't Do *That*."

In the verse, Lennon delivers up a classic inner phrasing form of *aabb*:

First, the listener hears a musical gesture (a)

followed by its repetition and rhyme (a)

followed by a new musical gesture (b)

followed by its repetition and rhyme (b).

The *aabb* verse phrasing form is symmetrical and familiar. The repetitive rhythmic structure makes it very easy for the listener to grasp the ideas, both lyrically and rhythmically.

Primary Bridge

▶ *Harmonic Phrasing*

At the onset of the primary bridge, the harmony changes, bringing the listener into a totally new sonic world. We move from G blues to G major.

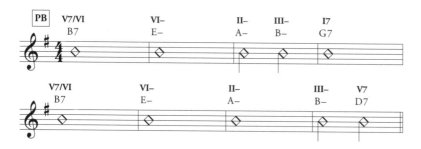

Fig. 2.3. Primary bridge harmonic phrasing

Throughout the entire verse, which is in G blues, we are inundated with F♮s in both the melody and the harmony. The F♮, which is the lowered 7th in G blues, plays a key role in establishing the bluesy sound. (Along with the 3rd, the 7th is considered a distinguishing tone in any chord. In blues mode, the 3rd and the 7ths are lowered.) The change to the F♯ in the primary bridge—and a very prominent F♯ at that—emphasizes that the key is no longer G blues. In combination with the major 3rd, B, the F♯ establishes the bridge's G major sound. Lennon does briefly retain the bluesy F♮ in the G7 in bar 4, but other than that, the entire bridge is truly major.

The primary bridge, in contrast to the bluesy 12-bar verses, is only eight bars long. The inclusion of an 8-bar bridge pushes the song more into the pop song category, as in Fig. 2.4:

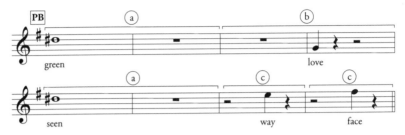

Fig. 2.4. Primary bridge melodic phrasing

Based on the form of the verse/refrain sections so far, one would expect that Lennon would deliver up the more standard and *abab* format in the melodic phrasing:

- theme 1 ⓐ
- theme 2 ⓑ
- repeat theme 1 ⓐ
- conclude by repeating theme 2 again ⓑ

But Lennon has something more creative planned. With the rhymes "green" and "seen" linking up the ⓐ sections, the listener tends to expect a rhyming 2-bar ⓑ phrase with the word "love." Instead, the lyric splits in half, forming two 1-bar phrases.

The accelerated harmonic and melodic rhythm created by the use of these 1-bar phrases helps propel the bridge forward to the next repetition of the verse/refrain. The short phrases make the section seem to move faster, even though the underlying rhythm and tempo remain steady. As an added mark of genius, Lennon included rhyme ("way" and "face") on those ⓒ phrases to make them even more powerful as they jet away back to the verse.

PROSODY

Melody: Verse

The structural tones in the verse melody support the demanding title, "You Can't Do That." The melody features the 4th and lowered 7th scale degrees (C and F♮) throughout, among prominent appearances of the 3rd and lowered 3rd degrees (B♮ and B♭):

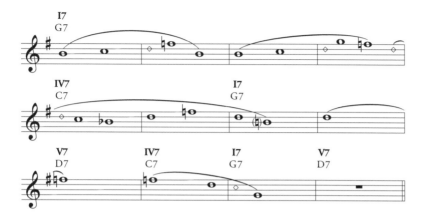

Fig. 2.5. Verse melody structural tones

The two opening phrases are somewhat similar. They both begin on B and move up by just a half step to C. The C gives a gritty, dissonant sound against the B, which is the 3rd of the G7 chord.

At the top of that first phrase, the bluesy F♮ overrides the F♯ in the key signature. The answering second phrase tops out a step higher at the tonic G before settling on the same bluesy F♮ for the phrase ending. At bar 5, B♭ makes its first appearance as a contrast to the now-familiar B♮ and gives a bluesy flavor in combination with the C7 chord. Both the F♮ and B♮ reappear before the end of that long phrase.

The most exciting melodic aspect in the song is now about to happen. Upon reaching the D7 chord in bar 9, Lennon's blistering lyric "because I told you before" is set on the F♮, once again conflicting bluesily and wonderfully with the F♯, which is the 3rd of the D7 chord. The high point of the melody occurs when Lennon shouts the lyric "Ohh," again on the same F♮ at bar 10. This time, it is over a C7 chord, which produces a dissonance—a tension—that is even more strident and exciting than the preceding D7 bar.

This part of the melody is a rock singer's paradise. Lyric, harmony, and melody all come together in a superb blend of 1950s r&b and 1960s rock 'n' roll. Lennon's mastery of musical climax and resolution makes it a killer song to perform and to listen to, because it arouses such emotion and excitement.

Melody: Primary Bridge

After all those F♮s, it's about time we heard an F♯ or two. And boy, do we get it in the bridge! The oft-repeated F♮ heard throughout the verse is the 7th of the G blues mode. Here, McCartney sings high harmony vocals on the F♯ while Lennon sings a third below on the chromatic melody note D♯. The addition of vocal harmony at this point adds a level of depth to the melody that supports the deeper message of primary bridge lyric. With the change to major, the F♯ drives the urgency of the song; it begs for resolution to the tonic note G. Lennon brilliantly wields its unstable and forward-moving nature to support the deepening lyric content at that point. Let's look at the structural tones in the primary bridge:

Fig. 2.6. Primary bridge structural tones

After Lennon's D♯ in the melody pushes upwards a half step to the unstable E (scale degree 6 in the key of G), the song moves to the E minor triad. As a tonic substitution (VI minor in the key of G), the E minor provides a temporary sense of rest but not a true tonic resolution. As the song progresses to the fourth bar of the bridge, the melody finds its way to tonic note G. Lennon reintroduces the bluesy G7 here, and the harmonic progression continues to avoid real resolution. The introduction of the note F♯ in the B7 and B minor chords in bars 1–3 would seem to promise that the chords would move to G major, but the progression doesn't completely deliver. The progression resolves to G7 instead, which contains an F♮.

The same melody begins the second line of the bridge, but this time it moves to a final bar, in which Lennon literally screams the unstable F♯ with the lyric, "They'd laugh in my face!" With the unstable, forward-moving F♯s, the angry passionate lyric, and the increased momentum of 1-bar phrases, the bridge successfully fulfills its role: It goes crashing back into the third and final verse for the last word of hopeful resolution.

SUMMARY

Typical teenage angst and jealousy. "Stop talking to that guy! Was he flirting with you?" It's a timeless topic for pop songwriting. Lennon's use of it shows that he understands the emotions we all share. Lennon took up the mantle of the angry young rocker in those days. With "You Can't Do That," he distilled those jealous, confused teenaged feelings into a sizzling bluesy rocker.

The lyrical refrain is simply the title of the song, "You Can't Do That," with Lennon's insertion of the "Oh." The refrain's grinding F♮ against that bluesy C7 chord burns the title into our hearts as a serious warning. Lennon's use of the tried-and-true AABA form, so universally familiar, provides the perfect backdrop as he spells out his feelings and demands—1, 2, 3—in the three A sections.

But my favorite part, other than the gritty refrain, is the opening of the B section with the famous lyric "Everybody's green." Green? Of course: with envy. Delightfully indirect. It makes a superb contrast to the extremely direct and forceful import of the verse lyrics. This brand of contrast was to become a classic Lennon device.

If I Fell

Words and Music by John Lennon and Paul McCartney

If I fell in love with you, would you
pro- mise to be true, and help me un - der - stand.___ 'Cause I've
been in love be - fore and I found that love was more than
just hold - ing hands.___ If I give my heart to
you, I must be sure from the ve - ry start that
you would love me more than her. If I
two, 'Cause I could - n't stand the pain.___ And I___

would be sad if our new love was in vain. So I two. If I fell in love with you.

Verse 2

If I trust in you, oh please,
Don't run and hide.
If I love you too, oh please,
Don't hurt my pride like her.

Verse 3

So I hope you see that I,
Would love to love you.
And that she will cry,

Coda

When she learns we are two.
If I fell in love with you.

BACKGROUND

Title	If I Fell
Recording Date	February 27, 1964
Meter	4/4
Key	D major
Song Form	AABA
Phrasing	Intro verse: *aab/aac*
	Verse 1: *ab*
	Verse 2: *abac*
	Verse 3: *ab*
	Primary Bridge: *ab*
Recording	*A Hard Day's Night*
	1964 EMD/CAPITOL

"If I Fell" is a curious song indeed. A throwback to the song forms of the 1920s and 1930s, it includes an introductory verse that sets the stage for the song proper. However, this intro verse is not in the same key as the rest of the song. Because of the unusual key relationship, this song stands in a category by itself among Lennon's Beatles ballads. Written for the movie *A Hard Day's Night*, it was one of his earliest ballads. He said it was a precursor to "In My Life." (See chapter 4.)

The song was recorded on February 27, 1964 with the same instrumentation seen in the movie: John on acoustic guitar and lead vocal, Paul on bass guitar and harmony vocal, George on electric 12-string guitar, and Ringo on drums.

The song was first heard in America on the album *A Hard Day's Night* on June 26, 1964. The album was not released in England until July 10, 1964. Though it was never released as a single in England, it *was* released as a single in America on July 20, 1964, cut with Paul's "And I Love Her" on the flipside.

STRUCTURE

Song Form

"If I Fell" follows classic AABA form, and in that way, is much more reminiscent of Lennon's "This Boy" (1963) than "In My Life," which uses the traditional verse/refrain format. However, it includes an introductory verse that is unlike anything else in the song—and unlike anything else Lennon had ever written. Because the intro is so very different, the best way to study this song is to look at the introductory verse separately, then consider the rest of the song.

▶ Introductory Verse

The short introductory verse actually sets up or leads into the song itself. While Lennon and the other Beatles often used instrumental introductions, it was rare for them to use introductions with distinct harmony, melody, *and* lyrics.

In that first eight bars, Lennon strings a sequential melody over a descending chromatic chord progression. (By sequential, I mean that the melody repeats the same rhythms, only with different notes.) He shifts the melodic pattern by half steps, rather than according to a particular scale, making it difficult to discern what key the tune is in until the fourth bar.

The descent from the starting E♭ minor chord down to D major, and further down to D♭ major, gives the listener the impression that something is amiss. The melody is as ambiguous as the protagonist is confused. In the lyrics, the singer faces a complex but common challenge in love affairs—remaining true to the one you love. The simultaneous descent of both the chord progression and the melody throughout this section emphasizes the song's feeling of depression and confusion.

▶ Song Form

After the introductory verse, Lennon adheres to the standard AABA song form:

A	A	B	A
Verse/Refrain	Verse/Refrain	Primary Bridge	Verse/Refrain
10 bars	10 bars	5 bars	10 bars

Lyric Content

Lennon's ballad "If I Fell" is a story of love and dilemma. It is sung by a male to a female. He declares his love, but indicates that he *already has* a girlfriend! In its three verses and bridge, the song outlines a common dilemma:

- Confession of feelings
- Fear of rejection
- Evaluation of the consequences
- Plea bargaining

In the first verse, the singer says he will give her his heart, but he wants to be sure that she will give him more love than he gets in his current relationship. It is the classic "having-your-cake-and-eating-it-too" scenario. Don't we all want such security in life and love?

The singer continues in verse 2, fearing rejection. He pleads with the girl not to "run and hide"—not an uncommon response, I would think—and then further begs her not to damage his pride.

He amplifies his concerns in the B section, or primary bridge. He begins to acknowledge the consequences by indicating that uprooting himself from his present relationship could become extremely complicated. He speaks of the pain that he would experience if—that key word from the title—their efforts were to be in vain.

The concluding third verse wraps up his message: he is serious about going forward. He would "love to love her." However, the concluding lyric line of the song expresses the "all's fair in love and war" sentiment. He notes that his present girlfriend will not look upon this new union favorably. For her, tears will be the inevitable conclusion.

The song's lyric delivers up admissions that, at best, are difficult and uncomfortable to make. The song expresses something many would be afraid to express themselves. It strikes a chord. Such honesty bears the mark of a classic: great songs utter the inutterable.

PHRASING

Introductory Verse and Verses

> #### Introductory Verse: Harmonic Phrasing

Now we investigate the question: what is the key of this introduction? As shown in the example below, the chords start on the II minor (Eb minor) chord, then descend to bII (D major), and finally arrive at I (Db major) at the third bar. It isn't until the arrival of VI minor (Bb minor) in bar 4 that we get a sense that the key is actually Db major.

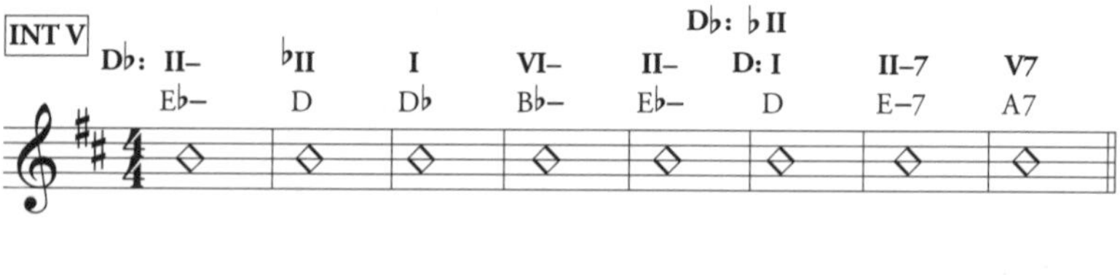

Fig. 2.7. Intro verse harmonic phrasing

The return to Eb minor at bar 5 further confirms the key. Here, both the chords and melody from the beginning are repeated. However, this time, Lennon introduces E–7 and A7. These chords are the II–7 and V7 of the new key, D major, which is the actual key of the song proper.

This modulation from the key of Db major up to D major creates an uplifting effect as the song begins, foreshadowing hope for the resolution of the confused feelings expressed so far in the lyric. As is typical in songs of the early twentieth century, this brief 8-bar introduction never returns again.

⬧ Verse: Harmonic Phrasing

The first four bars of the verse outline a stepwise chord movement up and down the D major scale, moving through I, II minor, III minor, and II minor, until the song arrives at the dominant V chord, A7:

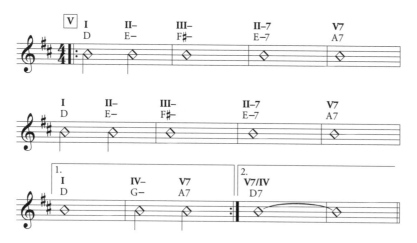

Fig. 2.8. Verse harmonic phrasing

Lennon repeats these four bars in the second line, creating an 8-bar section by the end of line 2. Then there are two endings—two bars that each create the 10-bar verse section.

The first ending closes off the verse with the tonic D major chord, followed by a turnaround. The second ending, by contrast, is open. It utilizes the chromatic secondary dominant D7, which propels the verse into the primary bridge.

⬧ Introductory Verse: Melodic Phrasing

The melodic phrasing for the introductory verse is very dramatic, in support of the emotionally charged lyric. The 8-bar section consists of no less that six separate phrases that give the sense of accelerated motion, as if the singer is short of breath or anxious.

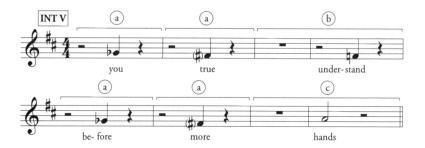

Fig. 2.9. Intro verse melodic phrasing

The resulting analysis is *aab*/*aac*. The repeating Ⓐ phrases are balanced with Lennon's move to a slower-feeling 2-bar phrase at the end of line 1. The frantic pace picks up again with a move back to the original 1-bar phrases, but slows again with the new Ⓒ phrase. The uneven phrase lengths help give a sense of the singer's emotional instability.

▶ *Verses: Melodic Phrasing*

Each of the three verses is set to melody differently, which produces three completely different effects and wonderfully emphasizes the differences in the lyric content. In the first verse, the character confesses his feelings to his beloved. In the second, he fears that she will reject him. Finally, in the third verse, he pleads with her. Through phrasing and rhyme, Lennon creates a different musical environment for each verse, and underscores the message conveyed in each. Lennon uses the same number of bars in each verse but breaks up the phrasing differently.

Verse 1

Verse 1 is really a vehicle for the singer to "spill his guts" in a careening 3-bar + 7-bar phrase pattern. This phrasing pattern is not repeated for the other two verses.

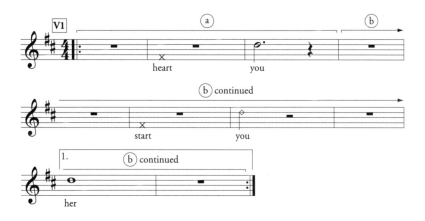

Fig. 2.10. Verse 1 melodic phrasing

Note the use of internal rhyme with the words "heart" and "start." This would be a classic internal rhyme setup if Lennon had composed the verse in a typical 8-bar layout. However, there are two extra bars at the end, producing an atypical 10-bar verse. The result is that "heart" and "start" perform a musical sleight of hand, outlining an asymmetrical rhyme scheme but giving the impression of symmetry:

- The unusual phrase lengths produce an *asymmetrical* rhyme pattern. The lyric "heart" winds up in the second bar of the 3-bar phrase, while "start" is placed in the third bar of the 7-bar phrase.
- The placement of both words at bars 2 and 6 give the *illusion of symmetry*, because the listener expects another 8-bar phrase just like the intro verse.

Lennon places the word "you" in classic rhyme position: the third bar of each 4-bar segment. Of course, the problem is that "you" and "you" are not rhymes, technically. Lennon's solution is to extend the verse past the expected 8-bar form and deliver up "her" as the concluding lyric.

While this verse is particularly complex in analysis, it sounds smooth when performed. Verses 2 and 3 are much less complex, both in analysis and sound than verse 1. With an artful balance of symmetrical and asymmetrical rhyming, Lennon manages to mask the differences between the verses and resolves each in a completely unique fashion.

Verse 2

The pattern for verse 2 (2 + 2 + 2 + 4) produces the effect of lurching forwards and pulling backwards in uncertainty as the singer considers his alternatives. Verse 2 is made of up four separate lyric phrases with a rhyme pattern that emphasizes the short phrases. Asymmetrical rhyme at "you" and "two" is continued with the lyrics "hide" and "pride" at bars 4 and 9. All of this internal rhyme further emphasizes the differences between each of the verses.

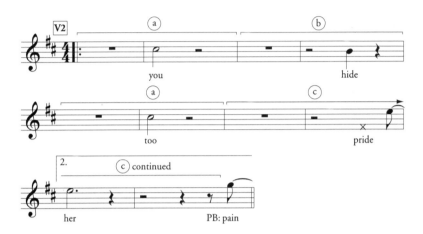

Fig. 2.11. Verse 2 melodic phrasing

After rhyming "pride" with "hide," Lennon continues with two words, ending the line with "like her." This illusion reveals that the singer is nearing resolution, but is not quite there yet. The resulting phrase analysis is abac. The ⓐ phrases end on beat 1, while the ⓑ phrase ends on beat 3. Using phrases of increasing length can give a sense of deceleration, and in this case, prepare our ears for the bridge, which moves much more slowly. In fact, as we will see, the entire bridge is just one long phrase.

Verse 3

Verse 3 gives the illusion of two standard 4-bar phrases, though in reality it is actually a 4-bar + 6-bar setting. That is because Lennon actually extends the lyric, and therefore the phrase, into the bridge.

In the final verse, Lennon uses both internal and external rhyme over long phrases. Internal rhyme again accentuates uneven phrasing and underscores the emotional content of the lyric. This became one of the Beatles' signature lyric-setting devices:

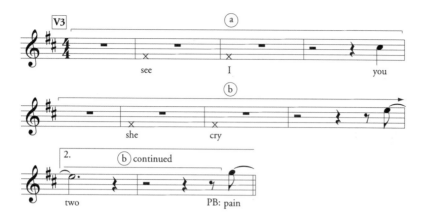

Fig. 2.12. Verse 3 melodic phrasing

Primary Bridge

▶ *Harmonic Phrasing*

Lennon keeps the primary bridge short. The bridge outlines a I–IV cadence:

Fig. 2.13. Primary bridge harmonic phrasing

This I–IV cadence is called a plagal cadence. The sound of the plagal cadence is commonly heard in the old "Amen" chords in traditional hymns and gospel music. In this key, the plagal cadence occurs in the move from the G major to D major chord. However, the G minor chord reappears, creating a slightly darker version of this well-known cadence to support the bittersweet tone of the lyric.

The A7 creates an open ending to the bridge, propelling it back to the beginning of the verse section. The lyric and melody remain active, however, increasing the momentum right to the end of the fifth bar. The sense of motion that results connects the bridge strongly to the start of the verse, as we will see in the next seciton.

▶ *Melodic Phrasing*

The primary bridge is a study on how to make a 5-bar bridge sound like a 4-bar bridge. Five is an unusual number in the world of popular music. Thousands upon thousands of songs are fashioned from phrases that are divisible by the number 2: 4-bar, 8-bar, 12-bar, and 16-bar phrases. In the Western world, our ears are trained to this sort of symmetry. When a writer utilizes an odd number of phrases or lines in a song section, it really changes the whole flow of the song.

Fig. 2.14. Primary bridge melodic phrasing

Because the first bar of the bridge is actually the last bar of the verse, Lennon simply applies a standard 4-bar phrase to the existing single bar at the end of the verse. The bar has a dual function, serving as the end of the verse and the beginning of the bridge at the same time. This forms a musical "dovetail joint" between the verse and the bridge. The resulting phrase analysis is a simple *ab*—a 1-bar phrase followed by a 4-bar phrase—creating the 5-bar bridge.

PROSODY

Melody: Intro Verse
The overall picture of the melodic structural tones in the introductory verse looks like this:

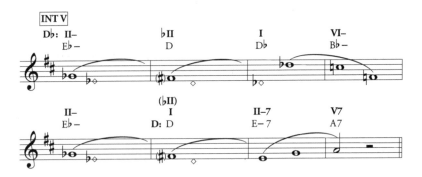

Fig. 2.15. Intro verse structural tones

The melody seems filled with eddies of confusion as it moves downward, then leaps wildly up an octave, then down again to a return of the first motive. It concludes with a rather bland, confused return to the middle—which is the perfect setting for the emotional content of the lyric that opens the song, as shown in the following example.

The melody in the introductory verse moves in running eighth notes, a pattern that is repeated exactly at bars 5 and 6:

Fig. 2.16. Intro verse melody

There is also a syncopated figure (♪ ♩ ♪) employed at bar 4. A descending melody sustains the effect of depression and confusion:

Fig. 2.17. Descending syncopated melodic figure

This same figure returns at bars 7 and 8, this time ascending and giving a sense of hope that he might be able to solve his confusion. The most outstanding part of the melodic and lyric line of this unusual introduction is the "help me" lyric at bar 3. As the singer makes a direct plea for help, the melody leaps an entire octave and holds the high Db for three full beats.

Melody: Verse

The verse melody slows down the pace, using half notes and dotted half notes. Ah…this slowed pace represents the smooth song of love that he will sing to the new one in his life:

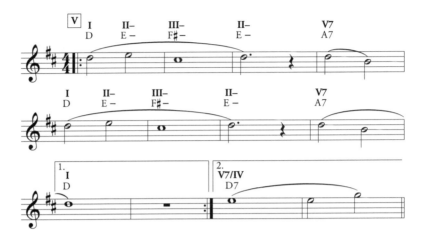

Fig. 2.18. Verse structural tones

The melody in the opening three bars of the A section is quite simple and static. The first phrase starts and ends on the stable tonic Do (D), with a brief movement to the surrounding unstable notes, Re (E) and Ti (C♯).

The second phrase up to the first ending again starts and ends on the stable and strong Do, as the singer proclaims the opening lyrical statement. The same phrase, this time moving into the second ending, is wide open. It ends on the extremely unstable Re (E) as the verse moves directly into the primary bridge.

Melody: Primary Bridge

As discussed above, Lennon begins the primary bridge by changing the last note of the verse melody from Do to Re. Coupled with the use of D7, it makes Re (E) sound like the 9th of the D7 chord. The use of the 9th above the band gives a lush sound to open the bridge. This emphasis on the dominant in the second ending amplifies the movement and resolution to the G chord.

At the very end of the second ending, the melody has moved upward from its initial setting on the unstable Re to another unstable Fa, as seen in fig. 2.19. Four bars later in the primary bridge, it finally resolves to the stable Mi, which is F♯ in this key.

Fig. 2.19. Second ending structural tones

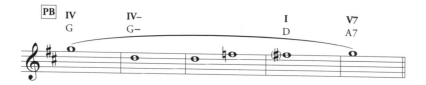

Fig. 2.20. Primary bridge structural tones

Though the melody resolves at this point, the lyric doesn't finish up until bar 5. To move back into the verse effectively, Lennon withholds the rhyming of "pain" with the word "vain" until it returns to the unstable G in the melody. So we have:

- Phrase 1 (1-bar), ending on unstable note G with the lyric "pain."
- Phrase 2 (4-bar), first arriving at the note F♯ resolving the G from phrase 1, but then introducing the lyric "love." The listener expects the line to rhyme at that point, but it does not.
- Final melody note G is left unresolved melodically, but resolved lyrically with the rhyming of "pain."

All of this resolution—and lack thereof—emphasizes the protagonist's confusion.

Notice that the bridge melody is much more active than the verse melody. The tonic Do appears at seven points in the verse, but is virtually nonexistent in the bridge. The bridge introduces chromaticism (notes outside the key) to a tune that up to now has been completely diatonic. This completely supports the lyric content of the bridge, in which the singer considers the consequences of his actions.

The constant use of that extremely stable Do usually produces a melody that is not very forward moving. But as I pointed out earlier, Lennon uses forward-moving chords to provide the momentum lacking in the melody.

The melodic rhythm used to connect the third verse back to the bridge is the same syncopation pattern (♪ ♩ ♪) that appears in the rhyming portion of the introductory verse. In addition, Lennon ends the third verse with this same gesture at the song's conclusion. This helps to bring a sense of balance and wholeness as the song draws to a close.

SUMMARY

Lennon concludes the song with a 4-bar coda. This brings a sense of covenant to the somewhat ambiguous title. (Lennon once announced this song in concert as "If I Fell Over.") "If I Fell" is certainly an incomplete title, and it's not completely clear until the very last line of the lyric that he is talking about falling in love.

Lennon avoids saying "fell in love" throughout the entire song except as the very first line in the introductory verse and the very last line in the coda. He doesn't include the title within the song proper at all, using it only as a setup in the intro, and a "get-out" in the coda. Here again Lennon shows his propensity to tease the listener. He mentions the things that falling in love involves—giving one's heart, trusting, et cetera—but never mentions the title line in the song itself.

So how does he handle the melody and harmony of this coda lyric, when he finally comes round to the critical "if I fell in love with you" line? Well, I would say brilliantly. For the darker, more uncertain part of the lyric—the "if I fell" part—he selected chords and notes not from D major, but rather from the darker parallel key of D minor: the G minor chord and the B♭ note. For the more hopeful and positive part of the lyric—"with *you*"—there is no other choice than the most stable chord in this key to convey that message. Of course, it's D major, the I chord.

The melody at this point heads upward in plodding quarter notes, suggesting he will climb any mountain or swim any ocean to make this relationship happen. On top of that, the last note is F♯, the 3rd of D (Mi). At last, here is the resolution of that left-over G from the bridge. This is significant, because G is Fa in the key, and Fa usually resolves to Mi. Without the coda, the Fa at the end of the verse would remain unresolved. Very well crafted!

I am quite sure Lennon had no idea of the mechanics of how these stable and unstable resolutions and lurching 4- and 5-bar phrases contributed to the overall prosody of melody and lyric. But it's quite obvious that he did have an innate ability to create the perfect musical setting for the difficult dilemma displayed in this lyric.

I Call Your Name

Words and Music by John Lennon and Paul McCartney

(Continued on following page)

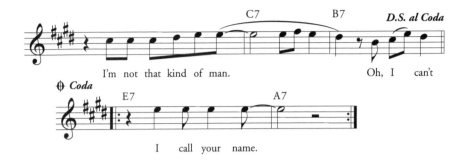

I'm not that kind of man.   Oh, I   can't

I   call   your   name.

Verse 3

Oh, I can't sleep at night,

but just the same,

I never weep at night,

I call your name.

BACKGROUND

Title	I Call Your Name
Recording Date	March 1, 1964
Meter	4/4
Key	E major
Song Form	AABA
Phrasing	Verse 1: *aa*
	Verse 2: *abc*
	Verse 3: *abab*
	Primary Bridge: *abcb*
Recording	*Beatles: Past Masters, Volume One*
	1988 EMD/CAPITOL

Lennon identifies this song as one of his earliest songwriting efforts. He has indicated that "I Call Your Name" is one of his favorites and was around before there was any Beatles group. Before the Beatles, though, he just had the first sixteen bars, which comprise the A section of the song. Lennon first brought the song into Abbey Road Studios on Sunday, March 1, 1964. The Beatles recorded seven takes, and the song was finished and ready for mixing.

Oddly enough, "I Call Your Name" was *never* released in England as a single or on any album. Rather, it was only released on June 10, 1964 as part of the *Long Tall Sally* EP (mono), a record album with four songs, two on each side. The Beatles released thirteen EPs in England. Only three EPs were released in America. Never released as a single in America, "I Call Your Name" can be found on the American album, *The Beatles' Second Album*, released on April 10, 1964. The song also appears on *Past Masters, Volume One*, released March 7, 1988 in America only.

The style of the song recalls the 1920s music that his mother so loved. Lennon had performed several songs in this style before "I Call Your Name." In Hamburg, he and the Beatles recorded "Ain't She Sweet," a Jack Yellin song from 1927. Also, at their audition for Decca Records in January 1962, the Beatles recorded another "old-style" song of Lennon's called "Hello, Little Girl." That song was another example of Lennon's earliest songwriting efforts. It remains unreleased to this day.

STRUCTURE

Song Form
"I Call Your Name" is in the classic AABA form.

A (V1)	A (V2)	B (PB)	A (V3)
Verse/Refrain	Verse/Refrain	Primary Bridge	Verse/Refrain
12 bars	12 bars	8 bars	12 bars

Lyric Content
The lyric conveys a familiar story: Boy loses girl; he wishes he had her back; he laments his predicament. Lennon strikes an immediate connection through his passionate title, "I Call Your Name." The title conjures up a variety of desperate romantic scenarios. From the opening line, "I call your name, but you're not there," the listener knows that the singer has been abandoned and the situation is serious.

PHRASING

Verse

▶ Harmonic Phrasing
The four chords that make up verse 1 are all dominant 7th chords, which create a happy and bluesy atmosphere. Used in succession, a chain of dominant chords are called **extended dominants**. Extended dominant chords were used frequently in songs written in the 1920s and 1930s.

Fig. 2.21. Verse 1 harmonic phrasing

This first verse winds its way through the 7th chords, ending on the dominant of the key, B7. Because the dominant chord has such a forward-moving feel, the section feels wide open. It directs movement toward the start of the second verse.

By contrast, verse 2 ends with a plagal cadence:

Fig. 2.22. Verse 2 harmonic phrasing

Note the substitution of the A, A minor, and E7 chords at the end of this section. Those are the very chords that create the plagal "Amen" cadence mentioned in our exploration of "If I Fell." This closed cadence delivers up a feeling of stopping briefly before verse 2 launches into the primary bridge.

The contrast Lennon chose to use in the harmonic setup of these two verses—the first open, the second closed—is a classic setup used for many years by many songwriters. Lennon chose the same closed harmonic progression found in verse 2 as the setup for verse 3. It provides a strong final punctuation to the AABA form.

▶ Melodic Phrasing

Lennon treats each of the lyrics in the three verses, or A sections, differently. The first verse contains two long lyrical statements. The first is a statement; the second, a question:

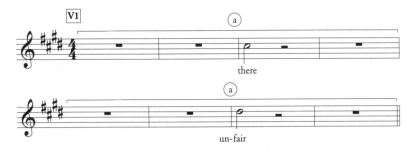

Fig. 2.23. Verse 1 melodic phrasing

These long phrases reinforce the forlorn nature of the opening verse, drawing out the lyrics like a lone wolf howling at the moon. The second verse, by contrast, introduces shorter phrases, introducing a sense of restlessness and forward motion into the bridge. This perfectly supports the stirring lyric at that point: "I can't sleep at night. I can't go on."

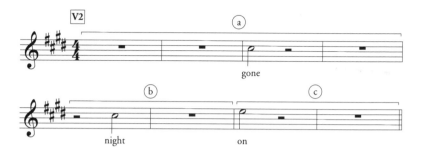

Fig. 2.24. Verse 2 melodic phrasing

The shorter ⓑ and ⓒ phrases provide movement both in lyric and melody as the section proceeds to the bridge.

Verse 3, the lyric's conclusion, is the most symmetrical of all:

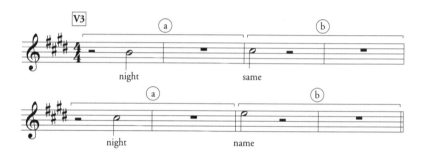

Fig. 2.25. Verse 3 melodic phrasing

The *abab* lyric form finally coincides with the melodic phrasing. All three verses are made up of four 2-bar melodic phrases. In verses 1 and 2, Lennon pulls and stretches the lyric over the melody in unexpected ways, creating the howling-wolf effect in verse 1 and the restless forward motion in verse 2.

In the final verse, with symmetrical 2-bar phrases occurring in both the melody *and* the lyric, the song phrases finally reach resolution. While the lyric phrasing of verses 1 and 2 subdue the effect of the melodic phrasing, the lyric phrasing of verse 3 embraces it. The last verse contains the most hopeful line of all: "I never weep at night." The melody, lyric, rhythm, and harmony come together in this final verse to give rise to the hope that everything will work out well in the end.

Primary Bridge

▶ Harmonic Phrasing

Like the verses, the chord progression for the primary bridge provides great forward motion—but with a twist. Instead of beginning the bridge on E7 like the verses, Lennon begins on the subdominant A7:

Fig. 2.26. Primary bridge harmonic phrasing

The bridge ends on a dominant chord, which is the perfect setup: wide open, so the song will make its way back to the tonic E7 at the top of verse 3.

▶ Melodic Phrasing

Lennon had the first half of this tune for several years before he finally reckoned it into a song. It seems logical that, in trying to create contrast in writing new sections, he would turn to shorter phrases as one of the solutions:

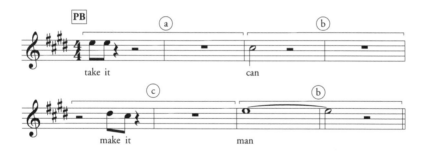

Fig. 2.27. Primary bridge melodic phrasing

The consistent 2-bar phrases in the primary bridge give immediate balance to the wandering harmonic and phrasal moves of verses 1 and 2. However, he retains the feel of uncertainty within the 2-bar phrases, because the inner phrasing has a jerky, unexpected phrase pattern that creates great forward motion.

Since the rhyming couplets "take it" and "make it" are placed on two different beats (beats 2 and 4 respectively), the resulting phrasing is an unexpected *abcb*. Had Lennon rhymed them both on beat 2, the result would have been rather pedestrian, with virtually no forward motion at all. The bland ⓑ phrases provide lyrical and rhythmic stability, with the lyrics "can" and "man" set on the extremely stable beat 1 of their respective bars.

PROSODY

Melody: Verse
In verse 1, the phrase endings of the melody make a steady movement from B up to D♯:

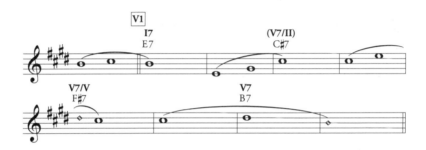

Fig. 2.28. Verse 1 structural tones

This rising melody and its plaintive questioning lyric makes a perfect combination. Even in his early years as a songwriter, Lennon had an excellent grasp on the mechanics of combining music and lyric.

Another unique aspect of this song's melodic phrasing is **back-heavy phrasing**. Back-heavy phrasing occurs when the melody begins before the chord progression. In such a case, the melody tends to lead to the chords. (By way of contrast, the first two songs discussed so far, "You Can't Do That" and "If I Fell," are excellent examples of **front-heavy phrasing**. The melody of both of these songs departs from the chords.)

The back-heavy phrasing in "I Call Your Name" is very easy to spot when looking at the music itself. In fig. 2.28 above, note that all of the melodic phrases begin in the even-numbered bars and finish up as each new chord is introduced.

According to standard 8-bar verse conventions, odd-numbered bars are strong, while even-numbered bars tend to be weak. With back-heavy phrasing, chords generally occur on the strong bars and the melody occurs on the weak bars. The classic structure of back-heavy phrases emphasizes the ends of lyric lines. The emphasis occurs for several reasons:

- The odd bars are the strongest anchors in rhythmic form.
- New chord changes occur at each of the odd bars.
- Each lyric line ends in an odd bar.

All of these factors work together to punch up the end of the lyric lines ("name," "not there," blame," "unfair"). These four words alone give the listener a sense of the song story immediately.

The second verse is essentially the same, except that the melody rises all the way to the tonic E, resolving to the D♯ left hanging at the end of the first verse:

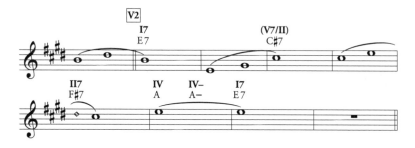

Fig. 2.29. Verse 2 structural tones

Melody: Primary Bridge

Reflecting Lennon's tendency in lyrics to explore both sides of an issue and often resolve to middle ground, the bridge melody moves between neighboring tones before settling on the D♯. After all of the bridge phrase have concluded on either tonic or the 6th degree, Lennon splits the difference and ends the entire bridge section on the note located *between* these two, D♯:

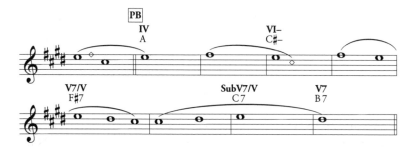

Fig. 2.30. Primary bridge structural tones

In the first four bars, Lennon totally avoids the use of the D♯. In bars 5 and 6 he uses it as a teasing, passing tone that foreshadows the section's ending. Finally in the very last bar, he embraces it. As discussed earlier, D♯ is the most unstable note from the key of E. It is no surprise that Lennon weaves it prominently into the most climatic lyric of the bridge, "I'm not that kind of man!"

SUMMARY

Even in Lennon's early songwriting efforts, we see a budding expert at writing for the people. First of all, the melodic range—only one octave and a step—makes the song very singable by almost anyone. And the nature of the song's repeating melodic rhythm makes it more of a sing-along than a tune meant for listening.

Though the song is composed entirely of 2-bar melodic phrases, the lengthy 8-bar harmonic phrasing provides the "string" on which the pearls of melody are strung. Lennon's clever application of the lyric and rhyme gives great contrast in every verse. This helps to create interest and pulls the listener right into the story.

The bluesy dominant 7th chords in the verse create an atmosphere that is at once rather happy but still holds a pang of lost love, as explored in the lyric. This is because the nature of dominant 7ths is at once major and at the same time dissonant; their strident unresolved sound always pulls forward for resolution.

The arrival of the C♯ minor chord in the bridge conjures the perfect darkness to express the singer's true turmoil. Since this is the only minor chord used in the song, it really stands out. The darker minor chord and the lyric, "I don't know who can," combine to create a cloudy night of confusion as the singer searches for daylight.

Lennon makes a shrewd choice in his connection from the end of the bridge into the hopeful last verse. He uses the unexpected C7–B7 chord progression to support that last plaintive D♯ in the melody. By bringing the bridge to such a dramatic conclusion, Lennon manages to keep the D♯ ringing in the listener's ear until the very end of the next verse, where it resolves upward to the long-awaited tonic note, E.

It's the perfect way to bring the song to a real conclusion. All songwriters are very aware of the time limits of a song. There's just a few lines to say all of what one wants to say. In this song, Lennon completes the presentation of his story in just twelve lyric lines for the verses and four lyric lines for the bridge. Even though this song is one of Lennon's earliest efforts from the late 1950s, he knew that he had something with this one. He brought it to final fruition in this famous recording from 1964.

A Hard Day's Night

Words and Music by John Lennon and Paul McCartney

(Continued on following page)

feel-ing you hold— -ing me tight! Tight!— Yeah!—

Verse 2

You know I work all day,
To get you money to buy you things.
And it's worth it just to hear you say,
You're gonna give me ev'rything.
So why on earth should I moan,
'Cause when I get you alone,
You know I'll be O.K.

BACKGROUND

Title	A Hard Day's Night
Recording Date	April 16, 1964
Meter	4/4
Key	G Mixolydian and G major
Song Form	AABA
Phrasing	Verse (A): *aabbc*
	Primary Bridge (B): *abc*
Recording	*A Hard Day's Night*
	1964 EMD/CAPITOL

Lennon wrote "A Hard Day's Night"—with some assistance from Paul McCartney—by request of Walter Shenson, who was the producer of the Beatles' first film. The film had recently been renamed *A Hard Day's Night*, changed from the original title, *Beatlemania*. United Artists was pressing Shenson to get the group to write a title song for the movie. Lennon decided he was up for the challenge.

Overnight, on demand, Lennon managed to churn out a pop classic! The composition of "A Hard Day's Night" must have been one of the turning points in Lennon's own realization of just how good a writer he was becoming.

The song was recorded on April 16, 1964 and was released on the soundtrack album in America in late June. A few weeks later, it was released on single in America and on single and LP in England.

STRUCTURE

Song Form

Still in the early days of his songwriting career, Lennon once again stuck with the tried-and-true AABA song form, but with a twist: there are only two verses of lyrics. Both the first and third A's have the same lyrics. This repetition is critical because *only* the first verse contains the title. In performance, the song form is AABA/BA. The primary bridge repeats once, but verse 1—as well as the title—repeats a total of three times:

A	A	B	A	B	A
Verse 1	Verse 2	Primary Bridge	Verse 1	Primary Bridge	Verse 1
12 bars	12 bars	8 bars	12 bars	8 bars	12 bars

Lyric Content

In two short verses and one primary bridge, Lennon successfully presents the form and substance. The first verse exploits two clichés: "working like a dog" and "sleeping like a log." By preceding these two clichés with the title of the song, Lennon transforms these phrases into most of the first verse. Because the title is repeated twice in this opening verse, the verse feels a bit like a chorus.

The next two rhyming couplets let the listener know that the singer is speaking to his girlfriend. His workday has ended, he's home with her, and he's going to feel alright.

The second verse does not contain the title of the song. Verse 2 is only sung once, while verse 1 is sung three times during the course of the song. With the mention of the word "money" in verse 2, the listener becomes aware of the singer's desire to provide for his beloved. Further, he indicates that being with her makes all his hard work worthwhile.

The primary bridge lyric focuses entirely on the wonderful feeling he has at home and away from work. Everything at home just seems to feel "right." And home is where he can hold his baby "tight." Classic pop romance lyric, but well-turned here in this driving bridge section.

PHRASING

Verse

▶ *Harmonic Phrasing*

"A Hard Day's Night" begins with an unsettling—and now famous—G7sus4 chord with a D in the bass. The chord is struck and held by the three guitarists as well as the piano—a very unusual beginning, to say the least. The chord immediately captures that feeling of "hitting the wall" when one has gone beyond one's limits. G7sus4 does contain the tonic note G, which gives it a certain stability. However, it also contains two extremely unstable notes, C (the 4th) and F♮ (♭7th). This combination of stable and unstable tones creates just the right atmosphere for a song about having a hard day:

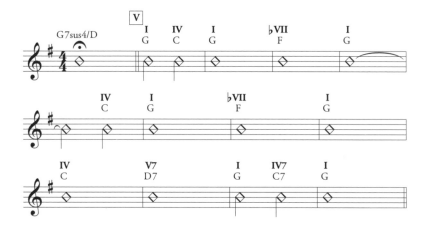

Fig. 2.31. Verse harmonic phrasing

The opening three verse chords (G, C, G) at first reflect the key of G major. But with the introduction of F major at bar 3, we find that Lennon has chosen to set the song in the key of G Mixolydian. With its bluesy ♭7th, the Mixolydian mode actually flattens out the sweetness normally associated with the major mode. The more droning sound of the flatted 7th works well with the import of Lennon's verse lyric about a hard day at work. The verses establish an atmosphere reflecting the monotony of the workaday world.

The mode shifts back to a straight-ahead G major at bar 10 with the introduction of the D7 chord, which contains the competing F♯. The only difference between G major and G Mixolydian is the F. The G major needs an F♯ to fully establish the major mode, while the G Mixolydian needs an F♮ to fully establish the Mixolydian mode. Lennon retains the bluesy edge by sneaking a C7 chord (bar 11) into the final cadence, which contains the also bluesy note, B♭.

▶ *Melodic Phrasing*
The phrasing of the verse is a study in asymmetry. Note that the following example has two different analyses: *aaa* and *aabbc* (as shown in fig. 2.32).

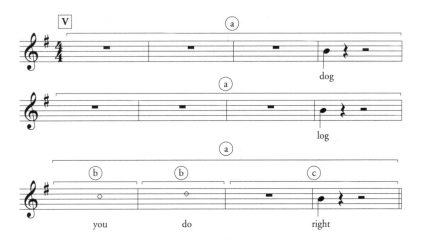

Fig. 2.32. Verse melodic phrasing

Lennon goes for longer phrases in the verses. The first 4-bar phrase ends on bar 4, beat 1 with the word "dog." It's not unexpected to hear a companion 4-bar phrase next, ending with "log" in the same place. So far, the form is *aa*.

The asymmetry comes with the third and final 4-bar phrase. Three, not four? That's asymmetry. This creates an *aaa* analysis. With the missing fourth phrase, the verse should seem unbalanced or unresolved rhythmically. But Lennon has a clever twist to keep that from happening: internal rhyme. The internally rhyming "you" and "do" breaks up the third 4-bar phrase into a 1 + 1 + 2 combination that deflects the asymmetry and focuses attention on the rhymes. It creates an alternate analysis of *aabbc*. By the time we hear the last 2-bar phrase after the two short 1-bar bits, the section feels resolved.

Primary Bridge

▶ *Harmonic Phrasing*

The 8-bar bridge introduces contrast. Set in the darker minor mode, it is a seemingly ironic setting for such a positive lyric. This works well because over the course of the bridge, the harmony moves from the implied B minor tonality to a straight-ahead G major tonality:

Fig. 2.33. Primary bridge harmonic phrasing

The bridge ends with a well-placed and familiar harmonic progression: a classic I-VI minor-IV-V progression. This propels the progression forward into the final D7–G cadence, which brings us back into the verse.

▶ *Melodic Phrasing*

The primary bridge offers a square 8-bar section. On some levels it is divided into 4-bar units, but as you see below, the lyric and the melody divide the second phrase and create an accelerating 1-bar phrase as the section closes:

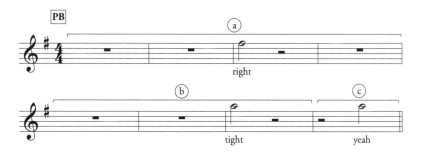

Fig. 2.34. Primary bridge melodic phrasing

Were it not for that last lyrical punctuation of "tight, yeh!" in the eighth bar, the bridge would come off as a somewhat lackluster, ho-hum affair, with "right" and "tight" rhyming together at their respective third bars. That would definitely work, but the creation and insertion of that last 1-bar phrase. It adds just a little jet propulsion toward the beginning of the next verse.

PROSODY

Melody: Verse

The verse melody is somewhat static. In the first two lines, the melody rarely leaves the D, except for brief excursions, as seen in fig. 2.35:

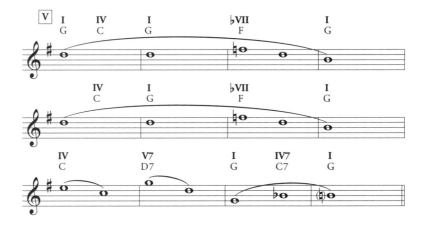

Fig. 2.35. Verse structural tones

The first two bars of the third line of the verse form a mini transitional bridge. Refer to the example below and notice that the melody and chords move up in the second bar. This upward motion creates and supports all the forward momentum in the lyrics. Lyrically, there is internal rhyme in those two bars. Harmonically, there is a cadence from C to D. Melodically, the unstable, forward-moving melody soon resolves to tonic at bar 3.

Fig. 2.36. Mini transitional bridge

Referring back for a moment to the first line in the verse, shown in fig. 2.37, the answering phrase at the third and fourth bars opens with a jerky but totally prosodic setting of the lyric "working." It concludes with a frantic melisma on the word "dog." Using melisma (singing many notes for a single syllable) emphasizes the lyric.

Fig. 2.37. Melisma in "Hard Day's Night"

Placing the lyrics "hard," "night," "working," and "dog" on beat 1 gives them the greatest lyrical emphasis. These four words alone are enough to conjure up a sense of urgency that supports the title, "It's Been a Hard Day's Night."

▶ *Melody: Primary Bridge*

The melodic range of the bridge is much higher, providing contrast and release from the verse melody. The screaming high A at the end of the section was so high that McCartney had to sing the bridge while Lennon sang the verses:

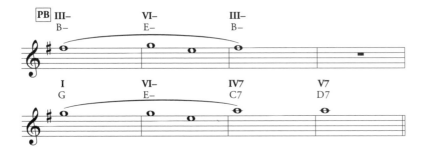

Fig. 2.38. Primary bridge structural tones

The F♯ that begins the primary bridge comes as a surprise, because it supports the tonality of G major rather than of G Mixolydian, which was exploited in the verse sections. The change is so dramatic it just takes your head off! Lennon did a little foreshadowing of it in the last part of the verse. But to select the least stable note from the G major tonality, after totally inundating the listener with F♯s in both the melody and harmony during the verses, is a dramatic move that carries the listener to a whole new musical plane.

The static melody of the bridge builds tension perfectly toward the climax at the word "home" in the second line, which begins a half step higher on the tonic G. Lennon doesn't let the G resolve the bridge, however. Two dramatic and extremely unstable A's finish off the bridge melody.

SUMMARY

The marriage of melody to this lyric showcases Lennon's ability to musically capture the experience of a difficult day (or night). From the very beginning, the lyric title is set with long notes encompassing a half bar per word, suggesting an image of a plodding, routine day at work. At the same time, the rhythm pushes forward, anticipating the second bar of the verse by a half a beat. This anticipation gives a sense of the urgency of getting the job done.

The song hits a nerve with most listeners: a hard day at work; dealing with people all day; waiting patiently for a return to euphoric isolation with the one you love, away from the world. It is an excellent musical portrait of mundane life. Capturing it so perfectly is the essence of what makes a great pop song. While later in his development Lennon explored avant-garde vehicles for song, "A Hard Day's Night" truly exemplifies his ability to distill the everyday issues of life and successfully present them in the pop song idiom. Though John Lennon never learned to read music, it is obvious as we explore his songs that he certainly knew how musical notes communicate.

CHAPTER 3 1964, Part II

The second half of 1964 found Lennon beginning to explore the verse/chorus form while continuing to retain roots in the familiar AABA form. In this chapter, I will discuss two songs from each form.

While the verse/chorus format was relatively new to the Beatles' writing style, the band had long been performing many verse/chorus cover songs by the r&b artists to whom Lennon listened constantly for influence and inspiration. Covers such as "Twist and Shout" and "Dizzy Miss Lizzie" used the verse/chorus format that had become a standard pop form during the 1950s and 1960s. In addition to those two great classics, Lennon and the Beatles had performed other verse/chorus cover songs including: "Boys," "Please Mr. Postman," "Honey Don't," "You've Really Got a Hold on Me," "Money," and "Carol." The Beatles recorded and released groundbreaking versions of all of these songs over the course of their first four albums.

Even though performing and recording these songs was having some influence on Lennon's writing style, he did not fully embrace the form and continued to write AABA songs. In dialogs about songwriting, both Lennon and McCartney refer to what they called the "middle eight." That was the term they used for the eight bars that comprise the primary bridge in the AABA form:

A	A	B	A
Verse/Refrain	Verse/Refrain	Primary Bridge	Verse/Refrain
		"the middle eight"	

Lennon and McCartney both used the AABA form in their early songs, though Lennon did try his luck at the verse/chorus format as early as 1963. With co-writer McCartney, Lennon churned out the famous "yeh, yeh, yeh" hit, "She Loves You," as well as "I Want to Hold Your Hand." Both of these songs have a chorus, although in both cases, the chorus chord progressions are through-composed. That is, they have no repeating chords and therefore lack the tonal center that is typical of chorus harmony.

The absence of a tonal center makes the choruses feel as if they are part of the verse, rather than the more typical harmonically closed, independent chorus unit. In both of these songs, the so-called choruses were too long to be a refrain and too short to be a chorus. These two songs reveal Lennon the composer in transition. Like a chick breaking out of its shell, he was halfway in the old AABA world but moving into the verse/chorus world.

In his early period, Lennon did compose two songs that had strong choruses, "It Won't Be Long" and "Tell Me Why." These are the earliest examples of Lennon, as a solo writer within the Beatles, embracing the verse/chorus format. As we will see in this and subsequent chapters, he used that format with increasing frequency throughout his career.

Having discussed the four AABA songs from the first half of the historic year 1964, we will now look at four songs from the second half of that year:

"Baby's in Black"
"I'm a Loser"
"I Don't Want to Spoil the Party"
"I Feel Fine"

In the first two songs, "Baby's in Black" and "I'm a Loser," Lennon takes a cue from his r&b influences. Both songs appear on the *Beatles for Sale* album. The rest of the Lennon contributions for that album and the rest of 1964 return to the tried-and-true AABA format. This is the case indeed with "I Don't Want to Spoil the Party" and "I Feel Fine," both of which contain the characteristic "middle eight."

Baby's in Black

Words and Music by John Lennon and Paul McCartney

Verse 2

I think of her,
But she thinks only of him,
And though it's only a whim,
She thinks of him.

BACKGROUND

Title	Baby's in Black
Recording Date	August 11, 1964
Meter	6/8
Key	A major
Song Form	Verse/Chorus with Primary Bridge
Phrasing	Verse: *ab*
	Chorus: *aab*
	Primary Bridge: *a*
Recording	*Beatles for Sale*
	1964 EMD/CAPITOL

"Baby's in Black" is one of the little-known staples of the Beatles repertoire and is a true Lennon/McCartney song. The song was the only one included in the Beatles' live performances on all three world tours from 1964–1966. It has a distinct country-and-western flavor, and it is the first song Lennon and McCartney had written *together* since "I Want to Hold Your Hand," composed nearly a year before. It is the one song in this book that is a true Lennon/McCartney collaboration.

"Baby's in Black" was the first song recorded for the *Beatles for Sale* LP, and it is one of the strongest tracks on the album. Of cosmetic interest, it is one of the few songs in which Lennon and McCartney always shared a microphone in the characteristic guitar neck disposition: Lennon to the left and McCartney to the right, as if to support the song as a collaborative effort.

The most interesting thing about the song is that it marks the beginning of the end of Lennon and McCartney's 50/50 songwriting efforts. Review the early 1962–63 material, and you'll find that many of the originals were composed eyeball-to-eyeball. Songs like "I Want to Hold Your Hand," "I'll Get You," "She Loves You," "From Me to You"…all those great songs were cowritten. But when *A Hard Day's Night* came along in 1964, Lennon and McCartney seemed to retreat from each other, writing nearly everything separately for that album.

"Baby's in Black" is really the *only* song on the *Beatles for Sale* album that the pair cowrote. According to William Dowdling in his book *Beatlesongs* (New York: Fireside Books, 1989), "Eight Days a Week" was credited as being cowritten, but that remains a mostly McCartney song. You won't find another true 50/50 effort until "Wait," on the *Rubber Soul* album (1965).

"Baby's in Black" was recorded on August 11, 1964 and released in England on the *Beatles for Sale* album on December 4, 1964. The song was released in America on the forward-looking American cousin of *Beatles for Sale*—the *Beatles '65* album—released on December 15, 1964.

STRUCTURE

Song Form

Lennon and McCartney wrote this song with a verse/chorus format, something new for Lennon. With the exception of "She Loves You," Lennon had not yet ventured into this soon-to-be standard form. The song is actually a three-section version of the verse/chorus form known as "verse/chorus with primary bridge." The usual performance of such a form, as heard today, is as follows:

Verse	Chorus	Verse	Chorus	Primary	Verse	Chorus
1		2		Bridge	3	

Sometimes there is a solo between the primary bridge and the verse, but you get the idea. First comes the verse, then the chorus. "Baby's in Black," however, does the reverse:

Chorus	Verse	Chorus	Verse	Primary	Chorus	Solo	Primary	Chorus	Verse	Chorus
	1		2	Bridge			Bridge		1	
6 bars	7 bars	6 bars	7 bars	4 bars	6 bars	6 bars	4 bars	6 bars	7 bars	6 bars

In the modern version of the verse/chorus pop song format, the chorus usually repeats only three times, unless the song ends with a repeating chorus. As you see from the above illustration, "Baby's in Black" hits the chorus no less than five times. This is an unusual setup but it serves this song well. Songs like McCartney's own "Can't Buy Me Love" use the chorus/verse format.

One of the reasons the chorus can be repeated so often in "Baby's in Black" is that it is short—only six bars long. In fact, as we expand our look into the song's form, we find the following:

Chorus = 6 bars
Verse = 7 bars
Primary Bridge = 4 bars

Each of these sections has an uneven length and none of them ever quite feel at rest. This unbalance provides a lively setting for this song about a person whose emotions are on the skids.

Just a brief word about meter. At the famous Shea Stadium concert in August 1965, Lennon introduced the song as a waltz. The song is set in 6/8 time, which often sounds like a very quick waltz:

ONE–two–three–FOUR–five–six

This song does in fact sound a little like a country waltz, but both the quick tempo and Ringo's two-to-the-bar drum feel push the meter from waltz feel into 6/8. As a result, each bar of 6/8 sounds a little like two bars of 3/4, or "waltz" time.

Lyric Content

The lyric content is very straight-ahead and focused. The singer dejectedly is thinking of someone he loves, knowing that her mind is on someone she's recently lost. She can give no attention to her suitor's advances, and he is distraught.

PHRASING

Chorus

▶ Harmonic Phrasing

The harmonic progression that accompanies the chorus is a standard country blues chord progression: I–V7–IV7–V7–I–IV–I–V.

Fig. 3.1. Chorus harmonic phrasing

The progression moves at a steady one chord per bar, except for the cadence and turnaround in the fifth and sixth bars. There, an acceleration in harmonic rhythm adds even more propulsion into the coming verse section.

▶ Melodic Phrasing

Throughout all three of its sections, the melody of "Baby's in Black" is made up of 2-bar phrases. The opening 2-bar phrase sets the dejected tone:

Fig. 3.2. Opening 2-bar phrase

The full analysis of the chorus section is *aab*:

Fig. 3.3. Chorus melodic phrasing

Verse

▶ Harmonic Phrasing

The verse section, by contrast, is an extremely unbalanced seven bars long. The chords are held much longer than in the chorus section. Comprised of mostly I and IV chords, the resulting verse progression is as follows:

Fig. 3.4. Verse harmonic phrasing

▶ *Melodic Phrasing*

The 7-bar verse is subdivided into an asymmetrical *ab* pattern.

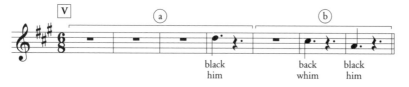

Fig. 3.5. Verse melodic phrasing

This asymmetry helps propel the verse forward to the next verse or into the bridge. It seems upon first hearing that the verse is going to be a 6-bar section like the chorus—but there's an extra bar! Note the asymmetrical internal rhyme at the sixth bar of each verse (verse 1 = "back"; verse 2 = "whim"). This choice is a wise one, indeed, since the ends of each of the phrases are *exactly* the same word (verse 1 = "black"; verse 2 = "him").

The verse's extra bar delays momentum for a moment, holding it back like the upswing before the down. This gives the song a nice sway forward. Before you know it, you're singing the chorus again. Most listeners probably find the 6-bar chorus and 7-bar verse a little off-kilter. This imbalance makes the sections seem to swagger back and forth into each other.

Primary Bridge

▶ *Harmonic Phrasing*

Finally, the 4-bar primary bridge provides an interesting contrast. There is no chord repetition, and this is the only time in the song that this happens:

Fig. 3.6. Primary bridge harmonic phrasing

The bridge introduces the VI minor chord (F♯ minor) for the first time, along with the exhilarating chromatic B7 chord. I say exhilarating, because the B7, which introduces notes not in the key, sets us up for a resolution to E but instead deceptively resolves to D.

(Lennon was to use a similarly successful deceptive resolution in "In My Life." See chapter 4.)

One might hope the primary bridge would deliver up the missing 8-bar section, but actually the bridge presents its own character, one that is totally different from the preceding sections. The contrast in the bridge is yet more evidence of Lennon's natural ability to map out the musical hills and valleys of his songs.

> ### Melodic Phrasing
The bridge lyric consists of a single line. In fact, it is a single question. It appears to be only four bars long, but in a classic Lennon twist, both the lyric and the melody reach their conclusion not at the fourth bar of the bridge as expected, but rather at the first bar of the chorus's return. This is the same "overlap" treatment used earlier in "If I Fell." The result is one long (a) phrase for this short section:

Fig. 3.7. Primary bridge melodic phrasing

The use of internal rhyme gives the illusion that the bridge will consist of two 2-bar phrases. However, the section ends with a 1-bar overlap at the lyric "made." This bar completes the section and creates the final 5-bar form for the bridge.

PROSODY

Melody: Chorus
In this particular song, the two-part harmony is integral to the melody. The top part is sung by McCartney, the lower by Lennon. In country music, the top part of layered harmony vocals is very often heard as a "high harmony." In this song, the lower part is the melody in the chorus and verse sections, and the higher part seems to take over as the melody in the primary bridge.

As the song opens with the chorus, the lower voice (Lennon's part) starts off as the melody. As you can see from the illustration, Lennon's part descends a full octave over the six bars of the chorus. The melodic descent of an octave supports the protagonist's emotional descent into depression:

Fig. 3.8. Chorus structural tones

The upper voice (McCartney's part) begins a third higher and provides the expected resolution to Do by the end of the chorus. In bar 3, McCartney's use of the C♮, the bluesy minor 3rd, in his sighing melodic descent from Sol down to Do, adds more melancholy to the sad lyric.

Melody: Verse

Both voices hang on their melodic notes much longer in the verse section than in any other. The upper voice moves to G♮, the main "blue" note in the key of A. This ♭7 injects a bluesy, pang-filled flavor into the melody. Though the verse melody begins to head upwards, its ultimate destination is downward to its final resting place at Do and Mi respectively in the seventh bar:

Fig. 3.9. Verse structural tones

Melody: Primary Bridge

The melodic treatment in the bridge is highly effective. The top voice represents the desperation of the bridge lyric as it jumps erratically between the high A and the F♯, finally resolving to the stable E. The chromatic descending linear lower voice engenders a sense of resignation to the song's scenario, coming to rest at the C♯ at the beginning of the chorus:

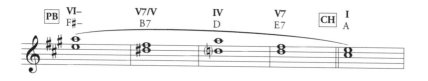

Fig. 3.10. Primary bridge structural tones

The lyric in the bridge brings the most direct pleading in the entire song. The choice of the oscillating top voice combined with the grounded linear line in the low voice creates an excellent setting for the lyrical mix of wild emotion and a plea for resolution.

Listen to the recording and note George Harrison's guitar solo. Even the solo, which occurs over the 6-bar chorus section, helps establish the song's unbalanced, downcast feel. Harrison plays the gnarliest country-style guitar solo you ever heard to such sweetly triadic chords as I , IV, and V. By the time he's finished, one feels dragged over the coals and ready for the first bridge outta here—which of course is exactly what Lennon and McCartney give us.

SUMMARY

Both the verse and chorus, with their alternating 6-bar and 7-bar sections, provide perfect prosody with the lyric content. The marriage of music and words captures the feelings expressed and feelings withheld. Through the imbalanced phrase and lyric sections, you can literally see and feel someone pacing about a room, abruptly turning and moving in anxious despair.

In the context of the entire Lennon/McCartney catalog, "Baby's in Black" remains a sort of diamond in the rough. Never released as a single, nor heralded with the likes of "I Want to Hold Your Hand," "In My Life," or "Come Together," it takes its humble place as a watershed for Lennon in his exploration of the chorus in his own writing.

I'm a Loser

Words and Music by John Lennon and Paul McCartney

(Continued on following page)

-er, and I'm not what I ap - pear—— to be.——

Verse 2

> Although I laugh and I act like a clown,
> Beneath this mask I am wearing a frown.
> My tears are falling like rain from the sky.
> Is it for her or myself that I cry?

Verse 3

> What have I done to deserve such a fate,
> I realize I have left it too late.
> And so it's true pride comes before a fall.
> I'm telling you so that you won't lose all.

BACKGROUND

Title	I'm a Loser
Recording Date	August 14, 1964
Meter	4/4
Key	G major
Song Form	Verse/Chorus
Phrasing	Verse: *ab*
	Chorus: *aab*
Recording	*Beatles for Sale*
	1964 EMD/CAPITOL

As we move along to explore Lennon's acoustic side, the first whistle stop is the outstanding "I'm a Loser." Recorded for the *Beatles for Sale* album on August 14, 1964, Lennon has identified this song as a part of his acoustically influenced "Dylan period." The influence is clear in the song's harmonica solo section and ending.

John had confided to some of his inner circle that the song had its real genesis in a March 23, 1964 meeting between Lennon and British journalist Kenneth Allsop. Allsop suggested that Lennon move past the usual banal pop lyrics to pursue a more autobiographical path. Lennon had explored this approach earlier, to some extent, with two lesser-known original contributions to the *Please Please Me* album: "Ask Me Why" and "There's a Place," the latter of which I consider to be the precursor to "Strawberry Fields Forever." The Beatles had enjoyed great success with the standard boy/girl pop formula, but as the folk movement eclipsed the musical mainstream with more heady topics, the timing was right for them to begin to explore deeper topics of their own.

The song was released on the *Beatles for Sale* and *Beatles '65* albums, and on the *Beatles for Sale* EP, released on April 6, 1965.

STRUCTURE

Song Form

"I'm a Loser" seems to begin with an introductory verse à la "If I Fell," except that this opening section is rubato, or without a steady tempo. Unlike most introductory verses that never return (as in "If I Fell"), however, this opening section is actually a condensed version of the coming chorus.

Though this song is one of Lennon's acoustic creations, he chose the more pop-based verse/chorus format instead of the folk-based AB form:

Intro	Verse	Chorus	Verse	Chorus	Verse	Verse	Chorus	Verse
6 bars	16 bars	8 bars	16 bars	8 bars	Solo: 16 bars	8 bars	8 bars	Fade

Both "Baby's in Black" and "I'm a Loser" represent Lennon's earliest explorations of the verse/chorus format. As you can see, it winds up to be a pretty standard setup. Of course, there are a few Lennon twists. Among the interesting form anomalies are:

- Lennon uses only six, instead of eight, bars from the chorus as the introduction.
- The 16-bar verse is actually a double verse, consisting of two 8-bar sections that are musically identical. The norm is a single verse.
- The solo verse sections include the return of the trusty Lennon harmonica for the first eight bars. The solo section is also repeated at the end of the song for the fade-out. A chorus ending would have been more conventional.

Lyric

The opening lyric during the introduction is searing. It sets the scene beyond the shadow of a doubt: the singer declares right up front that he is a loser, and in fact, is a charlatan. A real attention-getter.

Lennon continues his compelling if somewhat disconnected story over the three verses. In verse 1 the singer characterizes his failed attempt at love as the girl having won. In fact, as you see, this pivotal lyric at the end of verse 1—that he should have known she would win—sets up the first chorus. Of course, the girl didn't really win anything. She just wasn't interested. But this lyrical notion of a victor, used only at the end of that first verse, is enough to give the chorus lyric its impact in presenting the opposite: a loser.

The introspective second verse lets the listener peer into the singer's heart. He reveals that he is living a life of emotional deception, pretending to be happy when he really is overcome with grief and confusion. Just at the end of the verse, he brings the girl back into it as justification for the feelings he has expressed.

In the final verse the singer begins to recede into himself, offering a moral as the song moves into the final chorus: a great fall is always preceded by prideful actions. Pretty deep stuff for a pop song.

PHRASING

Verse

▶ *Harmonic Phrasing*

The song is set in the key of G major, with a twist. The playful little chord progression upon which the verse melody is set darts back and forth between G major and G Mixolydian. The interplay between these two modes was to become a Lennon signature:

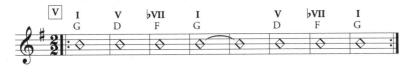

Fig. 3.11. Verse harmonic phrasing

The dominant chord in the second bar helps to establish the G major mode. The F major triad in third bar, however, establishes G Mixolydian mode. (See also "You Can't Do That," chapter 2.) Lennon loved this major/Mixolydian harmonic underpinning and used it throughout his writing career.

▶ *Melodic Phrasing*

As we combine the melody and lyric to decipher the song's phrasing, we note that Lennon has used a rather long 4-bar structure for the opening phrase of the verse section. The melody moves playfully around the stable B that begins and ends the phrase:

Fig. 3.12. Verse melodic section

The result is a 4-bar phrase, labeled ⓐ :

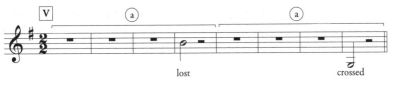

Fig. 3.13. Verse melodic phrasing

The second phrase of the verse is answered with another 4-bar ⓐ phrase, as illustrated in the example above. When this is repeated for an entire round of the 16-bar verse, the resulting verse phrase is a very square *aaaa* format.

Lennon often employed song sections that contained an odd number of bars. In this song, the use of the standard, square 16-bar format (4 + 4 + 4 + 4 = 16) provides a "humdrum-I'm-numb" background that heightens the impact of the lyric. In contrast to it, the lyric seems extremely dramatic.

Chorus

▶ *Harmonic Phrasing*

The chorus is entirely in G major except for an F major triad in bar 8. This gives us a hint of the modal interplay that will return in the verse:

Fig. 3.14. Chorus harmonic phrasing

The use of the more pop/jazz A minor-to-D chord changes that open the chorus is another complete turnabout from the more folk-influenced chord progression of the verse.

▶ *Melodic Phrasing*

The melodic phrasing for the chorus section provides even more contrast than the harmonic progression. Lennon moves to 2-bar phrasing in this section for an exciting and accelerated effect:

Fig. 3.15. Accelerated melodic phrasing

As you can see from the example below, the resulting phrasing for this section is *abab*:

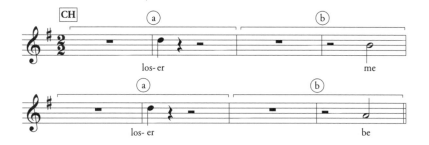

Fig. 3.16. Chorus melodic phrasing

Lennon simply repeats the phrasing exactly to complete the famous chorus for this song, adding only a single new lyric line to finish off the chorus—a modest but extremely effective technique.

PROSODY

Verse

The lyric for the verse is set into a square 16-bar section, but it is really heard as two repeating 8-bar sections. The harmonic rhythm for both sections is steady, with one chord per bar except at the turn-around in the chorus. The extremely square phrasing winds up being a perfect lens for this slightly detached song of cloaked despair. The happy, 8-bar sections function as the mask of happiness the singer wears while his feeling of loss rages within the lyric.

The melody for the verse begins so sweetly. Starting on the stable third note of the key, B, the melody moves upwards in an easy step-wise progression to D, which is emphasized by its placement on beat 1. Then, it moves back down to the restful and stable B in the fourth bar:

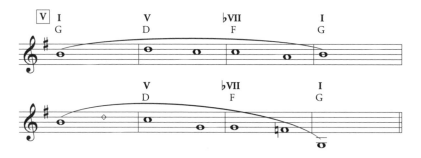

Fig. 3.17. Verse structural tones

The note D is emphasized in the second bar by its placement on beat 1. Then, it moves down to C in the third bar and finally returns to the restful and stable B in the fourth bar.

The second phrase begins exactly the same way, but suddenly the melody lurches downward with a bluesy feel at the F♮ in the seventh bar. Then the melody ends on the low tonic G, creating a dramatic outline of despair: it spans more than an octave in just a couple of bars. Most of Lennon's melodies are usually in the middle to high vocal range. It is extremely unusual indeed to find such a low note used in a song. (In fact, this is the lowest note Lennon ever wrote in any of his songs!)

This lower G resolves both the melody and the lyric. The two higher Gs at bars 6 and 7 do not provide final resolution, because they are played over the unstable D major and F major triads. Neither of those chords provide stability for the tonic note in this key. However, the lyric is unfinished at that point anyway, so these chords provide the necessary motion to finish both the lyric and melody in bar 8. The freefall melody is the perfect setting for the lyrics that end each of the two 8-bar verse sections—with such strong messages as losing, frowning, crying, and regret, respectively. (See verse lyrics on pages 71–72.) If these lyrics had been set to a melody that rose up to tonic, the effect would not be nearly as powerful.

Chorus

In the chorus melody, Lennon moves the starting pitch to the top of the song's range. This is the unstable E, which is La in the key. Its unstable nature creates playful motion up and down from its stable counterpart D before settling on the B once again by the fourth bar:

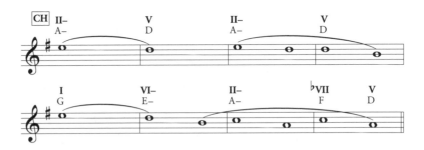

Fig. 3.18. Chorus structural tones

In the second and answering 4-bar phrase, the melody again makes an immediate stepwise descent to the unstable 2nd degree, A. With the insertion of two cadential chords—F major and D major—the song quickly pushes back into the verse.

At first the melody is set with A minor and D. The melody notes, E and D, are swallowed up in the two chords because they are chord tones. However, those same notes rest atop the new chords, G major and E minor, as nonchord tones in bars 4–8. This use of nonchord tones in the melody spotlights the lyric—which happens to be the title at that point—even more the second time.

That brings us to the other curious thing about the chorus: the melody for the title line has *two* different harmonic settings. While this is not completely unknown in the song repertoire, it is very unusual. Most pop songs using the verse/chorus format generally set the same lyric, melody, and harmony as a unit when repeating the title.

This early effort of Lennon's to master the chorus format shows he still had some work to hammer out. Its open ending (the unstable melody and harmony in bar 8) makes this section function slightly more like a connecting bridge than a stand-alone chorus. But the lyric is chorus all the way. Lennon straddles the fence on this one while he maps out an approach to writing these new kinds of song sections. Still in all, an extremely effective work.

SUMMARY

The motion in this song is quite unusual; it is a role reversal from the usual verse/chorus setup. We have a verse that closes down twice— way down to that low G! It's not uncommon to have a closed verse, but in this case the chorus is open and accelerated, as well—always ready to move quickly back to the verse again. Lennon's harmonic and melodic choices create all forward motion…so how does he end the song? Well, the Beatles themselves provide two answers. Listen to the recording and notice the classic fade-out during the second guitar/harmonica solo section.

The only other answer for a song with this structure would be an instrumental ending or coda section. I have seen a live performance of this song by the Beatles in which they did just that. They ended with the guitar solo as per the record, creating an instrumental outro. Then, they played a G major triad after the final F–D cadence.

Lennon's natural ability to reflect his feelings of honesty and confusion are displayed here in "I'm a Loser." Such self-effacement is a courageous topic for a star to tackle at the very moment of worldwide adulation. The song remains an excellent autobiographical vehicle by which Lennon lets us peer into his true heart for a moment, diverting our attention away from the illusory "Beatle John."

I Don't Want to Spoil the Party

Words and Music by John Lennon and Paul McCartney

Verse 2

I've had a drink or two and I don't care.

There's no fun in what I do if she's not there.

I wonder what went wrong,

I've waited far too long.

I think I'll take a walk and look for her.

BACKGROUND

Title	I Don't Want to Spoil the Party
Recording Date	September 29, 1964
Meter	2/2
Key	G major
Song Form	AABA
Phrasing	Verse (A): *aabba*
	Primary Bridge (B): *abab*
Recording	*Beatles for Sale*
	1964 EMD/CAPITOL

"I Don't Want to Spoil the Party" is another of Lennon's songs that reflect the influence of country and western music. The song is classic traditional songwriting form—with a few Lennon curve balls along the way.

John indicated in interviews that this was a "deeply personal" song (Dowdling, 1989). Recorded by the group on September 29, 1964, right in the midst of Beatlemania, Lennon was finding it difficult to maintain the witty, charming, ever-entertaining Beatles image required at the many parties and gatherings on the Beatles' expansive social agenda. According to Steve Turner in his book, *A Hard Day's Write* (New York: Harper Collins Publishers, 1994), Lennon and the rest of the Beatles were always looking for a respite from the chaos of fame. On tour, recharge time was frequently unavailable. The lyric from this Lennon song was inspired by these experiences. The song is at once an accessible pop classic and an autobiographical account of his deeper, road-worn emotions.

The song was recorded on September 29, 1964 and released in England on the *Beatles for Sale* album. It also appeared on the American *Beatles '65* album in December 1964, released for the holiday market.

Song Form

Lennon returns to his use of the classic AABA form. In this song, each A represents a verse/refrain, and the B represents the primary bridge. The lyric that often accompanies this form includes three verses, but this one employs only two verses. Lennon repeats the first verse in place of writing a new third verse, spotlighting the title once again before it disappears forever. In the Beatles' recorded performance, the final form is as follows:

A	A	B	A	A	B	A
Verse 1*	Verse 2	Primary Bridge	Verse 1*	Solo	Primary Bridge	Verse 2
16 bars	16 bars	12 bars	16 bars	16 bars	12 bars	16 bars

The asterisk (*) indicates the only two title statements in the course of the song.

Lyric Content

The refrain or title setting occurs only at the beginning of the first verse. Usually, a refrain occurs in every verse, whether it be at the beginning or the end. The refrain gives the song a sing-along character; that's the line that we can all join in to sing. However, because the refrain only occurs once, this song fits better in the listen-to category.

The story tells us of a fellow who is at a party without his girl-friend. There has been some difficulty between them, we find, but he still hopes for her to appear. Meanwhile, he is in a state of confusion. He leaves the party to find her. Lennon has spun his personal search for a respite into a song of unrequited love.

PHRASING

Verse

▶ *Harmonic Phrasing*
First, let's inspect the harmonic chord progression:

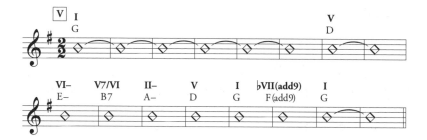

Fig. 3.19. Verse harmonic phrasing

The verse begins on the tonic chord and remains there for a full six bars before moving to the dominant D7. The first 8-bar section is then answered with a contrasting 8-bar section. In the first four bars of the second half of the verse, the harmony progresses quickly through several chords. This rapid harmonic rhythm provides great motion and a sense of anxiety to support the lyric at that point. The protagonist declares that the party offers nothing to him and that he will disappear.

The second four bars of this second part are made up of a I–♭VII–I cadence on the tonic G. An example of his signature Mixolydian cadence, it delays the full arrival on the tonic. Second, this bland cadence supports the somewhat ambiguous lyrics.

> *Melodic Phrasing*

True to its classic 16-bar setup, the lyric of each verse is set to a traditional structure that is, for the most part, divided into four 4-bar sections:

Fig. 3.20. Verse melodic phrasing

To achieve contrast and some forward motion, Lennon's lyric splits the next 4-bar unit into two 2-bar phrases. The final phrase is exactly like the first two, as the verse comes home to itself and returns to its opening phrase structure. The final rhyming word in the verse, "know," creates closure and punctuates the phrase ending with a rhyme of phrases 1 and 2.

Though the lyric content and rhyme is different for verse 2, the structure of the lyric, melody, rhythm, and harmony is the same as that of verse 1.

Primary Bridge

▶ Harmonic Phrasing

The chord progression at the primary bridge is a splendid contrast to the verse section. (The dark lines that bookend the bridge are called **repeat signs**; they indicate that the section repeats.):

Fig. 3.21. Primary bridge harmonic phrasing

The primary bridge begins on the tonic, but unlike the verse, the bridge has an open ending with the very forward-moving V chord, D. The use of the chromatic A major triad at the fourth bar introduces a nondiatonic C♯ to the mix to spotlight the lyric "still." This harmonic choice articulates the integral lyric at that point to say, "I *still* love her."

Lennon composed a 12-bar bridge, a departure from the more typical 8-bar form. The bridge is divided into two repeating 6-bar sections, as shown below:

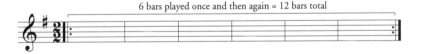

Fig. 3.22. Primary bridge with two repeating 6-bar phrases

▶ Melodic Phrasing

The phrasing structure of the primary bridge is classic but unusually executed. Its length is twelve bars, which is often associated with blues. When used in blues, the 12-bar form usually is divided into three 4-bar sections. Lennon, however, divides the twelve bars into alternating 2- and 4-bar sections. This creates two larger, balanced 6-bar sections that repeat. The expected phrase construction in 12-bar blues is this:

|| 4 bars | 4 bars | 4 bars ||

But the phrase construction for "I Don't Want to Spoil the Party" is this:

|| 2 bars | 4 bars | 2 bars | 4 bars ||

The result is *abab* phrasing for the bridge, as illustrated below:

Fig. 3.23. Primary bridge melodic phrasing

PROSODY

Verse

As we examine the verse a bit closer, we find that it contains a very static melody based predominantly on the note D. D is a stable note (Sol) in this key, and its constant repetition acts as a great tension-builder while a fast-moving melodic rhythm creates a percussive volley that helps propel the lyric and story. The verse section, as illustrated below, is divided into three 4-bar and two 2-bar melodic phrases:

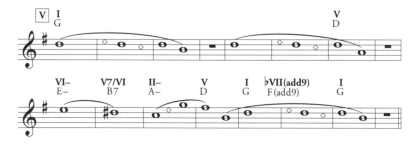

Fig. 3.24. Verse structural tones

Let's look at the 4-bar phrases first. Though the melodies for the first phrase (first four bars) and the last phrase (last four bars) are exactly the same, they have two totally different effects. In the first phrase, an ever-so-slight movement forward is created by ending on the semi-stable note B in bar 4.

When the same melody repeats in the last phrase, Lennon puts the brakes on by using a harmonic cadence of G to F(add9) to G. At the same time, he presses the accelerator by using the slightly forward-moving B for the melodic ending at bar 15. This musical treatment wholly supports the context of Lennon's ambivalent lyric, musically saying "I want to stay . . . I want to go . . . Is she coming? Have you seen her?"

While the first and last phrases provide stability of sorts, the second phrase (bars 5–8), with its conclusion on the unstable A (Re), creates the kind of forward motion that is usually found in verses. The harmonic progression, static on the tonic chord for a full six bars, provides a welcome change to the unstable D7. This keeps the verse from coming to a dead halt.

Lennon creates an excellent lyric spotlight in these phrases by inserting the unstable note E (La) in the second bar of each phrase. This showcases the most important verse lyrics:

Fig. 3.25. Verse melodic segment

Lennon uses this powerful unstable note to emphasize these lyrics from verse 1: "party," "disappointment," and "gone." Just those three words alone give the listener the sense that something is amiss.

Turning now to the four bars that comprise the third and fourth phrases of the verse, we find plenty of movement. The two 2-bar phrases really begin to churn things up. Here's a close-up of that 4-bar section:

Fig. 3.26. Verse structural tones, phrases 3 and 4

This is the most active part of the verse. The move to 2-bar phrases creates acceleration after the more slowly moving 4-bar phrases. To compound the action, both phrases contain the most unstable melodic endings for the entire verse section: D♯ (bar 2) and F♯ (bar 4)—and they rhyme!

The D♯ at the end of the first phrase is completely outside the key of G and is interacting with the unstable E to create the most unstable phrase of all. The second phrase returns the melody to G major, but instability still reigns, because the phrase ends on the most unstable note in this key, F♯ (Ti). The D♯ and the F♯ spotlight these rhyming lyrics over the course of the song: "here" and "disappear," and "wrong" and "long." Lennon sustains the confusion by leaving the F♯ hanging in the air and melodically unresolved during the verse.

Primary Bridge

The delayed resolution doesn't last long, though. At the primary bridge, what do we find? G! Twelve of them, in fact. In just the bridge melody, both the melody and harmony resoundingly strike the note G and hammer the tonic chord, G major. In a way, this is the resolution the verse melody was begging for:

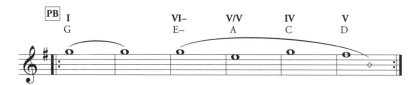

Fig. 3.27. Primary bridge structural tones

The bridge tends to sound and function a little bit like a chorus. First, it arrives at tonic in both the melody and harmony, and second, the melodic rhythm slows down, moving to four whole notes at four beats each!

This kind of treatment tends to have a static feel and is more commonly found in choruses. Very often choruses contain long-note statements of the title with lots of movement toward tonic in both harmony and melody. Bridges, whose usual role is to connect sections, usually have faster harmonic and melodic rhythm. Further, this bridge includes a repeating lyric—again, just what one might expect from a chorus.

The main thing that keeps this section in the "bridge" category is the unresolved F♯ over the dominant D triad at the end of the section. The dominant chord provides a sense of movement back into the tonic-centered verse, as is the function of the typical primary bridge.

SUMMARY

Many times in this song Lennon mixed modes, and this was very effective in the overall connection of music and lyrics. Most of the verse section has a happy, major (Ionian) flavor until the ambiguous Mixolydian flavor of the last four bars. For example, the final harmonic cadence in the verse section is:

G major to F major to G major

Technically, this is no big deal. It happens all the time in songs. The thing is, immediately preceding the first G major chord is a D7 chord that contains an F♯. The F major triad obviously contains an F♮. The 7th degree, in this case F♯, strongly establishes the major (or Ionian mode) sound. The ♭7, or F♮ in the key of G, helps to establish the Mixolydian sound.

The use of the less cheery Mixolydian sound enhances the uncertainty of the situation described in the lyric. The music chosen for this song is so sweet and delightful, it hardly sends out a message of confusion—until we examine the melody carefully. Then we find that the entire song remains unresolved, as does the lyric. It is yet another exhibition of Lennon's innate grasp of perfect prosody.

In a way, Lennon's straddling solution of creating a choruslike bridge goes well with the impact of the lyric. In the lyric, there is some resolution and some movement, but everything is stilted somehow. The lyrics create a scenario that reveals the singer's restlessness at a party. Lennon's choice of unresolved melody and harmony supports this premise entirely.

And so we see the true meaning of the lyric. The story works on multiple levels. Behind the party narrative, interviews indicate that Lennon was using "I Don't Want to Spoil the Party" as a metaphorical vehicle to explore his own discomfort in social situations during those Beatlemania days. The song is an ode through which he indirectly addresses the unrealistic "celebrity" expectations placed on him as a living, feeling human being.

I Feel Fine

Words and Music by John Lennon and Paul McCartney

Verse 2

Baby says she's mine, you know,

She tells me all the time, you know,

She said so.

I'm in love with her and I feel fine.

Verse 3

That her baby buys her things, you know,

He buys her diamond rings, you know,

She said so.

She's in love with me and I feel fine.

BACKGROUND

Title	I Feel Fine
Recording Date	October 18, 1964
Meter	2/2
Key	G major
Song Form	AABA
Phrasing	Verse (A): *abc*
	Primary Bridge (B): *aa*
Recording	*Beatles: Past Masters, Volume One*
	1988 EMD/CAPITOL

The Beatles' recorded version of this great John Lennon song is one of the most "electric" moments in rock history. The song begins with Paul McCartney plucking an A on his Hofner bass—but it quickly escalates into otherwordly, screaming feedback. With John's Gibson J-160E acoustic guitar positioned carefully in the studio to receive the note and produce the tension-building sawtooth distortion, the song blasts off when John plays the main instrumental figure on another guitar, his trusty Rickenbacker electric. What is so ironic about this startling, electric feedback introduction is that it is accomplished on an acoustic guitar. Leave it to Lennon to come up with a creation like that!

The striking feedback makes a terrific beginning to one of Lennon's most accessible songs. It's the kind of sound one might expect to hear in "Strawberry Fields" or "Walrus"—but the listener instead is immediately treated to an uplifting lyric and melody.

Lennon said that he wrote this song in the recording studio, based on the now-famous guitar riff that is now so strongly associated with the song (Dowdling, 1989). It was recorded on October 18, 1964. The single was released on November 23 in America and on November 27 in England. The song featured each of the Beatles on their respective instruments, including John on lead vocal and Paul and George on backup vocals. The song remained available only as a single until December 1966, when it appeared on the *A Collection of Oldies* album released only in England. It was later re-released on March 7, 1988 in America on *Past Masters, Volume One*.

STRUCTURE

Introduction
The song begins with an instrumental introduction that contains the same rhythmic figure used in the verse melody. The figure is shown at right:

Fig. 3.28. Intro melody

It's a very clever figure built into a bluesy context. Harmonically, the line implies the traditional V7–IV7–I movement associated with the blues style. The repeating figure is two bars long. It descends and repeats three times, creating an 8-bar introduction.

The repeating 2-bar figure is structured so that the first bar (shown in bars 1, 3, 5, and 7) features the root of each 7th chord, while the second bar (repeated in bars 2, 4, 6, and 8) provides a classic "4-3" dissonance associated with rock and folk melodies. (The melodic sequence of a 4th moving to a 3rd was used by many songwriters in the twentieth century.)

As the riff descends, the last two repetitions establish G as tonic. The D7 and C7 chords that precede it function as the common progression, V7–IV7–I. The G7 repeats twice and dominates as tonic.

Song Form

The song form for "I Feel Fine" is classic AABA. The performance form for the recording is AABA/AABA. The fourth A contains the lead guitar solo, the fifth A repeats verse 2, and the sixth and last A repeats verse 3. The form is illustrated as follows:

- Song Form

A	A	B	A
Verse 1	Verse 2	Primary Bridge	Verse 3
10 bars	10 bars	8 bars	10 bars

- Performance Form

A	A	B	A	A (solo)	A	B	A
10 bars	10 bars	8 bars	10 bars	10 bars	10 bars	8 bars	10 bars

Lyric Content

"I Feel Fine" is simply a song of the exhilaration of newfound love. She's good to me, she's happy, she's mine, and it feels great.

Lennon does provide an interesting lyrical thread, however, by using two key words continually throughout the song: "baby" and "you know." The repetition of these words provides a playful competition with the title itself. Normally, the verse does not include very much repetition; that is usually reserved for the title section of the song. Lennon's use of such repetition was to become a mainstay of many of his song lyrics.

There are actually only three verses, but in the Beatles' performance, the second and third verses are repeated, creating five separate uses of both the title and the word "baby." Lennon uses repetion to build… to build… to build… (Enough already!)…to build tension. (See what I mean?) Since the phrase "you know" is repeated twice in each verse, the listener is treated to this very Lennon-esque tension builder a total of ten times. Quite noticeable since the total length of the song is only 2:18!

PHRASING

Verse

▶ Harmonic Phrasing

The harmonic progression for "I Feel Fine" is blues based, featuring the familiar I7, IV7, and V7 blues chords (G7, C7, and D7 in this key). A typical 12-bar blues progression is this:

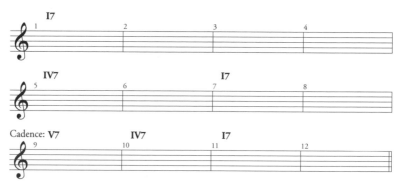

Fig. 3.29. Typical blues harmonic progression

While the 12-bar structure is standard for such blues harmonies, Lennon adds his mark by fashioning an unusual 10-bar blues to create a pop hit.

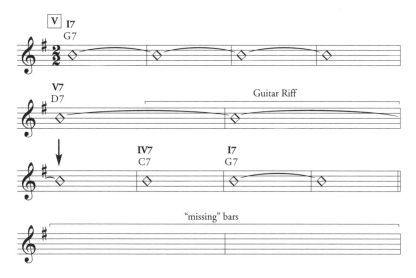

Fig. 3.30. Verse harmonic phrasing

Compared to the typical blues progression in fig. 3.29, the harmonic rhythm pattern is most unusual—but extremely effective. The extra bar of D7 at bar 7 is what makes Lennon's unusual blues setup so effective. (See arrow, fig. 3.30.) This bar functions both as the last bar of the 3-bar D7 phrase and as the first bar of the final cadence (D7 to C7 to G7). The result is a beautifully dovetailed harmonic phrase that gives the D7 a double duty—thus completing the blues progression, but in a deceptively condensed fashion. This definitely bears the Lennon stamp.

▶ Melodic Phrasing

The phrasing of the lyric splits the 10-bar verse into three parts:

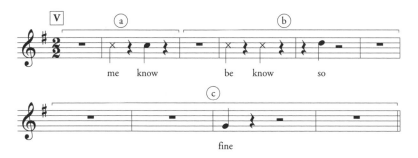

Fig. 3.31. Verse melodic phrasing

The resultant *abc* form shows a slight phrase deceleration. That is, shorter phrases move to loooooonnnger phrases. . . . This coincides exactly with the smooth lyric phrasing for the refrain and title: "I feel fiiiiine."

Despite the phrasal deceleration, internal rhyme keeps the verse persistently moving forward. The rhymes of "me" and "be," both set on the strong beat 1 of their respective bars, are very effective toward this end. Also the infectious "you know" is repeated once, and is set on the slightly stable beat 3, while the rhyming "so" is set on the forward-moving beat 2.

Lennon succeeds in bringing the verse to a satisfying conclusion by setting the last word of the title, "fine," on beat 1 of that strong ninth bar. Many songwriters, including Lennon, go to great lengths to see that their title rhymes with another line in the song. Oddly enough, that doesn't happen here. In this song, while Lennon uses lots of internal rhyme to create forward motion in the verse, the lack of it in the refrain helps spotlight the title.

Primary Bridge

▶ *Harmonic Phrasing*

The harmonic progression for the primary bridge is a wonderful contrast, strictly in G major rather than G blues:

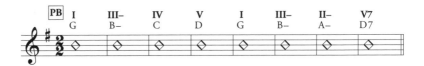

Fig. 3.32. Primary bridge harmonic phrasing

In the bridge, the first four bars are repeated to create a standard 8-bar bridge. The only difference between the two 4-bar sections is that the C triad is replaced with the softer A minor triad at the end. Lennon's substitution of the mellow minor triad provides a most subtle change to distinguish the two halves of the bridge.

The harmony in both sections follows standard harmonic tendencies: the verse sections close with tonic, while the bridge section is left open with a dominant that pulls the bridge forward into the next verse.

▶ *Melodic Phrasing*

The lyric of the bridge also splits the music into two 4-bar phrases. The rhyming lyrics "girl" and "world" reinforce the two parts:

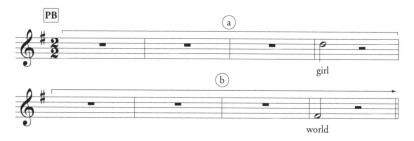

Fig. 3.33. Primary bridge melodic phrasing

Here Lennon employs a lyrical overlap to connect back to the third verse. The lyric in the second phrase of the bridge doesn't actually end until the first phrase of the third verse, with the now-familiar "you know" phrase.

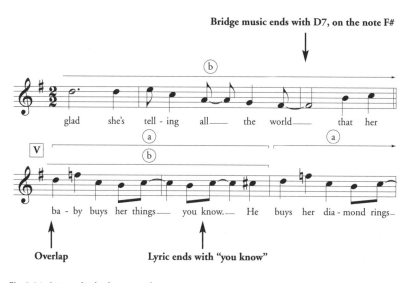

Fig. 3.34. Primary bridge/verse overlap

The ultimate effect is that the 6-bar lyrical phrase is strung over the end of one section and the beginning of another: The music of the verse begins, but the bridge lyric overlaps into the verse music for another two bars. This overlap only happens coming out of the bridge into the third verse. The overlapping lyric creates much melody motion, and doubles the feeling of intensity. As a result, this proves to be the most exhilarating part of the song.

The phrasing of the bridge is a stroke of genius. Lennon manages to transform a rather square 8-bar bridge into a 10-bar overlap by simply continuing the lyric into the next section. The result is a 4 + 6 combination instead of the expected 4 + 4.

PROSODY

Verse

With the lyric phrasing as a guide, the first six bars of the verse are divided into a 2-bar phrase followed by a 4-bar phrase. The final phrase moves from D down to the tonic note G, stopping off for a bluesy B♭ on the way down:

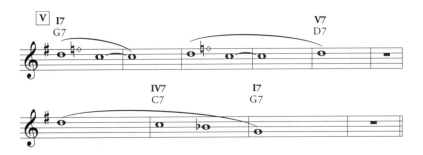

Fig. 3.35. Verse structural tones

When the melody finally enters after the intro at the beginning of the verse, the C is in slight conflict with the B in the G7 chord for a series of melodic suspensions that remind me of someone skipping stones across a lake. The 4-3 (Fa to Mi) suspension in the melody seems to skip and float as the C interacts with its resolution note, B. This is the same 4-3 resolution heard earlier in the song's musical introduction. Like many great composers, Lennon develops a melodic motif and peppers it throughout the song. He uses a pinch of the melody in the introduction to foreshadow its later entrance, without stating the melody explicitly.

The use of the bluesy F♮ in the verse melody and its infectious grind, in conjunction with the floating C, creates the melodic excitement needed to support this lyric. The G7 chord continues as the only chord in the harmonic progression for a full four bars. Because the harmony is somewhat static, the melody really has to deliver. And, it does so effortlessly in Lennon's engaging, suspension-filled melody. During this section, he uses that suspended C no less than six times, sometimes resolving down to B before finally moving up to D in bar 5 of the verse.

The final 4-bar phrase that states the title (line 2) offers up the tonic by the end of the phrase. Lennon has finished teasing the listener with the unresolved, suspended 4th and calls for melody, lyric, and harmony to come together to close the verse. Before the final tonic, however, he strikes a typically Lennon-esque bluesy B♭ on the way down for the finish. This contrasts the bright and upbeat B♮s from the earlier phrases in a classic Lennon fashion.

Primary Bridge

The melodic rhythm slows dramatically to half notes at the primary bridge, emphasizing the lyric, "I'm so glad." Long notes emphasize lyrics, particularly when set in juxtaposition to faster-moving lyrics that occur before or after.

Fig. 3.36. Slowed melodic rhythm spotlights lyrics in primary bridge

The first phrase is melodically static, emphasizing the melody note D, briefly flirting with the E and C above and below it:

Fig. 3.37. Primary bridge structural tones

The second phrase, by contrast, ends with a melodic flourish that spans an interval of a seventh in a single bar:

Fig. 3.38. Primary bridge melodic flourish

This melodic flourish ends on the unstable F♯ (Ti), creating a direct, jet-propelled movement right back into the verse. This unstable F♯ (Ti) finally resolves to G (Do) at the end of verse 3.

SUMMARY

"I Feel Fine" is one of the happiest songs I've ever heard in my life. The skipping-stones-on-a-sunny-day melody in the verse contrasts beautifully with the melody of the exuberant bridge, which tacks the lyric up like a heart carved in a tree near the ol' swimmin' hole.

The most powerful bar in the song is the overlap from the last bar of the bridge into the third verse. There is so much action there. It shoots out of the bridge and rushes into the verse as if coming out of a loop on a roller coaster ride. The melody quickly descends the gargantuan span of a seventh in only one bar. This is a surprise, as such as large down-leap would be more normally be used to set a rather sad lyric. However, Lennon's carefully crafted lyric is not finished by the end of the bridge. Like a roller coaster, its rapid descent only prepares us for the next ascent. To reach completion, it revs up unexpectedly as it connects with and captures the optimistic, skipping verse melody that follows.

This song really *is* like a ride on a roller coaster—or a rocket! From the moment you hear that first bass note, so soft, so subtle, so natural—followed by its transformation into jarring feedback—you are drawn into its otherworldly yawp of primal vibration. The odyssey continues until the end of the song…yet the song doesn't really end. It fades out, as if it were speeding back into the cosmos. After a ride like that, who could possibly *want* it to end?

CHAPTER 4   1965

The year 1965 proved to be a year of expansion in the area of song form for John Lennon. Until this year he relied mainly on the standard form of the twentieth century up to that point: AABA. However, as we will explore in this chapter, Lennon had begun to embrace many new forms:

- Verse/Chorus with Primary Bridge
- Verse/Refrain
- ABA
- AB (a variation on the verse/refrain form)
- Verse/Chorus with Instrumental Interlude

Lennon, ever searching for new ways to express himself in song, successfully experimented with folk forms even more than he did with blues. His astute sense of the pop idiom enabled him to incorporate and transform other song forms to fit in the pop realm. In our view from the twenty-first century, we can see and hear that, in the process, Lennon in fact expanded the scope of all songwriting. Despite his proclivity for experimentation, he kept the need for pop simplicity foremost in his mind. Though most of Lennon's songs contained complexities both in music and lyric, he was always aware that ultimately a simple, modest theme would be the one that would resonate with the largest audience.

The songs we will examine from this historic year are:

"Ticket to Ride"
"You've Got to Hide Your Love Away"
"Norwegian Wood"
"Day Tripper"
"In My Life"

Each song, in its own way, will reveal a steadily maturing songwriter. Written over a short eight-month period in 1965, these songs provide an excellent inside view of Lennon's new approach to form.

Ticket to Ride

Words and Music by John Lennon and Paul McCartney

(Continued on following page)

chapter 4 · ticket to ride

featured in the Motion Picture HELP!
Copyright © 1965 Sony/ATV Songs LLC
Copyright Renewed
All Rights Administered by Sony/ATV Music Publishing, 8 Music Square West, Nashville, TN 37203
International Copyright Secured All Rights Reserved

think twice,   she ough-ta do right   by   me.   I

Coda   A

My   ba-by don't   care.

Verse 2

She said that living with me is bringing her down, yeah!

For she would never be free when I was around.

She's got a ticket to ride,

She's got a ticket to ride,

She's got a ticket to ride but she don't care!

BACKGROUND

Title	Ticket to Ride
Recording Date	February 15, 1965
Meter	4/4
Key	A major
Song Form	Verse/Chorus with Primary Bridge
Phrasing	Verse: *aab*
	Chorus: *aab*
	Primary Bridge: *aaab*
Recording	*Help!*
	1965 EMD/CAPITOL

Lennon claimed that "Ticket to Ride" was the first heavy metal record in pop history. While that assertion might be up for dispute, it is certainly true as far as the Beatles' repertoire is concerned. The song's 12-string guitar introduction automatically lightens its impact, but the strident beat and feel of the song is heavier than any previous Beatles song.

As the story goes, it was Paul who came up with the song's characteristic syncopated drum pattern. His emphatic bass line and screaming high harmonies also contributed greatly to accomplishing Lennon's heavy-metal vision for this song (Dowdling, 1989).

"Ticket to Ride" was included in the Beatles' second movie, *Help!* The song was released as a single in England on April 9, 1965 and in America on April 19. Both sides of the single were one-hundred-percent Lennon songs: Side A was "Ticket to Ride" and side B was "Yes It Is, " John's attempted rewrite of "This Boy" (1963). Previously, John and Paul had split the A-sides and B-sides. "Ticket to Ride" also appeared on the *Help!* album, which was released later that summer on August 6, 1965 in England and exactly one week later in America.

STRUCTURE

Song Form

The form for "Ticket to Ride" is an interesting variation on the AABA format. It is one of the earliest pop songs to push the envelope on this standard form. The song is an embryonic form of the verse/chorus with primary bridge format, though it sounds very close to the standard classic AABA. Both the verse and chorus are eight bars long, creating a 16-bar section that may be thought of as an A section. The "middle eight" takes the form of the 9-bar primary bridge, which may be thought of as B. The modern interpretation of this form is:

A	A	B	A
Verse/Chorus	Verse/Chorus	Primary Bridge	Verse/Chorus
8 + 8 bars	8 + 8 bars	9 bars	8 + 8 bars

Lyric Content

The lyric tells the story of a young man who appears to be losing the affection of his girlfriend. In the two verses, the singer tells of his sadness at the imminent departure of his lover, for he had made her feel imprisoned.

The bridge lyric, however, counters with an "instant karma" warning. He advises her to be sure that she has thought everything through completely before taking action. This lyrical strategy is found in many of Lennon's songs. He delivers a story or observation passionately in the verse, but then balances it in the bridge with the opposite side of the story. As we shall see throughout his works, Lennon had a proclivity for embracing contradiction as a means of expressing the mixed emotion that so often accompanies humanity's deepest experiences.

PHRASING

Verse

▶ Harmonic Phrasing

The harmonic chord progressions for the verse and the chorus are diametrically opposed. That is, the verse utilizes a slow harmonic rhythm and ends with open harmony. The chorus, in contrast, utilizes a fast harmonic rhythm and ends closed. The slow harmonic rhythm in the verses creates a contemplative mood as the lyric muses, "I think I'm gonna be sad," and "she said that living with me is bringing her down." Note the slower harmonic rhythm in the verse:

Fig. 4.1. Verse harmonic phrasing

Staying on the single chord builds tension and creates an effective build-up to the heavy rock sound that Lennon unleashes in the chorus. The tension continues to build at bar 5, with the move from the A triad to the A7 chord. The final II–V cadence (B minor to E7) sweeps the verse away from its grounded tonic to the chorus.

An oddity about the verse: the guitar lyric that is contained in the introduction continues over the first four bars while the A triad is being sounded:

Fig. 4.2. "Ticket to Ride" guitar riff

The arrows above the A and the B, the tonic and 2nd scale degrees, indicate the two most potent notes in the riff. The riff ends on the B, while the E eighth note acts as a pickup note to the repeated riff. Ending repeatedly on the B has two dramatic effects. Its repetition drives the verse forward like mad. Second, the note gives the A triad a more unsettled nature by creating an Asus2 (or A(add9)) feel. Suspended chords, abbreviated as "sus," lack the definitive 3rd of the chord and as a result always have a somewhat uncertain, ambiguous sound.

Lennon's combination of these two treatments—the long sojourn on the tonic chord and the interjection of the competitive sus2 guitar riff—causes the opening bars of the verse to generate tension and forward motion into the chorus.

▶ Melodic Phrasing

The phrasing employed for the verse section is simple, making the song very easy to sing along with after just one or two hearings:

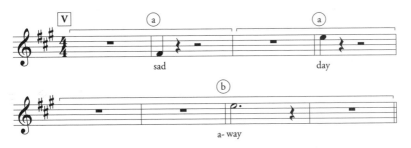

Fig. 4.3. Verse melodic phrasing

There is a good reason that "Ticket to Ride" is one of the most singable of all of Lennon's compositions: its symmetrical phrasing. Utilizing a standard 8-bar section, Lennon constructs the verse, beginning with two simple 2-bar ⓐ phrases. Then he answers those two phrases with a complementary 4-bar ⓑ phrase, creating an easily grasped *aab* inner form for the verse.

Both of the 2-bar statements create an accelerated effect, because they end on weak bars 2 and 4. The 4-bar phrase introduces deceleration, because longer phrases following a short phrase tend to slow the overall motion of the phrase. The 4-bar phrase also ends on the strong bar 7, supporting the deceleration slightly. This deceleration sends out a signal of change, which is the coming chorus section. The chorus arrives with a return to the accelerated phrasing pattern that began the verse.

Chorus

▶ Harmonic Phrasing

The harmonic progression for the chorus is much more active than the grounded verse section. The chorus is where the song takes off, making a splendid contrast to the verse.

Fig. 4.4. Chorus harmonic phrasing

Like many classic choruses, this one starts on a chord that gives movement, the tonic substitute, F♯ minor. It leads into a final cadence on tonic, A major. At the end of the chorus, the melody is on Do, the harmony is on the I chord, the rhythm of the melody ends on beat 1, and the lyric ends with a conclusive, "and she don't care." This provides well-defined harmonic closure to support closure in the song's other main elements: melody and lyric.

▶ Melodic Phrasing

The same *aab* phrasing is used for the chorus. This repetitive phrasing pattern lends an accessibility and familiarity that contributes to the popular and commercial success of this great song:

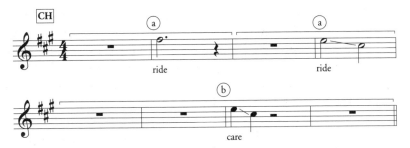

Fig. 4.5. Chorus melodic phrasing

Even though "ride" is treated with a melisma, I analyze the phrase as being two bars long, because when looking at words and music together, the phrase ends with the last syllable sung—not the last note sung. For instance, take a closer look at a 2-bar excerpt from the chorus:

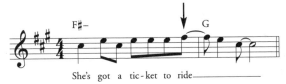

Fig. 4.6. 2-bar chorus excerpt

The phrase ends at the beginning of the G major bar, right where the singer sings the lyric "ride" with the F♯. Without the addition of new words or syllables, the impact of the continuing E and C♯ is greatly diminished. Together, the inner forms of the verse and chorus create a balance (*aab*/*aab*), which gives both sections a connection as a whole.

Primary Bridge

▶ Harmonic Phrasing

For the primary bridge, Lennon returns to a slower harmonic rhythm reminiscent of the verse. Like the verse, the bridge retains its opening D7 chord for several bars before moving to the E7. That elongated chord motion is a total departure from the chorus:

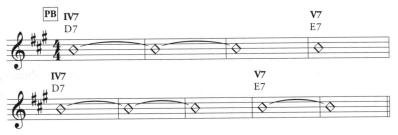

Fig. 4.7. Primary bridge harmonic phrasing

Lennon does not use the tonic chord at all in the primary bridge—quite common practice in composing bridges. As we have discussed in previous chapters, the tonic would slow down what is a typically forward-moving song section. In effective songwriting, choruses summarize and bridges move. Lennon chose only the simple and forward-moving IV7 and V7 chords, D7 and E7, for this section.

The primary bridge for "Ticket to Ride" is the only section that is nine, instead of eight, bars long. The extra bar suspends the bridge in mid-air, with the aid of the George Harrison guitar lick in those last two bars. Then, the bridge comes crashing down, once again back to the droning A triad of the verse.

◗ Melodic Phrasing

The bridge phrasing exercises both repetition and deception. Another uniquely Lennon trait surfaces: making two opposing ideas work together in perfect balance. As the bridge gets underway, repetition signals that this will be the classic *aaaa* format, but Lennon surprises us with an *aaab* structure instead:

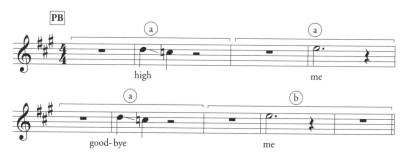

Fig. 4.8. Primary bridge melodic phrasing

After three ⓐ phrases, an extra bar is thrust upon the listener. This imposes a fleeting moment of chaos. It looks like an ⓐ, it sounds like an ⓐ . . . but with that extra ninth bar, we have a ⓑ. The extra bar sets up a moment of imbalance, and the unexpected guitar lick that leads the bridge back to the verse provides a twinkling, blissful suspended moment.

PROSODY

Verse

The verse melody marches proudly up through the chord tones of the tonic chord before slamming into that D in bar 1 on the lyric "gonna." Lennon puts both the melody and lyric right up front:

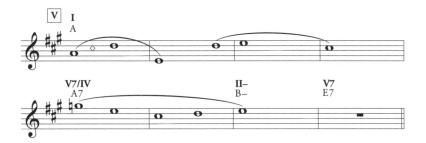

Fig. 4.9. Verse structural tones

The D in the melody brings the lyric "gonna" to the forefront; the lyric is spotlighted because the D is not present in the tonic chord A (bar 1). You may recall that Lennon used nonchord tones successfully both in "I Feel Fine" and "You Can't Do That" to spotlight lyrics. Both of those songs, in the key of G, featured the nonchord tone C with exactly the same effect.

After the first phrase, the D makes a playful, syncopated bounce ("today") up to the stable E before falling off to the C♯ in the second phrase (bars 2, 3, and 4). Then the melody makes a dramatic leap up a tritone to the high nondiatonic G (bar 4 going to 5). The last phrase moves back down, and ends with the same D-and-E interplay heard earlier in the second phrase.

Lennon was wise to design a melody with such great motion and activity. It works well against the static tonic pedal (repeated bass note) created by the sustained A chord (bars 1–6). It spotlights the lyric and creates tension as the melody progresses into the chorus.

Chorus

Lennon is passionate in his delivery of the chorus melody. Note that each subsequent phrase gets longer than the previous: first three notes, then four, then five. This creates a deceleration into the ending—the perfect prescription to bring the chorus to a conclusion.

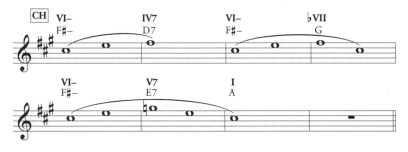

Fig. 4.10. Chorus structural tones

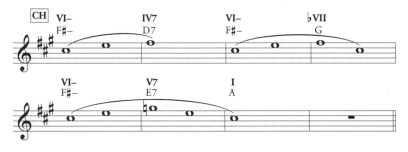 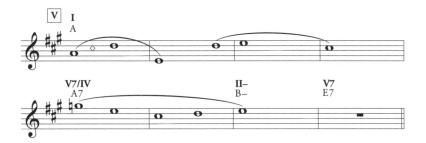

The first line of the chorus features two teasing movements up to the F♯. Each is set with the lyric "ride" from the title (bars 2 and 4). A very passionate moment is created in the second phrase, as the F♯ moves down to the C♯. Neither of these notes are chord tones of the nondiatonic G triad (bar 4). In this bar, F♯ becomes a stinging major 7th tension, while the stable C♯ acts as the melodramatic #11th tension. The melody then makes a final ascent to the bluesy G♮ before it falls away back down to the stable C♯ in bar 7 to close down the chorus. This fall-off approach to the melodic ending is an excellent support to the resigned lyric, "She don't care!"

Primary Bridge

Lennon's melodic treatment in the bridge utilizes a tried-and-true Lennon technique: the static melody.

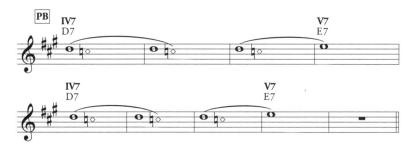

Fig. 4.11. Primary bridge structural tones

The static bridge melody contrasts well with the active verse and chorus melodies. For the bridge melody, Lennon simply exploits three simple notes: D, E, and C♮. The D, so skillfully used in the verse and completely omitted in the chorus, now makes a reappearance as the governing note in the bridge. The main contrast for the bridge melody is the introduction of the bluesy C♮. This contributes to the gospel/blues-flavored sound in this section and sets it apart from the other two sections.

Here again, Lennon brilliantly weaves motion and stasis into a complete, balanced unit. You will see in the lead sheet that Lennon introduces faster moving sixteenth-note rhythms for the lyrics "She oughta think twice," and "she oughta do right by me." The longer harmonic rhythm on the D7 chord provides stasis, while the C♮ and the sixteenth notes provide motion. It is another Lennon success—he has created the perfect bridge with just three notes and two chords.

SUMMARY

Using his expanded view of the standard AABA form as a backdrop, Lennon fashioned something quite new in "Ticket to Ride." Up until now the A in the AABA form always represented the standard verse/refrain. But in his effort to write a heavier rock song, Lennon began to think of the A as a verse/chorus combination.

Rather than having a simple, single statement of the title line, Lennon repeats the title three times. This repetition transforms the part from a refrain (single statement) to a chorus (three statements). The repetition also supports Lennon's desire to make this a heavier rock song. The repeated lyric creates an anthemlike sing-along.

Despite Lennon's desire for "Ticket to Ride" to be regarded as one of the earliest heavy-metal songs, the song does lend itself to lighter settings. Recall the famous 1969 soft rock cover of the song by the Carpenters. Recently, a student in my "Music of John Lennon" class at Berklee College of Music submitted a tantalizing reggae version of the song for her final project. Her version presented a delicate, subdued feel as well. It is the mark of a good song that it can be presented in many musical styles—and thus reach listeners from all walks of musical life.

"Ticket to Ride" remains one of the best known of Lennon's early rockers. Even when the song is performed today, it still makes a connection with young and old alike. Lennon mastered the ability to speak to us all—and his voice still echoes today, nearly forty years later.

You've Got to Hide Your Love Away

Words and Music by John Lennon and Paul McCartney

Verse 2a

How can I even try?

I can never win.

Hearing them, seeing them,

In the state I'm in.

Verse 2b

How could she say to me,

"Love will find a way?"

Gather 'round all you clowns,

Let me hear you say:

BACKGROUND

Title	You've Got to Hide Your Love Away
Recording Date	February 18, 1965
Meter	6/8
Key	A major
Song Form	Verse/Refrain
	Phrasing: *aabc/aabd/ee* (Verse/Verse/Refrain)
Recording	*Help!*
	1965 EMD/CAPITOL

This song was included in the summer 1965 movie, *Help!* Its instrumentation was different than any previous Beatles song. It had voice, 12-string acoustic guitar—and flute.

There are a couple of stories regarding the origin and meaning of the song. Some say that it appears to be a story of love lost and hidden feelings. The other is that John had written it for manager Brian Epstein, who was compelled to hide his gay lifestyle from the press and public.

"You've Got to Hide Your Love Away" is another Dylan-influenced song, though Lennon's decision to feature flute instead of harmonica on the recording was a marked deviation from the Dylan influence. Recorded February 18, 1965, this was the first time the Beatles enrolled outside musicians to play on their recordings.

Pete Shotton, Lennon's childhood friend from Liverpool and the original washboard player from Lennon's first group, the Quarrymen, was present as the song was being composed. It was Shotton who suggested the "hey's" that punctuate the song's refrain.

The song was released on the *Help!* album in England on August 6, 1965 and in America on August 13, 1965.

STRUCTURE

Song Form

The song is in G major and in 6/8 meter. It is a fine example of Lennon's folk-style writing. At first the song seems to be just a simple G major folk song that moves along in 4-bar segments, for a classic 16-bar verse. However, as one would expect, there is more afoot than the usual folk treatment. A wide-lens view of the form looks like this:

Verse/Refrain	Verse/Refrain	Coda
27 bars	27 bars	9 bars

However, if we zoom in closer, a more detailed picture looks like this:

V-a/V-b	Refrain	V-a/V-b	Refrain	Coda
9 bars/10 bars	8 bars	9 bars/10 bars	8 bars	9 bars

Lyric Content

The lyric, as mentioned briefly above, is about unrequited love. The first verse clearly reflects that. Since the song has only two verses, we don't experience the natural build of "beginning, middle, and end" that a three-verse song can supply. The second verse seems to reflect a series of feelings and questions, but in the totality of the lyric, Lennon opts to leave them unresolved.

In the closing line, calling for the gathering of clowns to join in the refrain, the singer seems to become one of the clowns himself. Perhaps he has called them in to cheer him up; perhaps he feels himself to be the clown—duped, deluded, a fool.

In the original version of the lyric as Lennon composed it, the original rhyming couplet for "wall" in verse 1 was supposed to be "two-foot tall." As the story goes, when Lennon first sang it for McCartney, he accidentally sang "two-foot small." Lennon decided he liked that better and kept it in (Dowdling, 1989).

Some of Lennon's images in this song are somewhat abstract. This ambiguity means the possibility of multiple interpretions—allowing the song to strike a chord in the hearts of many Beatles fans. The song remains a classic study in lyrical brevity.

Verses

▶ *Harmonic Phrasing*

Though this song is primarily in G, it is really in two keys. Again, it's Lennon's favorite combo: G major and G Mixolydian. The Dsus4 in bar 1 of the verse establishes the G major mode, while the F major triad adds the G Mixolydian flavor:

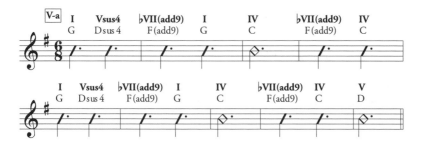

Fig. 4.12. V-a harmonic phrasing

Lennon presents the verse twice for a double verse form. But note that the first verse, V-a, is nine bars long. This is accomplished by simply repeating the initial four bars, creating an 8-bar unit, and then tagging on that extra bar with the D chord in it.

The second verse of the double verse, V-b, adds still another bar, creating a 10-bar section. Here, Lennon uses a harmonic progression with a descending bass line pattern (D, D/C, D/B, D/A) to link the verse to the refrain:

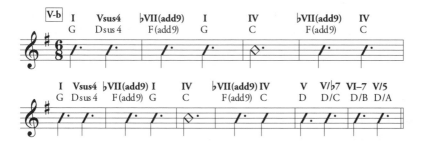

Fig. 4.13. V-b harmonic phrasing

chapter 4 · you've got to hide your love away

▶ *Melodic Phrasing*

Lennon's choice of 6/8 meter creates a lullaby-style, to-and-fro feel. The 6/8 meter tends to be heard as two quick bars of 3/4 waltz time, 1 2 3 4 5 6.

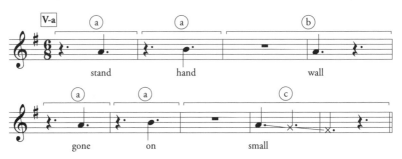

Fig. 4.14. V-a melodic phrasing

Regarding the melodic phrasing, Lennon's use of 1-bar, 2-bar, and 3-bar phrases in the first verse creates a relatively complex *aab/aac* phrasing pattern. The 1-bar phrases provide a balanced, accelerated motion in the first two bars. These phrases are lightly punctuated on the weaker beat 4 with the rhymes "stand" and "hand." Lennon then balances this with a complementary 2-bar phrase that has the nonrhyming lyric "wall" on strong beat 1. It sets up the expectation of rhyme (with "wall") in the next line.

Line 2 seems at first to be an exact repeat of line 1, as the lyric picks up the ending rhymes ("wall" and "small"). However, Lennon lengthens the answering phrase in the second line from two to three bars, creating a decelerating deception in true Lennon style.

Leading up to the ⓓ section of V-b, the listener expects to hear a 3-bar ⓒ phrase, as was heard in the V-a (first verse) section. But Lennon crafts the final phrase of V-b into a 4-bar phrase—the only one in the verse sections—creating an *aab/aad* inner form for the second of the two verses:

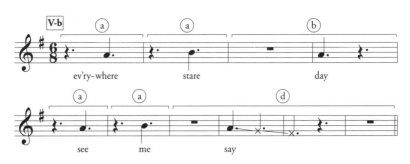

Fig. 4.15. V-b melodic phrasing

The effect of such deception is to spotlight that section itself—because it is so different than what has come before—and also to lead into the upcoming section. In this case, the refrain and title setting are what's coming next.

Refrain

Since this is the first verse/refrain song we have examined, let's review the basic differences between a refrain and a chorus. As we discussed in chapter 1, a refrain is a *part* of the verse, whereas the chorus is a separate section that *follows* the verse. A chorus stands alone. Necessarily, the refrain is usually much shorter than the verse that contains it, while the chorus is usually about as long as the verse.

Refrains and choruses do have one thing in common: They both usually contain the title line of the song. The verse/refrain format is a mainstay of folk-style songwriting.

▶ Harmonic Phrasing

The refrain employs just the standard I, IV, and V chords (G, C, and D) from G major:

Fig. 4.16. Refrain harmonic phrasing

The most classic folk harmonic treatments in the whole song are the suspended 4ths and 2nds added to the D major triads in the refrain. The addition of suspensions eliminates the major 3rd of the D triad in favor of the 4th and 2nd, respectively. The suspensions add motion to an otherwise static triad. This treatment tends to leave the refrain open, coinciding perfectly with the content of the title "Hey, You've Got to Hide Your Love Away," which is the lyric at that point.

▶ Melodic Phrasing

The refrain is the most accessible and singable of all the song's sections:

Fig. 4.17. Refrain melodic phrasing

One simple 4-bar phrase is repeated to formulate the 8-bar refrain for an *aa* format. All elements are in unison here: the lyric is repeated, the chord pattern is repeated, the melody and rhythm are repeated. This is a truly infectious folk-style refrain. It is a classic double refrain à la Dylan, with a double statement of the title, plain and simple. It works well for the rather lengthy 19-bar double verse.

PROSODY

Verses

Lennon's treatment of the musical form, combined with the structure and rhyme in the lyric, skews and transforms the song into something much more interesting.

In the view of verse 1 below, note how the melody in the first bar ends on the unstable A, then moves up to the stable B in the second bar. The third phrase creates forward motion, because it ends on an unstable note and is harmonized with chords that are also unstable, F(add9) and C (♭VII and IV in this key):

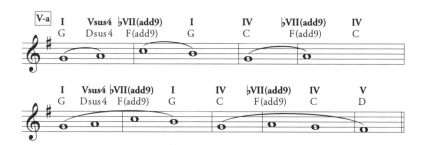

Fig. 4.18. V-a structural tones

The verse is divided into two similar 4-bar phrases. The whole-note structural tones in fig. 4.18 show that the same melody is in play twice: in the first four bars of line 1 and the first four bars of line 2. There is a difference, however: In the second four bars, the melody ends on the extremely unstable F♯ (Ti), keeping the verse from closing down by creating forward motion similar to that of the A in the first line.

The V-a and the V-b sections adhere to the same melodic format:

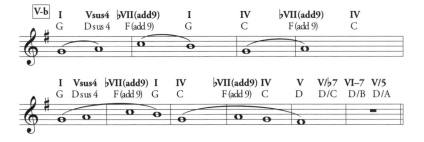

Fig. 4.19. V-b structural tones

The only difference is one of form. The V-b section has an extra bar that concludes the entire verse section. The ultimate prosodic effect of the two verses is that they characterize the confusion and despair expressed in the lyric. In most songs, all of the verses are exactly the same length. The changing lengths provide an unstable feel that coincides with the lyrical confusion. This is the same effect created by the constantly shifting phrase lengths and by ending each of the verses on suspended dominant chords.

Refrain

The unstable F♯s that end both halves of the verse sections are pleading for resolution to the tonic G…and Lennon delivers. But the melody in the refrain is not the sweet, playful melody of the verse:

Fig. 4.20. Refrain structural tones

Immediately, the refrain melody races up to a high G and down to a low G in the very first bar. The octave leap spotlights the beginning of the refrain, and emphasizes the tonic G as a resolution of the F♯ of the previous section.

By the second bar of the refrain, the melody has soared up to a D and then abruptly dropped all the way down to the D an octave below. This creates a melodic range of an octave and a half in only two bars. It is reminiscent of the verse melody from "I'm a Loser." The two octave leaps in the refrain spotlight the rhyming words "hey" (on the high G) and "away" (on the low D). In both songs, a despairing lyric is coupled with melodies that descend a great distance to melodically represent that despair.

The verse and refrain melodies interact perfectly with each other because the two sections create both contrast and continuity. The verse melody, almost a little lullaby, takes the listener on a rather agonizing lyrical journey through the questions of life and love. The dramatic and forceful melody in the refrain, in contrast, is the bugle call for a prudent retreat. Lennon successfully captures the conflicting emotions portrayed in the lyrics to match the melody of each section.

SUMMARY

This song has two open sections. When it comes time for the ending, the composer winds up in a similar predicament as encountered in "I'm a Loser": how to end the song? Again, Lennon resolves it brilliantly.

First, he creates an instrumental outro for flute and guitar, based on two repetitions of the 4-bar harmonic phrase from the verse. This approach brings the song's rhythm, harmony, and phrasing to a strong conclusion. However, the flute's last note is D, Sol. Although the D is a stable note in the key of G, it doesn't provide the strong closure that the tonic note Do would. The listener is left feeling somewhat unresolved as the song concludes.

We have seen earlier how the high G is used in the refrain to set the lyric, "Hey!" This punctuated high note is just the wake-up call the song needs to herald the arrival of the refrain. Upon inspecting the rest of that lyric line, one might wonder which lyrics Lennon will spotlight next. With the exception of "away," each word in this lyric is monosyllabic, giving the composer license to accent any one word chooses—and it's not immediately clear which word is most important to the song's overall message.

Lennon's placement of the word "hide" on beat 1 suggests that something is to be hidden. But what is it? Next, he gives the word "your" a slight accent with rhythmic syncopation. As a result, both "hide" and "your" are accented up front. One might expect that the word "love" might be emphasized as well, since that appears to be the subject of the song. However, Lennon chooses to hide the word "love" away and spotlight to the last word "away" by placing it on strong beat 1 and setting it with the lowest note in the song (low D).

The words "hide" and "your" pick up all the rhythmic action, leaving the word "love" tucked away almost unnoticed—which supports the whole point of the song! Love remains safely tucked away. The lyrical treatment is yet another great intuitive move by Mr. Lennon.

Norwegian Wood (This Bird Has Flown)

Words and Music by John Lennon and Paul McCartney

I once had a girl, or should I say she once had me.

She showed me her room, is-n't it good, Nor-we-gian wood. She

asked me to stay and she told me to sit an-y-where. So

I looked a-round and I no-ticed there was-n't a chair.

I sat on a rug, bid-ing my time, drink-ing her wine.

We talked un-til two, and then she said, "It's time for bed."

A

(Sitar Solo)

B

She told me she worked in the morning and started to laugh,
I told her I didn't and crawled off to sleep in the bath.

A

And when I awoke I was alone, this bird had flown.
So I lit a fire, isn't it good, Norwegian wood.

Title	Norwegian Wood (This Bird Has Flown)
Recording Date	October 12, 1965
Meter	12/8
Key	E Mixolydian and E melodic minor
Song Form	ABA (variation on Verse/Refrain)
Phrasing	A: *aaabb*
	B: *aa*
Recording	*Rubber Soul*
	1965 EMD/CAPITOL

This song remains one of the most popular album cuts from Lennon's Beatles repertoire. Never released as a single, "Norwegian Wood" somehow managed to cut right through the others to become one of the most popular tracks from the 1965 *Rubber Soul* album.

John once summed up the lyric with the word "gobbledygook." His intention was to write a song about one of his love affairs during the Beatlemania period (1963–1966) without addressing it directly. Classic Lennon. It is a smoky, hazy story that matches perfectly with the tone and import of *Rubber Soul*.

"Norwegian Wood" was the first Beatles song that made use of the sitar, the gourdlike stringed instrument from India with which George Harrison was beginning to experiment. The result was an interesting transformation from the usual Beatles instrumentation of two guitars, bass, and drums.

John wrote the song in St. Moritz, Switzerland in February 1965 while on holiday with his first wife Cynthia. It was first recorded for the *Rubber Soul* album on October 12, 1965. The album was released December 3, 1965.

STRUCTURE

Song Form

"Norwegian Wood" is a very concise song indeed. A transformed version of the simple verse/refrain format, the song paints a vivid picture of a somewhat surreal love affair. It seems to start off as a typical AB form, but Lennon instead fashions a rare variation—ABA:

A	B	A	A (Sitar Solo)	B	A
4 bars	4 bars	4 bars	4 bars	4 bars	4 bars

Lennon's use and treatment of this form produces some interesting results. At first the listener hears AB. When the second A occurs, the listener expects another B to follow. When a third A section replaces the expected B, the whole song form immediately shifts from a simple AB form to the more complex ABA form.

Further, at the beginning of the second and final statement of the ABA form, Lennon inserts the curious and unprecedented sitar solo. Lennon supports the unusual nature of the music, lyrics, and arrangement by providing supporting deception in his use of form. This creates what seems like a backward finish to the song. After the solo, the lyric returns at the B section. The listener is left with BA to conclude the song.

Lyric Content

The title, "Norwegian Wood (This Bird Has Flown)," piques our curiosity right from the start. Wood? Birds? What could this song possibly be about? With the mention of a "girl" in the very first line, we think that it might be some sort of love song.

Throughout the song, the lyric seems to be a continuous thread, without repeat. The title appears only once at the very beginning and once at the very end, and there is really no traditional refrain, as in "You've Got to Hide Your Love Away" or "Come Together."

"Norwegian Wood" is the story of a young man who is invited to a young woman's room. There, they drink wine and talk until the wee hours. For an instant, we get the idea they might become lovers. But she informs him otherwise. The morning brings a rather unresolved situation. The protagonist wakes after the girl's departure to find himself alone. He decides to hang for a while and light a fire…presumably of Norwegian firewood. Paul McCartney's contribution to "Norwegian Wood" was the suggestion of the fire, though he has indicated that his vision was actually to burn the down the flat.

As he presents the story, Lennon moves quickly from one image to another and constructs a somewhat surreal lyrical collage. As surreal as the story appears to be, it strikes a nerve. We all can identify with having been in a situation that seems to be moving in one direction but then suddenly turns into something else.

PHRASING

A Section

▶ Harmonic Phrasing

The first half of the song's verse is in E Mixolydian:

Fig. 4.21. A section harmonic phrasing

The A section is the shortest in Lennon's repertoire—only four bars long. The droning static E major tonic triad only briefly visits the D major and A major chords, both of which contain the D♮ (♭7) that imparts the E Mixolydian flavor. The mode itself by this time was becoming part Lennon's harmonic repertoire.

▶ Melodic Phrasing

The rhyme scheme in this song seems backward in comparison to the typical Lennon setup of two quick rhymes followed by a nonrhyming phrase. This song instead opens with two nonrhyming phrases followed by two quick, asymmetrical rhyming phrases. This pattern continues throughout each of the A sections. The rhyming creates a sense of double punctuation, bringing the section to an abrupt halt each time it is repeated.

The flow and phrasing of the song couldn't be more straightforward, however. In the first verse, Lennon sets up a rhyming couplet in the ⓑ phrases with the words "wood" and "good" to punctuate the end of the verse:

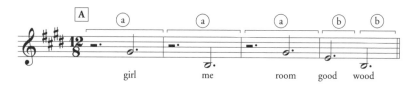

Fig. 4.22. A section melodic phrasing

However, in the second verse, Lennon incorporates the rhyming couplet twice in each verse. The presence of two rhyming couplets in each verse provides more forward motion, as they are placed in the weaker second and fourth bars.

The title/refrain line ("Isn't it good, Norwegian wood") is noticeably absent in verse 2, especially when it was so nicely foreshadowed in the line before ("biding my time, drinking her wine"). This teases the listener and keeps them engaged:

Fig. 4.23. A section, verse 2 melodic phrasing

For the third verse, Lennon combines the structures of verses 1 and 2. Like verse 2, verse 3 has the double rhyming couplets ("alone" and "flown," followed by "good" and "wood"). But the third verse recalls the opening verse and finally brings back the title/refrain line, "Isn't it good, Norwegian wood." Lennon's choice of phrasing brings him back full circle to where he began. The repeating phrase patterns give the listener a consistent framework through which to gaze into the series of veiled images painted by the verse lyrics.

B Section

▶ *Harmonic Phrasing*
The B section could at first be heard as E Dorian, except for the B7 in the chord progression at the end, which is a true melodic minor chord.

Fig. 4.24. B section harmonic phrasing

It is peculiar that the A section closes with the tonic chord E, while the B section remains open. It is a departure from the classic AB (verse/refrain) format to the less-common ABA format, as discussed earlier. The open B section leads back to the closed A section, creating a balanced three-part form.

▶ *Melodic Phrasing*

The melodic phrasing of the B section is much squarer: two 2-bar phrases. Ending both phrases in the second weaker bar gives some forward motion, but the fact that there are two of them gives some balance to the section and slows the motion:

Fig. 4.25. B section melodic phrasing

In the end, the B7 dominant chord in the harmony, along with the unstable A in the melody, keeps the section open and moving back to the tonic key of E in the A section.

PROSODY

A Section

The melody of the A section is a descending line that moves down an entire octave in the course of the opening 4-bar phrase. An exact repeat of the first four bars completes the A section, as illustrated below:

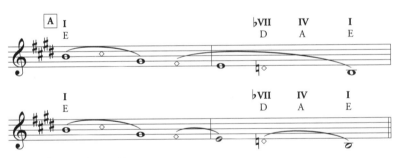

Fig. 4.26. A section structural tones

This descending melody lends an ominous flavor to the setting of the lyrics, which, though somewhat positive on the surface, are predominately ambiguous:

> *I once had a girl, or should I say she once had me.*
> *She showed me her room, isn't it good, Norwegian wood?*

Taking a closer look at that first 2-bar phrase, we notice that the three stable notes in the key (E, G♯, and B) are visited with one important note: D♮, or ♭7. The ♭7 in the melody signals a droning Mixolydian tonality. The second half of the second bar, however, contains predominantly unstable tones (D, A, and C♯). This spotlights the clever twist in the lyrics involved: "she once had me."

Fig. 4.27. Unstable tones spotlight a lyrical twist.

B Section

The melody for the B section is simpler. The melody is more static and descends only a single step from the 5th to the unstable 4th degree:

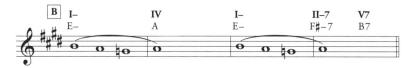

Fig. 4.28. B section structural tones

The appearance of the G♮ is the most significant event of the B section. After its modal interchange cousin G♯ played such a prominent role in the A section, the darker G♮ provides an instant change of atmosphere. Listen to the song and note how the change in the musical atmosphere corresponds to the lyric.

SUMMARY

It's not surprising that Lennon resorted to an instrumental outro to close the song. Although the song does close down musically, the lyric is somewhat ambiguous, both in lyric content and harmonic resolution. Ending with an instrumental outro gives the listener one last hearing of the singular sitar that has been scored out to play the melody. The song, after all, really ends with a question: "Isn't it good, Norwegian wood?" Lennon could not have picked a more ambiguous ending.

Lyrically, this song is very much a turning point for the folk-style ballad. In 1965, most folk ballads told a cohesive story. However, in this song, Lennon moves quickly from one lyrical image to another, leaving it up to the listener's imagination to complete the picture. The repetition of the melody in both sections gives support to the feeling that there will be repeating lyrics in the refrain; we expect the *lyrics* to repeat because the *melody* does.

Lennon tantalizes us with his magical title by delivering up only half of it in the first A section. The listener waits patiently for the return of this playful refrain. But it doesn't come. Instead the music and lyric lead the listener through a myriad of surreal images, like a dream come to life. Then quite unexpectedly in the very last line of the song, the listener is treated to one last hearing of the title.

The full title of the song is "Norwegian Wood (This Bird Has Flown)." The full title is not stated until the last A section, and then, in the seeds of what will later become a Lennon signature device, he states the title backwards. That is, a slighly modified version of the second portion of the title, "this bird had flown," comes at the end of line 2. Meanwhile, the first part of the title, "Norwegian wood," comes at the end of line 2. It is the last lyric heard in the song. Exhalation. Resolution, of sorts, at last.

"Norwegian Wood" is the pivotal song in Lennon's effort to use surrealistic imagery in pop lyrics. Earlier efforts like "Ask Me Why" and "There's a Place" from 1963 sow the seeds, but after the success of the Beatles' mainstream efforts, Lennon set this interest aside until the *Rubber Soul* album. In addition to the surreal "Norwegian Wood," that album includes "In My Life" and "Nowhere Man." Both of these introspective Lennon songs set the stage for a song like "Norwegian Wood."

Day Tripper

Words and Music by John Lennon and Paul McCartney

(Continued on following page)

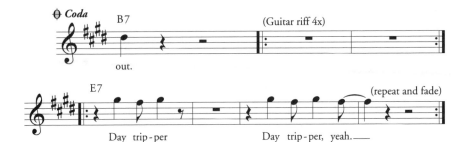

Verse 2

    She's a big teaser,

    She took me half the way there.

    She's a big teaser,

    She took me half the way there, now.

Verse 3

    Tried to please her,

    She only played one-night stands.

    Tried to please her,

    She only played one-night stands, now.

Chorus 3

    She was a day tripper,

    Sunday driver, yeah,

    It took me so long to find out,

    And I found out.

BACKGROUND

Title	Day Tripper
Recording Date	October 16, 1965
Meter	4/4
Key	E blues
Song Form	Verse/Chorus (or AB) w/Instrumental Interlude
Phrasing	Verse or A: *abac*
	Chorus or B: *abcd*
Recording	*Beatles: Past Masters, Volume Two*
	1988 EMD/CAPITOL

This song is an odd one. "Day Tripper" was written mainly because the Beatles needed another pot-boiler single for the winter sales period. By now, everyone expected the Beatles to have another big hit. This song *sort of* fit the bill, but was a riff-based song that didn't really go anywhere lyrically. Lennon himself did not consider "Day Tripper" to be one of his greatest songs, though its lasting popularity shows his indomitable influence as a solid rock 'n' roll writer and singer.

I heard Lennon say in a 1974 radio interview on WNEW in New York that the guitar lick that drives the song was inspired by Bobby Parker's song called "Watch Your Step." The influence is quite clear. However, Lennon's composition of the main guitar riff is definitely original, while still capturing the flavor of those great 1950s r&b hits.

The song was recorded in one day—October 16, 1965—in only three takes. The Beatles and George Martin made a decision to release "Day Tripper" and "We Can Work It Out" as the winter single and to not include either on the contemporaneous *Rubber Soul* LP. Both the single and the album were released on the same day(!): December 3, 1965 in England and three days later in America. It was quite unusual to simultaneously release a single and an album, particularly when the single was not part of the album.

Both songs eventually wound up on two completely different albums in England and America. In England, "Day Tripper" was released on December 9, 1966, on a completely different compilation album titled *A Collection of Beatles Oldies*. In America, it was released on June 20, 1966 on a compilation album called *Yesterday and Today*. This was the famous album with two covers, one of which was later withdrawn. The album's surface cover was a picture of the group around a steamer trunk. Perhaps the steamer trunk was a subtle hint, because if one carefully steamed off the album cover with a tea kettle, another cover was revealed beneath: a picture of the Fab Four in white lab coats with decapitated baby dolls and pieces of raw steak. This shocking photo was chosen by the Beatles themselves to break the every-mother's-son image that had overtaken them. The hidden picture was soon to become known as "The Butcher Cover" and quickly became a collector's item.

STRUCTURE

Song Form

The form for this song is elusive. Most hear it as a verse/chorus, but the music in the chorus has more of the elements of a bridge than a chorus. Lennon resolves the confusion in a most unusual way, as we shall see.

There is also another curveball in this song: an instrumental bridge. Instrumental bridges tend to be heard as interludes or solo sections, rather than as standard primary bridges, which contain lyrics that push the story along. The resulting form is:

Verse/Chorus	Verse/Chorus	Interlude	Verse/Chorus
8 bars + 8 bars	8 bars + 8 bars	12 bars	8 bars + 8 bars

The 2-bar guitar riff that opens the song is repeated four times in the 10-bar intro. The riff is sprinkled throughout the song. A twice-repeated version is used before the second verse, while the full version from the intro is used between the interlude and the third verse.

Lyric Content

After "Norwegian Wood's" complex surreal imagery, this song has a very simple lyrical message. It is a song about a young man who wishes to be in the company of a young woman. She seems to be indecisive at best and playing head games at worst. The verses lament the young man's efforts to make a comfortable connection with her. The chorus seems to herald his awakening to the truth of the relationship.

PHRASING

Verse (or A)

▶ Harmonic Phrasing

"Day Tripper" follows a blues-based harmonic progression. However, the song makes some unexpected harmonic journeys before its return to tonic.

As seen earlier, blues-based songs tend to work mostly with the I, IV, and V chords. The verse section lulls the listener into believing that it is a rather standard bluesy pop song, predominantly including the I7 and IV7 chords (E7 and A7) so strongly associated with blues and blues-based pop:

Fig. 4.29. Verse harmonic phrasing

▶ *Melodic Phrasing*

The melodic and lyric phrasing for the verse is well designed for the song's intended purpose: to be a blockbuster single. It is accessible and does not go the way of Lennon's more artistic songs. Like many rock 'n' roll blues songs, the verse starts with a short, lyrical statement that is either repeated exactly or varied slightly on the repeat:

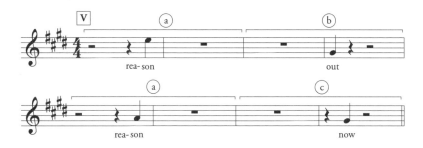

Fig. 4.30. Verse melodic phrasing

The phrasing seems to be classic blues: say something once, then say it again while you're playing a new chord. Lennon begins with a short, 2-bar statement ⓐ followed by an answering phrase ⓑ to complete the lyrical idea. As line 2 starts, we hear the same ⓐ phrase and expect a classic *abab* section. But again Lennon deceives us. The last phrase stretches out to beat 2 on the lyric "now." This creates a new phrase ⓒ. The result is the deceptive, classically Lennon-esque *abac* inner form for the verse.

Chorus (or B)

▶ *Harmonic Phrasing*

The area of gray is now upon us. As we move from the verse, we arrive at a chorus—or is it a B section? Usually a chorus provides a sense of harmonic arrival. But this chorus does not do that:

Fig. 4.31. Chorus harmonic phrasing

Harmonically speaking, the section acts more like a "second half," as if it were a B of an AB section. Reason? The F♯7 chord (II7 in this key) is a somewhat unexpected opening chord for a chorus. It has so many notes that are not in the key that it stands out dramatically, and thus creates the kind of instability that is usually associated with a bridge section.

Still, if the section had made its way to the tonic E7 by bar 7, it would have achieved a choruslike wrap-up. But notice the four chords that conclude the section: A7, G♯7, C♯, and B. There is *no* tonic resolution—and this makes the section more like a bridge. The G♯7 and C♯ chords have so many notes out of the key that they, in and of themselves, cause the section to move forward with great force. But forward to where?

Lennon resolves the B chord to tonic right at the introduction of the tonic-based guitar riff:

Fig. 4.32. Guitar riff resolves chorus

The great motion provided by the chords in the section makes it sound more like a primary bridge. It's a tough call: verse/chorus or verse/bridge? He transitions to the next section using the guitar riff. This clever dovetailing of the section back into the tonic-based guitar riff imparts resolution to the section. We have what seems like a chorus…but this conclusion is confounded by the melody.

❯ *Melodic Phrasing*

The phrasing for the unchoruslike chorus starts off in a very choruslike manner with the singers shouting, "she was a day-ay-ay tripper, one-way ticket, yeh:"

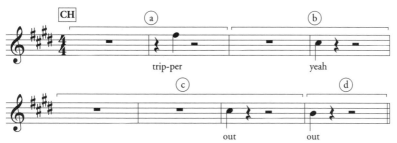

Fig. 4.33. Chorus melodic phrasing

In fact, line 1 has a similar form to the verse section: *ab*. However, unlike a typical chorus, there is no repeating melody, there are no repeating lyrics and only a few repeating rhythms. At line 2 both the melody and lyric join together in a headlong dash for the beginning of the next section, as one would find in a bridge section. Further, using a 3-bar ⓒ phrase followed by the 1-bar ⓓ phrase produces an inner phrasing form that is even more deceptive than the one found in the verse: *abcd*.

Usually chorus phrasing doesn't involve that much of the alphabet. The most common scenarios for choruses are *aaaa* or *abab*, employing just one or two rhythmic ideas. Lennon's chorus section works because he dovetails it into the guitar riff. With the instrumental riff and the choruslike melody, this is indeed a chorus…kind of.

PROSODY

Verse

Taking a melodic cue from r&b and blues, the entire verse comprises just one melodic riff that is varied and transformed subtly along the way. The verse melody is composed of mostly stable melodic tones (Do, Mi, Sol):

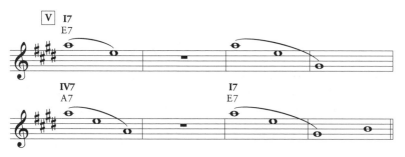

Fig. 4.34. Verse structural tones

This is a successful contrast to the chorus melody, which is composed of mostly unstable melodic tones (Re, Fa, La, Ti):

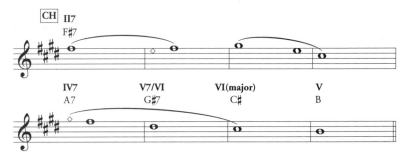

Fig. 4.35. Chorus structural tones

The stable tones create a sense of grounding in the verse, while unstable tones create forward motion in the chorus section. The verse becomes a rather subdued vehicle for the story line, while the chorus's unstable tones used for the chorus create a real sense of movement. This forward-moving chorus works perfectly for a song about someone taking a day trip. The unresolved verse creates an atmosphere of preparation and anticipation, while the churning chorus is in fact "going somewhere." Another 50-point bull's eye for Lennon in the prosody column.

SUMMARY

The striking opening guitar riff for "Day Tripper" signals that a great rock 'n' roll song is about to get underway. Carefully crafting the lick from the influences of those great 1950s r&b songs, Lennon carved out a niche for himself in the annals of 1960s rock.

This song promises in the beginning to go the standard way of most r&b-influenced rockers, which is:

- Original melodic/lyric statement on the I chord
- Same melodic/lyric statement on the IV chord
- New melodic/lyric statement back on the I chord
- New melodic/lyric statement on V–IV cadence
- Final wrap-up on the I chord

Instead, after taking the listener down the primrose path of I–IV–I (the first three steps from above), Lennon takes a sharp left turn and inserts a II7 chord, F♯7. One would have expected that Lennon would choose the last two harmonic steps above to create a standard blues/r&b form. As was his style, Lennon subverts the listener's expectation with a delicious deception. The song takes us on a wild and unexpected harmonic ride through several chromatic and diatonic chords. Unstable melody and harmony leave the listener hanging in midair, looking for a place to land. The chorus brings us in for a tonic splashdown with the return of the guitar riff, as the next verse starts the journey all over again.

Just a word about the third section of the song, which I have not mentioned yet. After the two verses and two choruses, there is a third instrumental section. At first it promises to be a standard primary bridge, as is often found in Lennon's songwriting. Lennon may have had nothing lyrically to add in the so-called bridge section and perhaps chose to fashion an instrumental interlude. This section is based on his now-famous guitar riff, played over the dominant chord for twelve bars. It becomes the showcase for George Harrison's solo, as well as for the Beatle-y three-part, close vocal harmony "ah's," which move up the scale six degrees before crashing back down into the intro again.

Using the forward-moving guitar riff as an introduction to each verse makes us wonder how the song will end. Up to this point, the guitar riff has led us into a new section. In live performance, the Beatles just stopped abruptly on the tonic. But on the recording, they used a fade-out. This was a great choice…and a powerful tool that leaves the listener straining for more.

In My Life

Words and Music by John Lennon and Paul McCartney

Verse 2

But of all these friends and lovers,
There is no one compares with you.
And these mem'ries lose their meaning,
When I think of love as something new.
Tho' I know I'll never lose affection,
For people and things that went before.
I know I'll often stop and think about them,
In my life I love you more.

BACKGROUND

Title	In My Life
Recording Date	October 18, 1965
Meter	4/4
Key	A major
Song Form	Verse/Refrain or AB
Phrasing	A: *abab*
	B: *abab*
Recording	*Rubber Soul*
	1965 EMD/CAPITOL

"In My Life," from the *Rubber Soul* album, is often thought of as a one-hundred-percent Lennon song. However, the song is one of the few Beatles songs with a dispute in authorship. In interviews, McCartney has said that he worked out the melody on the mellotron, while Lennon said that McCartney only worked out the melody for the "middle eight." (In this case, Lennon is referring to the B section.) My purpose here is not to resolve the true authorship of the song, but as with the other songs in this book, to look inside the song and see what makes it work. For discussion purposes, I will present it as a Lennon song.

Simplicity is one of the strongest traits found in Lennon's songs. As we will soon see, this song is a masterpiece of simplicity. The original concept for the song was a trip through John's childhood and neighborhood, a sort of collage of his past in Liverpool. But the lyric was turning out rather like a trying-to-be-clever laundry list of childhood memories. After setting it aside for awhile, Lennon tried another approach to the lyric, which led to the form we hear today.

Lennon supplied only vocals for this one. McCartney played bass and backup vocals, George played electric guitar, and Ringo, drums. Producer George Martin played the famous Elizabethan-style harpsichord solo at half speed. The recorded solo was then played back at double speed to connect with the original key and tempo, producing the crisp classical-sounding performance on the recording.

The song was first recorded on October 18, 1965 for *Rubber Soul*. It was released on that album in England on December 3, 1965 and in America on December 6. Recently in 2000, the British magazine *Mojo* voted it the "All Time Best Song" of the twentieth century.

STRUCTURE

Song Form
"In My Life" is structured in the verse/refrain format. In this form there is no primary bridge. Also, there is no chorus. It's really just a simple AB format, much like a folk song, in which the refrain is located at the end of the B section. The form of the song looks like this:

A/B	A/B	A/B
Verse/Refrain	Verse/Refrain	Verse/Refrain
16 bars (8 + 8)	16 bars (8 + 8)	16 bars (8 + 8)

Lennon wrote the entire lyric before the chords or melody. This in itself sets the form of the song, so I think we can safely say that Lennon had the standard AB, or verse/refrain, form already in mind in crafting the lyric.

Lyric Content
Since the lyric was composed first, let's have a critical look at the form and content that lies within. The most important lyric, other than the memorable title, is the word "places." This word occurs at the head of the both the A and the B sections in the first verse.

In the A section, Lennon gives a balanced description of "places," indicating that he remembers them and has experienced what we all experience when recalling places from our past: some of them change, some stay the same. This shows a true songwriter working his way into the hearts of his listeners.

It is a perfect setup for Lennon's entrance into the B section, in which he points out that places bring to mind different moments, and the people and friends who were there to share them. He continues in the B section that the people in his life have also changed—indicating that some are still around while others have passed on. This is an unusually poignant observation for a pop song.

In the second verse, we find Lennon expressing his undying love directly to one person. Though he refers to loved ones in verse 1, now he gives perspective: "Yes, I still love all the others who have been in my life," he seems to say, "but I love you above all." This change brings the message of the entire song into focus. Lennon was concerned when first writing the lyric that it would turn into a mere laundry list of people and places. He deftly prevented that from happening by moving from the more general first verse to a direct person-to-person statement in the second verse.

Leaving the canvas finished at that point was another great song-writing decision. It may have been very tempting to write another verse or to create another section of both music and lyric for this one, but he recognized that the song was complete. Nearly four decades since it was written, the lyric has stood the test of time.

PHRASING

Verse (or A section)

▶ *Harmonic Phrasing*
The A section (marked "V-a") is made up of two 4-bar sections that repeat:

Fig. 4.36. Verse harmonic phrasing

Lennon provides two surprise chords in the V-a section: A7 and D minor. The A7 is a version of the tonic chord that more readily resolves down to D major. Lennon then follows it with the D minor triad, which darkens and saddens the preceding D major triad. The D triads continue the motion, because 1) the D major chord is an unstable IV in the key, and 2) the D minor triad is nondiatonic, introducing the chromatic note F♮ into the game. The D minor chord also provides a more melancholy sound, matching the lyric perfectly at that point: "all my *life*" and "some have *gone*."

▶ *Melodic Phrasing*
The melodic phrasing once again follows a pattern of simplicity:

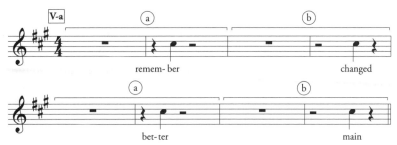

Fig. 4.37. Verse melodic phrasing

Lennon sets up a classic rhyme scheme by rhyming all the ⓑ sections, such as "changed" and "remain" in this example. This pattern is followed in both the V-a and V-b sections. The result is a song and story that are easy to follow.

Refrain (or V-b)

▶ *Harmonic Phrasing*

In the V-b section, the harmonic rhythm decelerates. While V-a contained two chords in almost every bar, V-b contains a steady one chord per bar throughout. This provides harmonic contrast between the two sections:

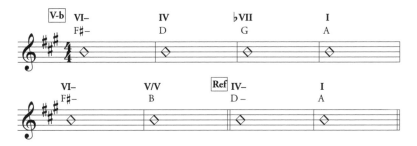

Fig. 4.38. Refrain harmonic phrasing

Throughout the song, there is a cadence to tonic every four bars. Of these four cadences, three involve the IV major or IV minor chord. The nondiatonic cadence from G to A in bars 11 and 12 provides a new level of harmonic interest:

Bars 3 and 4 = IV to I
Bars 7 and 8 = IV to I
Bars 11 and 12 = ♭VII to I
Bars 15 and 16 = IV minor to I

The most dramatic harmonic move is dead ahead: the well-placed VI minor chord moves with suddenness and exhilaration to B at the end of V-b. It functions as a secondary dominant—but it is left unresolved. B normally would be analyzed as V/V in this key. Normal movement would call for B to progress to E7, and then on to A major. But it resolves deceptively to D minor, right at the point where the title is sung. This harmonic surprise creates the perfect spotlight for the lyric and the perfect harmonic ending for this jewel of a song.

▶ Melodic Phrasing

Since there is so much change of both melody and harmony in the V-b section, Lennon is free to use the same phrasing that he used for the V-a section:

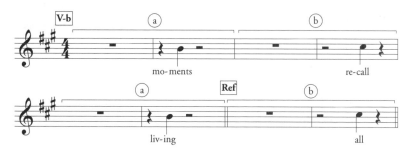

Fig. 4.39. Refrain melodic phrasing

The repetition of the phrasing makes it possible for almost any listener to sing along after just a couple of hearings. This, of course, is the goal of any pop songwriter: to have everyone singing their song.

The last two bars of the refrain include the song's conclusive lyrics, suggesting the song's ultimate message: "In my life, I've loved them all."

PROSODY

Verse (V-a)

It is interesting to note that all four of the melodic phrases of the V-a section end on the stable note C♯ (Mi in the key of A). The repetition of this stable note has the effect of stopping the motion of the song ever so slightly every two bars:

Fig. 4.40. Verse structural tones

We find forward motion and lyric spotlighting right from bar 1. The melody begins with the extremely unstable and pleasantly dissonant B (Re in this key). The B occurs on strong beats 1 and 3. The dissonance and rhythmic placement emphasize two important words—"places" and "I'll." The same thing happens again at bar 2 with the note E on the F♯ minor triad. Here, the placement accents the word "remember."

Refrain (V-b)

The melody of V-b increases the motion of the song in all aspects: harmonically, lyrically, and melodically. This is the first time that a phrase ends on the unstable Re, as we see in bar 2 of fig. 4.41. Re has a strong tendency to move toward Do. But Lennon diverts this resolution. In bar 4, he arrives at the tonic *chord* using not A, but once again C♯, as the melodic phrase ending.

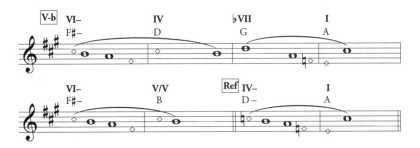

Fig. 4.41. Refrain structural tones

The tonic note A in bar 3 does create a fleeting melodic resolution for the B (Re), except that Lennon harmonizes it with a G triad. He then moves the melody up to the familiar C♯ that has ended every phrase so far. This treatment is repeated in the second 4-bar unit, but as the melody hits the refrain in the last two bars, Lennon moves to chromatic melody notes C♮ and F♮ to complete the song system. After all the C♯s in both sections so far, the C♮ in the melody spotlights the refrain.

SUMMARY

Note that the rhythm chosen for the melody of the V-a section is initially a string of plodding quarter notes that end abruptly in the second bar. At bars 3 and 7, however, he spotlights the lyric with a lovely melisma.

In contrast, the melody for the V-b section moves quickly into running eighth notes throughout, except at the phrase endings. This section ends with the restatement of the earlier melisma, spotlighting the title for the conclusion of the verses.

How does such a simple song get to be voted all-time best song of a century? No doubt it's because its simplicity balanced with just enough—but not *too* much—complexity thrown in for good measure. Ever had a simple salad with too much salt and pepper? It can really ruin the mix.

What Lennon has wrought in terms of simplicity is his use of:

- the simple verse/refrain form
- a simple and direct two-verse lyric
- a simple melody with a one-octave range
- simple arrangement of guitar, bass, drums, and a couple of voices

And what of the complexities? These include his use of:

- chromatic melody and harmony saved up for the second half of the song
- a subtle change of voice in the lyric between the two verses
- that outrageous harpsichord solo to ornament the arrangement

The song has one other interesting aspect: It seems to keep moving, right up to the end! Every single phrase ending occurs on the beat 3 instead of the strongest beat 1, giving it a persistent feeling of forward motion.

The version recorded by the Beatles has a dramatic grand pause at the end, at which point Lennon sings a 1950s-inspired high falsetto, in a drawn-out, rubato fashion. Time is suspended. This is then followed by the insertion of a 2/4 bar in order to get the last lyric, "more," to finally appear on beat 1. In fact, this is the only time in the whole song where a melody and lyric line conclude on beat 1! What we finally hear at that point is real rhythmic resolution of the whole song.

But what about melodic resolution? That is finally provided by the lead guitar lick at the very end of the arrangement—the final notes being La–Ti–Do, or F♯–G♯–A in this key. That A becomes the note the listener has been patiently waiting for all along. A gem. A jewel. Excellently crafted. 'Nuff said!

CHAPTER 5   1966

In 1966 there were dramatic shifts on many levels for John Lennon and the Beatles. For all of 1964 and 1965, the band had been working nonstop, bouncing from concert to concert like performing fleas. In 1964, the year Beatlemania overtook the world, the Fab Four cranked out a gargantuan amount of work. In England they produced four singles, two albums, and a movie. Playing catch-up in America, they released eleven singles and four albums—and those figures don't even include the re-releases. In 1965, the British releases totaled three singles, two albums, and yet another movie. America logged in with seven singles and four albums. This is an incredible amount of work for any artist to churn out in a two-year period.

There were more albums in America than in England because the original English albums contained fourteen songs per album. But in America albums were fashioned with different covers and different song collections, sometimes containing as few as eleven songs per album. Therefore, America was able to derive seventeen albums from the original thirteen English releases on Parlophone records.

The year 1966 was the last year that different albums were issued in different countries. The playing fields were on their way to being leveled worldwide. As they began to assert more control over the release of their songs and albums, the Beatles decided that all of their albums would be the same.

In both England and America only one album of new material was released: *Revolver*. "Clean-up" albums were released in both countries. In America, it was *Yesterday and Today*; in England it was *A Collection of Oldies*. Both albums were culled from the songs and singles not included on albums up to that point. In just one short year, the Beatles would assume total worldwide control of their complete artistic output in their songs and albums.

After three years of hectic Beatlemania, 1966 marked a slower, more contemplative period in Lennon's life. It was the first year that there was no Beatles movie. The Beatles stopped touring as of August 1966, giving each band member time to explore his own musical direction. Nearly every song written in this historic year has the stamp of new directions on it.

Lennon himself began to explore some of the more uncharted quadrants of the musical universe. In terms of form, he would move away from his classic AABA roots and begin to embrace the verse/chorus form more directly in songs like "Rain" and "Strawberry Fields Forever." He would begin to expand his songwriting style by incorporating such new techniques as mixed meter, mixed modes, and layered tape loops of unusual sounds played both forwards and backwards. He also began to use more abstract and introspective lyrics. We'll take a closer look at these changes by inspecting four songs from 1966:

"Tomorrow Never Knows"
"Rain"
"She Said She Said"
"Strawberry Fields Forever"

Each of these songs is a landmark in its own way. "Tomorrow Never Knows" has its backward tape collages and "Rain," its backward coda. "She Said She Said" uses mixed meter and lyrics from the *Tibetan Book of the Dead*, while "Strawberry Fields Forever" has its own studio legerdemain and spliced-together magic.

Tomorrow Never Knows

Words and Music by John Lennon and Paul McCartney

Verse 3
That you may see the meaning
of within,
It is speaking, it is speaking.

Solos

Verse 4
That love is all and love is
ev'ryone,
It is knowing, it is knowing.

Verse 5
When ignorance and haste may mourn
the dead,
It is believing, it is believing.

Verse 6
But listen to the color of
your dreams,
It is not living, it is not living.

Verse 7
So play the game "existence" to the end,
Of the beginning, of the beginning.

BACKGROUND

Title	Tomorrow Never Knows
Recording	Date April 6, 1966
Meter	4/4
Key	C Mixolydian
Song Form	Verse/Refrain
Phrasing	abb
Recording	*Revolver*
	1966 EMD/CAPITOL

Though Lennon's Beatles single "Rain" was released first, "Tomorrow Never Knows" was actually the first song to be adorned with the groundbreaking backward tape treatment. The song was brought into the studio for the first time on April 6, 1966.

Lennon called it his first psychedelic song, citing the *Tibetan Book of the Dead* as one of its big influences. The song does indeed have an eerie, cosmic edge as it hypnotically delivers up the seven two-line karmic couplets that comprise the lyric. "Tomorrow Never Knows" maintains this hypnotic atmosphere mainly due to production effects, though Lennon's choice to set the melody and harmony in Mixolydian mode strongly supports this mood.

Lennon said once that he had wanted to achieve the sound of thousands of chanting monks. To accomplish this, each of the Beatles worked at home on their Brennell tape recorders creating sound effects to add to the backdrop of the song. Though the sound effects did not sound exactly like chanting monks, they did provide and excellent backwash for the recording. The sound effects included the sound of seagulls (created by a distorted guitar) and an effect-enhanced wine glass. Many of the sounds were played forwards, backwards, speeded up, slowed down, or with a number of other effects, and were added to the rhythm track the next day.

Recording technology at the time allowed for a wide variety of possibilities, though Lennon and the Beatles had not yet had time to explore them. But with their hectic schedule of public appearances drastically curtailed in 1966, Lennon had more time to explore the use of new technology in his recordings. His interest in this subject, which began with this landmark song, would only grow as he progressed through his Beatles career.

The song was the very first recorded for the *Revolver* album. It was released in England on August 5, 1966 and three days later in America and worldwide.

Song Form

The song is set in basic 4/4 meter and is exceedingly simple. It has only one 8-bar section that repeats. The song is set in the classic verse/refrain format and contains seven verses altogether. Each verse ends with a double refrain that is different each time from the title. Usually in a verse/refrain song, the refrain contains the title, which is emphasized by constant repeats. But in this song, the title appears *nowhere*. Further, each one of the seven ending refrains presents seven different lyrical ideas. (See lyric sheet.) Through this technique, we see Lennon opening a brand new area of songwriting. Forget the repeated pop refrain; let the listener derive the meaning on their own without commercial repetition of a lyrical theme or title. Here is the form:

Verse/ Refrain	Verse/ Refrain	Verse/ Refrain	Verse/ Refrain	Keyboard Solo	Guitar Solo	Verse/ Refrain	Verse/ Refrain	Verse/ Refrain
8 bars	8 bars	8 bars	8 bars	8 bars	8 bars	8 bars	8 bars	8 bars

John indicated in numerous interviews and writings that he was fascinated with the number 9, mainly because his birthday was on October 9. John's magic number 9 appears in the form of this song:

4 verses + 2 solos + 3 verses = 9 sections

We shall see his obsession play out later in "Revolution 9."

Lyric Content

The opening lyric is a Zen-like beckoning to retreat into relaxation and a trip downstream. Then, a soothing refrain assures the listener that it is not really dying. In his own life, Lennon took to the Zen Buddhist philosophy that says that suffering is inseparable from existence. However, as the opening lyric subtly alludes, if one can eliminate ego, self-absorption, and worldly desire, a state of spiritual enlightenment beyond both suffering and existence can be achieved.

John has always said that a large portion of the lyric came from the *Tibetan Book of the Dead*. The book is not about death in the physical sense, but rather in the spiritual sense: a death of the ego. The lyric has a distinctly meditative nature, advising the listener to float away and listen to the music of one's soul; or to find the meaning of life and love within one's own heart. The lyrics tell of submission to the void, and of discovering the message from within.

After presenting all these intangible alternatives as a search for truth in life, Lennon ends the song with the message to live life to the very end…until it starts over again at the "beginning." He is echoing the Zen Buddhist philosophy of reincarnation, the rebirth of the soul into another body to begin the cycle of life anew. This ironic word is placed at the ending lyric, and it repeats over and over as the record fades out.

The song includes some classic Lennon-isms. The use of the words "color" and "living" in the same verse is a reference to television. At the time, NBC television referred to their network as the supplier of "living color." John was intrigued by the medium. When he wasn't appearing on television, one of John's favorite pastimes was to crash out in front of the telly.

This is a lyric that offers grounding but no resolution, consistent with its Zen-like nature. Its series of seven two-line verse/refrain expositions are concise, simple, direct, and thought provoking.

PHRASING

▶ *Harmonic Phrasing*

The song is set in C Mixolydian with a single C triad being sounded. The melody enters immediately on the 3rd of the chord. At the fifth bar of the verse, the C Mixolydian mode takes the day. Here, Lennon introduces the Mixolydian ♭VII chord, B♭ major:

Fig. 5.1. Verse harmonic phrasing

The bass remains on C, creating the semicadential chord B♭/C. Normally in this mode, B♭ moving directly up to C would create a perfect Mixolydian cadence. In this case, however, because the root remains as C, the B♭/C chord is actually heard as a C7sus4; the F in the B♭ triad becomes the suspended 4th with the C in the bass. The melody supplies the note E, which sits a third above the C to produce the C triad.

The Roman numeral analysis for B♭/C would be I7sus4. Therefore, the song really has just two different versions of the tonic I chord: I and I7sus4. This harmonic treatment is the perfect accompaniment for this dream-state lyric. By retaining the C in the bass throughout, Lennon creates a droning, hypnotic bottom for the song. The periodic and subtle changes generated by the upper movement of the notes E and F create an ambiguous sound canvas—is it C or Csus? At the same time, the very movement of these notes contributes a slight sense of motion in the harmonic structure. This slight movement helps support the all-important lyric by not getting in the way with lots of different harmonic changes.

In any case, we feel a sense of release from the grounded tonic C chord that begins the verse when it moves to the Bb/C chord bar 5. We also feel a sense of arrival back to tonic with the move to C7 at bar 7.

▌ Melodic Phrasing

The lyric for each verse is comprised of three phrases. The 4-bar section comprises the extremely short verse, while the consecutive 2-bar phrases contain a repeating refrain that presents a new lyric at each refrain:

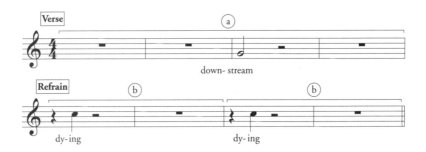

Fig. 5.2. Verse/refrain melodic phrasing

Without a repeating refrain, this is no sing-along. As soon as the listener is familiar with one refrain in this song, a brand new one is delivered up in the next verse/refrain section.

PROSODY

Melody/Harmony

In the first four bars, the melody comes off rather like a bugle call, as it descends in range utilizing only the stable tones Do, Mi, and Sol (C, E, and G). By contrast, the two answering phrases are shorter and stepwise, using two key notes in the scale: Te (a lowered 7th) and Do (Bb and C in C Mixolydian).

The continual interplay of the descending call-to-arms verse melody and its heavy lyrical message is balanced with the two ascending phrases in the refrain, which contain a lyric of hope or advice. This occurs in bars 5 and 7 below, where the lowered 7th resolves upward to the security of home-based Do (C):

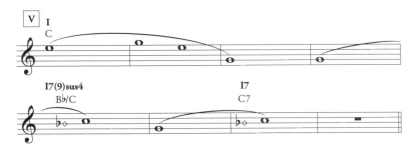

Fig. 5.3. Verse/refrain structural tones

Notice the way that the characteristic note from the C Mixolydian scale, B♭, further establishes the melody as C Mixolydian at bars 5 and 7. In fact, that fifth bar of each verse is rich with melodic and harmonic contrast. It is the perfect setting to spotlight the first of the double refrains.

SUMMARY

"Tomorrow Never Knows" was the first Beatles recording since "Eight Days a Week" to feature a fade-in. "Tomorrow Never Knows" also includes a fade-out. The fade-in and fade-out help create the song's "waves-upon-the shore" effect. With its drifting lines and refrains, the lyric seems to come out of nowhere. It washes up on the grounded C Mixolydian setting every time the progression moves from the B♭/C up to the C7.

The song's hypnotic nature makes it function as a sort of rocked-out cosmic lullaby. Admittedly, the lyrics are a bit heady, but the karmic advice is presented as a gentle tap on the shoulder. As the song steals away into the fade-out end, the listener is left with a sense of relaxed exhilaration and curiosity: "What is the meaning of this splendid feeling?"

With Lennon's newfound interest in combining studio wizardry and songwriting, "Tomorrow Never Knows" represents his realization of the variety of composing options now at his disposal. The song was a signal of new visions and new paths that would become increasingly present in his own writing, as we will soon see in "Rain," "Strawberry Fields Forever," "I Am the Walrus," and "Revolution 9."

Rain

Words and Music by John Lennon and Paul McCartney

If the rain comes they run and hide their heads. They might as well be dead. If the rain comes.—— If the rain comes. When the shines.

Rain,—— I don't mind.—

Shine,—— the wea-ther's fine.—

Verse 2

When the sun shines they slip into the shade,
And sip their lemonade.
When the sun shines,
When the sun shines.

Verse 3

I can show you that when it starts to Rain,
Ev'rything's the same.
I can show you,
I can show you.

Verse 4

Can you hear me that when it rains and shines,
It's just a state of mind.
Can you hear me?
Can you hear me?

BACKGROUND

Title	Rain
Recording Date	April 14, 1966
Meter	4/4
Key	G major
Song Form	Verse/Chorus
Phrasing	Verse: *abcb*
	Chorus: *aa*
Recording	*Beatles: Past Masters, Volume Two*
	1988 EMD/CAPITOL

"Rain" marks the first appearance of a soon-to-be signature compositional device for Lennon: the backward coda. It was as much a landmark for Lennon as was the fuzz-tone beginning of "I Feel Fine." The very first song treated to the backward tapes treatment, introduced by producer George Martin, was "Tomorrow Never Knows" from the *Revolver* album. "Rain" marks the second song to receive this special effect, but the first to include it as a separate coda.

The famous backward coda was actually an accidental discovery. It happened during John's late-night/early-morning playback of the day's recording session. In those days, the rough mixes of a session's work were given to the boys on "tails-out," 3" reel-to-reel audio tape. This meant that the tape first had to first be rewound and then played. John did not rewind the tape, and as a result he heard the entire session tape of "Rain" played backwards. John, soon realizing his mistake, sat in wonder as he listened to the mysterious cacophony. He was determined then and there to have the entire song released backwards!

As one can imagine, producer George Martin and bandmate Paul McCartney were not particularly supportive of this suggestion. A pop song released backwards into the pop music market under the Beatles' name? An extremely avant-garde suggestion, to say the least!

Eventually, a compromise was reached. The song is exactly three minutes (3:00) long. Two minutes and thirty seconds (2:30) were devoted to the normally recorded main body of the song, while the last thirty seconds (:30) were reserved for a variety of sounds, played both forwards and backwards, creating the backward coda.

The song, first recorded on April 14, 1966, was released only as a single in England on June 10, 1966. America got two versions: the single, released May 30, 1966 and as a track on the *Hey Jude* album, released on February 27, 1970. It was later released again worldwide on the *Past Masters, Volume Two* CD on March 7, 1988.

STRUCTURE

Song Form

The song is a move away from Lennon's AABA roots into the verse/chorus format. The song actually begins with a double verse, but there is a catch: The first verse is nine bars long and the second is nine and a half bars. All of the other verses are also nine bars long, in contrast to the more standard 8-bar section. There's that number 9 again!

Lennon expands the second verse by a half bar by adding a bar of 2/4 to the series of 4/4 bars. This metric change spotlights the upcoming section change from verse to chorus. At the point where another verse could begin, two beats go by and then the listener is regaled with the chorus intoning the song's title, "Rain."

This is the final form as performed by the Beatles in their recording from that summer of 1966:

Verse	Verse	Chorus	Verse	Chorus	Verse	Chorus	Coda
9 bars	9 1/2 bars	12 bars	9 bars	12 bars	9 bars	12 bars	Backward

As we have seen, Lennon had a knack for the AABA form. But just like "I'm a Loser," this song shows movement away from that classic form. Though the lyric for the chorus is sparse, Lennon managed to transform it into a true chorus. He did this by constructing a long, solid 12-bar section for the lyrics. Otherwise, those lyrics could have been introduced into a small 4-bar section, transforming the song into a verse/refrain format. Lennon divided his 12-bar chorus into two balanced 6-bar sections. The contrast of the unbalanced 9-bar verses against the balanced 12-bar chorus provides incredible spotlight for the title setting in the chorus.

Lyric Content

The story Lennon tells in this song is much different than anything released as a single up to this point. He did explore lyrical abstraction in his 1963 song "There's a Place," but even that was a love song of sorts. We have seen in "Tomorrow Never Knows" how Lennon began to move away from the standard boy/girl pop song lyrics. In "Rain," he continues the journey as he begins to explore deeper topics.

Of the four verses, the first two give a seemingly harsh assessment of the human condition: Those who run from the unknown are only running from the warming sun and the refreshing rain. They are living life without truly living. In the third verse, Lennon offers to show us and teach us an alternative. In the fourth, he ends the song with a question: do you understand?

Some listeners may find the lyric rather disturbing for a pop song. Lennon asks his audience to consider embracing life instead of hiding from it. The lyrics entice the listener to consider an encounter session with reality, rather than give in to the temptation to live an insulated life. But as Lennon offers: "I can show you that when it starts to rain, everything's the same." The gentle tone of the lyric helps keep the message subdued instead of preachy. It is a message one might want to whisper, rather than proclaim, lest it quickly become the newest bandwagon event. His is a simple plea for introspection.

PHRASING

Verse

▶ *Harmonic Phrasing*
The chord progression Lennon chose for this reverent ode is as simple as a summer shower: I, IV, and V.

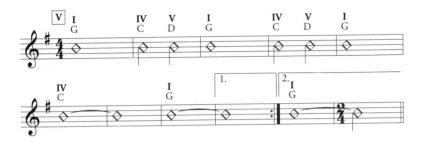

Fig. 5.4. Verse harmonic phrasing

It's no surprise that Lennon began the song with a 9-bar verse. He created a simple 2-bar harmonic phrase consisting of G, C, and D, and simply repeated it to fashion a 4-bar beginning. As he moves to what seems to be a third statement of the same chords, he hangs on the subdominant C triad for two whole bars, creating a plagal cadence into the tonic G major triad. Note in fig. 5.4 that the second ending contains an abrupt 2/4 bar that interrupts the plodding 4/4 meter and creates a 9 1/2–bar structure for the second verse.

▶ *Melodic Phrasing*

The phrasing for this song begins with a promise of simplicity and familiarity—three different phrases with one that is repeated:

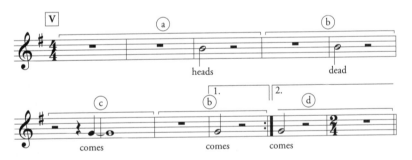

Fig. 5.5. Verse melodic phrasing

The use of the 9-bar section means that something has to be a little off-kilter. Note the beginning phrase, ⓐ, is three bars long, while the ⓑ and ⓒ phrases are two bars long. The resulting analysis is *abcb*, including the first ending. With the arrival of the second ending, Lennon adds another wrinkle by using the 2/4 bar. This creates an *abcd* section for the second verse.

Chorus

▶ *Harmonic Phrasing*

The chorus section stops the motion harmonically with the use of the pedal point on the tonic G throughout the entire section:

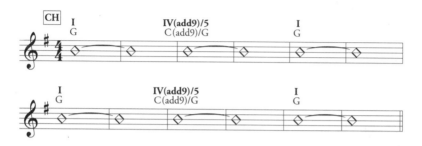

Fig. 5.6. Chorus harmonic phrasing

The 12-bar section is divided into two 6-bar units. The C/G chord is introduced halfway through each 6-bar statement. Moving to the subdominant C chord would normally give a lift to the chorus, because it provides a release from the tonic G. But retaining the note G in the bass C subdues the effect of the chord motion. This chord stability provides wonderful prosody with the descending melody and lyric at that point (he doesn't mind the rain) and creates the perfect contrast to the verse section.

As the chorus makes its entrance, an abrupt change in harmonic rhythm causes the whole song to seize up and come to a dead halt. The chords in the verse move at a rate of two to four beats (one or two chords per bar); the chorus slows to a harmonic rhythm of eight beats (one chord every two bars).

The chorus itself is comprised of only two chords, forming a IV–I plagal cadence. Unexpectedly, the chord progression gets stuck on that C/G for two full bars. The extended plagal cadence provides a very effective yet subtle punctuation to the faster-moving verse section. The minimalistic chorus, containing only two chords and eight words, creates an excellent spotlight for the title setting.

▶ *Melodic Phrasing*

The chorus contains two long 6-bar phrases full of warm and cozy droning chords and familiar repeating phrases. This creates the perfect arrival point for the song of the rain—a safe haven:

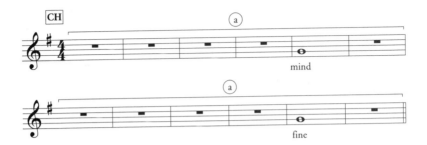

Fig. 5.7. Chorus melodic phrasing

The phrasal analysis is *aa*, as notated above. Compared to the unbalanced 2-bar and 3-bar phrases of the verses, the chorus's two long 6-bar phrases create a sense of balance. The unbalanced verse is great for spinning out the song's story, as its uneven phrase lengths provide lots of motion. The balanced chorus, by contrast, makes an excellent platform for the arrival of the song's message: "Rain, I don't mind. Shine, the weather's fine."

PROSODY

Verse

Lennon paints the verse melody from a limited palette, using simplicity itself. He first states both musical ideas back to back (bars 1–3), then repeats the second once again (bars 4–5). To conclude he simply repeats the first idea twice (bars 6–9). A perfect 9-bar verse is born:

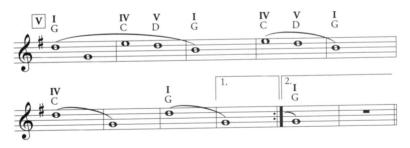

Fig. 5.8. Verse structural tones

The verse melody contains two main melodic gestures: the first encompassing bar 1; the second encompassing bars 2 and 3. In these three bars lie the entire verse melody.

The first five bars of the melody create great motion for the active part of the lyric by withholding its arrival at tonic. ("When the rain

comes, they run and hide their heads. They might as well be dead.")
By contrast the last four bars of the verse double-emphasize the dominant and tonic notes D and G, supporting the repetition at the end of the verse lyric.

Chorus

In the chorus melody, Lennon broke new ground. It was unlike any chorus melody he had ever composed. Instead of many notes and many syllables, he used very few syllables and many notes. This transformed the melody into a melisma—a treatment Lennon used often:

Fig. 5.9. Melismatic chorus melody (bars 1–3)

Melismas have been used in melody by nearly every composer from Bach to the Beatles themselves, but this one has a particularly Eastern flavor to it. Like much Eastern music, the chorus of "Rain" contains a droning tonic pedal below and a rhythmically active diatonic melodic line above.

The first four bars of the melody are made up of a little dance between the stable 5th degree of the key (D) and the unstable 4th degree (C). Lennon allows both the D and the C to dominate two full bars each before completing the lyric on the tonic:

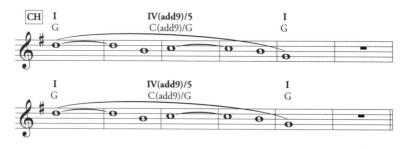

Fig. 5.10. Chorus structural tones

All three of these connect to form one long 6-bar phrase that is repeated exactly, except for the rhyming lyric, to create a 12-bar chorus.

Backward Coda

In the coda, a good percentage of the 4-track tape was also moving in the correct direction: forwards. But through a process of connecting several tape machines together, several signals could be sent simultaneously to a single track. To do this, continuous tape loops of varying lengths were created. (A tape loop is device that provides a continuous series of repeating sounds.) The Beatles created their tape loops by recording sounds onto a main reel of recording tape, isolating a specific area of sound by cutting the tape to a specific length, then splicing together the two ends of the tape to form a continuous loop.

The longer loops produced fewer repetitions of the sounds, while the shorter loops produced many repetitions. The loops were then threaded around the take-up reel, over the playback heads, and then around a waiting pencil that someone would hold in mid-air to maintain just enough tension. The tape loop would then make a three-point revolution around the reel, the heads, and the pencil, repeating endlessly.

The main vocal melody in the backward section is simply the very first three bars of the vocal from the first verse. The background vocals are backward, too. You can hear the Beatles singing "nair" instead of "rain."

In "Rain" Lennon asks the listener to address his or her inner thoughts and fears. Such a prospect might cause much turmoil. The backward coda represents this cosmic inner conflict—scary, but familiar.

Though Lennon really wanted to release the entire song backwards, he instead compromised by just using the backward coda. This was to become a signature compositional device for Lennon during this period. Later in 1966 he used it in "Strawberry Fields Forever," and again in 1967 in "I Am the Walrus." (Both of these songs and their backward codas are addressed later in this book. Lennon came closest to fulfilling his desire to release a "backward" song in 1968 when he composed "Revolution 9." Though "Revolution 9" is not really a backward song, it does sound like it's coming from another world. It too is addressed in chapter 7 of this book.)

SUMMARY

In "Rain," Lennon makes the abstract lyric easy to comprehend by repeating the lyric at the beginning and end of each verse. The flowing motion of the verse swirls into a great standstill as the chorus grinds to a halt on the tonic. But then the melody races forward, heraldlike, on a single syllable, literally proclaiming the two lyrical targets for the whole songs: "rain" and "shine."

"Rain" is a showcase for one of Lennon's favorite compositional techniques: minimalism. After the release of his first solo album,

John Lennon/Plastic Ono Band, he said that this song was his attempt to get minimal and trim everything down to basics, both in writing and production. Though "Rain's" layers of sound and backward/forward tape loops make the song quite the production, Lennon deftly accomplished his goal with the simple repeating verse lyric coupled with its extremely concise eight-word chorus.

She Said She Said

Words and Music by John Lennon and Paul McCartney

Verse 2

> I said, "Who put all those things in your head?
> Things that make me feel like I'm mad.
> And you're making me feel like I've never been born."

Verse 3

> I said, "Even though you know what you know,
> I know that I'm ready to leave.
> 'Cos you're making me feel like I've never been born."

BACKGROUND

Title	She Said She Said
Recording Date	June 21, 1966
Meter	4/4 and 3/4
Key	B♭ major
Song Form	AABA
Phrasing	Verse or A: *abc*
	Primary Bridge or B: *abcdb*
Recording	*Revolver*
	1966 EMD/CAPITOL

When Peter Fonda first listened to the Beatles' *Revolver* album and came to the song "She Said She Said," he knew exactly the origin of the song. After all, he was the song's inspiration.

As the story goes, while the Beatles were on tour in 1965, they stayed at a rented house in Benedict Canyon in the Los Angeles area. They traveled from there to gigs in Portland, San Diego, San Francisco, and Los Angeles. One afternoon, the Fab Four invited several celebrities over for a soirée. The luminaries included actor Peter Fonda.

During the party, Lennon overheard Fonda relating a horrific story to George Harrison. Fonda was telling Harrison that as a boy he had accidentally shot himself in the stomach. His heart had stopped beating three different times while he was on the operating table. He summed up the story to Harrison, saying he knew what it was like to be dead.

Lennon remembered the conversation and tried to formulate a song around Fonda's curious remark. He was getting nowhere with it, so he set it aside for awhile. Later, he was working on a song that also needed another section. Lennon decided to see if the two would go together. This new section proved to be the missing piece needed to complete "She Said She Said." Lennon said in an interview that he was delighted with the end result. Metrically speaking, it was Lennon's boldest move yet. He utilized two different time signatures: the original section is 4/4 time, while the new added section is 3/4 time.

"She Said, She Said" was the last song recorded for the *Revolver* album. John brought the song into the studio for rehearsal on June 21, 1966. The band completed the recording the same day, in only three takes. The world got its first hearing later that summer with the release of *Revolver* on August 5.

STRUCTURE

Song Form
The form of this strange song utilizes the most standard of the song forms, AABA:

A	A	B	A
Verse/Refrain	Verse/Refrain	Primary Bridge	Verse/Refrain
10 bars	10 bars	11 bars	10 bars

The meter is basic 4/4 meter until the arrival of the 11-bar primary bridge. At that point, the first two bars continue the 4/4 meter, but then abruptly shift to 3/4 time for the remaining nine bars.

Lyric Content
If the tale of Lennon, Fonda, and Harrison is true, the lyric does seem to encapsulate that very short encounter. The first verse reviews Fonda's statement, the second verse reveals Lennon's initial reaction to the remark, and the third verse describes Lennon's departure from the conversation because he found it too disturbing. The lyric in the primary bridge abruptly shifts to the past, abandoning the verse scenario altogether—a sudden flashback to his childhood when everything was secure and everything was alright.

PHRASING

Verse

▶ *Harmonic Phrasing*
This song, like "Tomorrow Never Knows" from the *Revolver* album, is set in Mixolydian mode. In this case, it's B♭ Mixolydian.

The verse's first three chords, Bb7, Ab, and Eb, give the impression of Eb major. The Bb and Ab function as V7 and IV of Eb, respectively. But as the song continues, we find that the Bb is actually the tonic, creating Bb Mixolydian instead of Eb major:

Fig. 5.11. Verse harmonic phrasing

▶ Melodic Phrasing

The lyric and melody divide the verse phrasing into three sections. Though all of the phrases end on beat 3, I analyze them as *abc*:

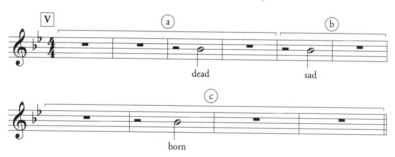

Fig. 5.12. Verse melodic phrasing

These different phrase endings cause the verse to speed up and slow down, swerving untamed into the final cadence. The effect is so great that Lennon had George Harrison echo the last melody line in the verse just to help shut it down properly. Without the echo, the melody doesn't close properly, because all the endings are on beat 3 instead of strong beat 1. Even though Harrison's guitar lick also ends on beat 3, Harrison's simple repetition on guitar imparts balance to the previous vocal phrase.

Primary Bridge

▶ Harmonic Phrasing

Where the verse is made up of more open cadences, the primary bridge begins in a land of comforting closed cadences. We get both classic Mixolydian cadences right off the bat in the first seven bars: B♭7–A♭–B♭7 and B♭7–F7–B♭7.

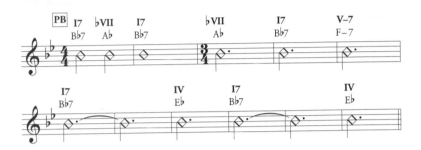

Fig. 5.13. Primary bridge harmonic phrasing

With the onset of the B♭7 in bar 6, the last six bars of the primary bridge pivot into two open cadences, both of which end on E♭, just like the verse. This provides the perfect harmonic setting for a daydream trip back in time to childhood, when all was right in the world.

▶ *Melodic Phrasing*

The phrasing for the bridge section is curious indeed. It consists of a series of 2-bar phrases with one 3-bar phrase inserted in the middle. The first 2-bar phrase is in 4/4 time, while the second phrase is in 3/4 time. Immediately, there is a major shift in the feel of the song:

Fig. 5.14. Primary bridge melodic phrasing

Lennon's excursion into 3/4 time continues with another 2-bar phrase at bar 3 of the bridge. This produces three completely different phrases: *abc*. Then the section is totally unbalanced with the introduction of the song's first and only 3-bar phrase. The last phrase at first seems to be a repeat of the decelerating 3-bar phrase, but Lennon chops off a bar, creating the section's final 2-bar phrase, ⓑ. This ⓑ phrase is a repeat of the second phrase pattern from this section and accelerates the primary bridge abruptly back into the top of the verse section.

The main portion of the bridge, the 3/4 section, was written after the verse. Lennon's novel solution to begin the bridge with two bars of 4/4 borrowed from the verse was ideal. Those first two bars literally function as the "bridge to the bridge."

The melodic phrasing for the bridge creates a pleasant conflict with the lyric and harmonic phrasing. On one hand, you have those pleasant cadences in the harmony and the talk of being a boy once again with the whole world "alright." On the other hand, Lennon sends the listener off into a tumbling world of 3/4 time. Set in juxtaposition to its counterpart 4/4 verse, the change to 3/4 in the bridge gives a sudden feeling of acceleration, as the downbeat comes quicker with each bar.

In the end, all four elements—lyric, harmony, meter, and melody—*do* come together to create a rather accurate world of a young boy: many things are safe and secure, yet the world is also full of unknowns.

PROSODY

Verse

The melody for the first six bars remains within the range of a 5th. In these opening phrases, the melody always begins and ends on the tonic note, B♭:

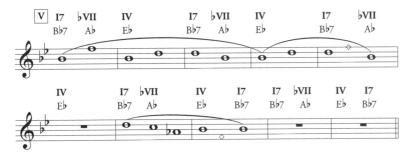

Fig. 5.15. Verse structural tones

To keep the melody of the verses moving forward against those B♭ stopping points, Lennon calls for the unstable A♭ chord to harmonize the B♭ tonic endings. This mildly dissonant tension begs for resolution.

To conclude the verse, Lennon begins the final melodic phrase on the stable 3rd, D, at the seventh bar. The melody quickly descends to the characteristic note of the B♭ Mixolydian mode, A♭. The unstable A♭ is quickly resolved upwards to the tonic B♭ in the next bar to give some closure to the verse melody.

Refer now to bar 8 on the lead sheet, and notice that the melody of the verse ends on tonic B♭, both harmonically and melodically. This *should* completely close down the verse. However, the rhythm of the melody cadences on beat 3, which keeps the section slightly open. This slightly open quality is the real reason for the aforementioned Harrison guitar riff heard in the last two bars of the verse.

Primary Bridge

Lennon does not expand the melodic range in the bridge. Rather, he provides a series of interesting melodic variations with the same melody notes already used in the verse section. The opening phrase of the bridge starts on stable note D, then moves to unstable notes E♭ and C before resolving to the tonic B♭. For the very next phrase he does the same thing—but *backwards!* The last two phrases emphasize all three of the stable tones in the mode: B♭, D, and F. But both phrases end on the unstable 4th degree, E♭. This is the perfect cast for molding a bridge that returns beautifully back to the verse.

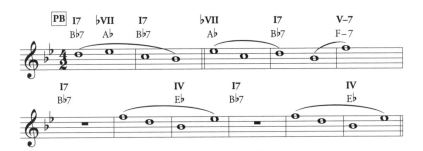

Fig. 5.16. Primary bridge structural tones

SUMMARY

On the original vinyl release of *Revolver*, "She Said, She Said" was the last song on the first side. "Tomorrow Never Knows" was the last song on the second side. Lennon no doubt had a hand in deciding to leave the listener with a Lennon song at the end of both sides.

In these days of compact discs, "She Said, She Said" comes sandwiched between "Yellow Submarine" and "Good Day Sunshine." The original vinyl LP setup left the song ringing in the mind of the listener until the record could be turned over.

The melody of the verse begins with the simple, almost childlike major-key stepwise melody, giving no hint of the Mixolydian harmony that accompanies it. It is only at the end, with the appearance of the Ab in the melody, that the song reaches a level of greater rhythmic and melodic complexity.

The real contrast is the constantly changing rhythmic structure of the bridge melody. The 4/4 and 3/4 meters underpinning the section provide even more rhythmic interest. It is fascinating that Lennon had had the 4/4 A section lying around for months before he found a bridge to finish it off. And then when he did come up with a bridge, he chose one composed in 3/4! It was a bold and astute move, as mixed meter was uncharted territory in 1960s pop songwriting. Another Lennon landmark!

Strawberry Fields Forever

Words and Music by John Lennon and Paul McCartney

Verse 2

No one, I think, is in my tree,

I mean it must be high or low.

That is, you can't, you know, tune in, but that's all right,

That is, I think it's not too bad.

Verse 3

Always know sometimes think it's me,

But you know I know when it's a dream.

I think a "no" will be a "yes," but it's all wrong,

That is, I think I disagree.

BACKGROUND

Title	Strawberry Fields Forever
Recording Date	November 24, 1966
Meter	4/4, 3/4, and 2/4
Key	A major
Song Form	Verse/Chorus
Phrasing	Verse: *abab*
	Chorus: *abcd*
Recording	*Magical Mystery Tour*
	1967 EMD/CAPITOL

"Strawberry Fields Forever" is regarded by many as Lennon's song-writing masterpiece. It is a landmark piece that, especially because of its release as a single, separates the earlier songs from his later work. Lennon, taking the experience he gained working with tape loops for "Rain" and "Tomorrow Never Knows," expanded his palette of sounds by asking producer George Martin to score brass and string parts for this song. The result was a sound unprecedented by any Beatles song.

The astute Martin took John's simple ballad and transformed it into a pop masterpiece. Rather than using the four trumpets and three cellos in a more typical lush, Hollywood fashion, Martin chose to exploit the success he had already achieved using classically influenced arrangements. (He had used a string quartet and a double string quartet with great success on Paul McCartney's "Yesterday" and "Eleanor Rigby.") For "Strawberry Fields" Martin supplied a very active, classically based cello line throughout, as well as heralding trumpets for the chorus.

John first recorded a version with the Beatles and afterwards asked producer Martin to develop a score for the song. In the process of doing this, there were several changes: strings, brass, a new key, and a slightly faster tempo. Upon reviewing both versions, John liked the beginning of the original version but the latter half of the second version. He asked Martin to see if the two could be linked together. With a raised eyebrow and probably not much hope of a usable result, producer George Martin indicated he would investigate Lennon's request.

Many stories exist as to how this played out. The most famous story is that the Beatles' original version was near the key of A, while the Martin-orchestrated second version was in the key of C. The magic of connecting the two versions was to speed one version up and slow one version down until the tempos and the keys synchronized.

The tapes of these sessions reveal that the original Beatles version is in the key of B while the orchestrated version is in the key of C. However, tape speed can affect keys, especially when one is working with copies of copies of bootlegs. If the above scenario is true, Martin may have slowed down *both* versions with his variable-speed tape machine until the two songs synchronized perfectly in tempo and key.

In any case, the final key of the official release is somewhere between A and B♭. Lennon was completely satisfied with Martin's final result, probably because the slowing of one or both versions created the dreamy, surrealistic atmosphere required to support the song's music and introspective lyric.

The song was first recorded on November 24, 1966. It was released in America as a single on February 13, 1967 and four days later in England. The song was never released on any album in England, but appeared on the *Magical Mystery Tour* album, released in America on November 27, 1967.

STRUCTURE

Song Form

After the brief mellotron introduction played by Paul McCartney, the first section heard is actually the chorus, not the verse. Set in the simple verse/chorus format, Lennon simply reverses the order from this:

Verse 1	Chorus	Verse 2	Chorus	Verse 3	Chorus	Coda

to this:

Chorus	Verse 1	Chorus	Verse 2	Chorus	Verse 3	Chorus	Coda
10 bars	8 bars	10 bars	8 bars	10 bars	8 bars	10 bars	Tape

This is the same reverse format that Lennon employed in "Baby's in Black." The listener is treated to four hearings of the marvelous chorus with this format. Opening with the call-to-action chorus gives an extra spotlight.

Lyric Content

The opening chorus lyric beckons the listener to come with. But whither? To Strawberry Fields: the idyllic respite from Lennon's youth in Liverpool, promising freedom from reality and inhibitions. He is referring to the real Strawberry Field, a Salvation Army orphanage located near his childhood home in Woolton, Liverpool. The main house, bedecked in Gothic Victorian splendor and located on mysterious, wooded grounds, captivated Lennon on his frequent trips there as a child. He recognized this as a place where he could be free—alone with his imagination and ideas.

In the first verse Lennon describes the "normal" world as a place where people trudge though life with averted eyes and retreat to social biases. "Rain" revisited. In the remaining two verses, he lets the listener into his inner world, a world in which he feels different and sometimes alone. At the same time he reveals acceptance of the world in its "blindness." Lennon's prescription for an escape from the world remains the same throughout the duration of the song: come on down...and recharge...here in Strawberry Fields...forever.

PHRASING

Chorus

▶ *Harmonic Phrasing*

The definitive copyrighted version of "Strawberry Fields Forever" is in the key of A, though the record is closer to B♭. I analyze the song here in A.

The harmonic progression delivers up a distinct A Mixolydian (big surprise there, huh?) flavor to it with the use of I to V–7 (A to E–7). By the end, Lennon moves clearly into the key of A major:

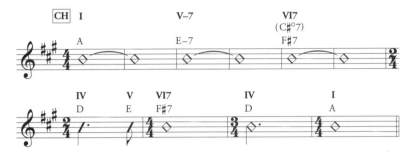

Fig. 5.17. Chorus harmonic phrasing

The most dramatic moment in the chorus is the entrance of the exhilarating F♯7 chord (VI7 of the key) and its move to the diatonic D major triad, IV in this key. In subsequent choruses, Lennon darkens the mood by reharmonizing the F♯7 with a C♯°7. The chorus concludes with a classic plagal cadence, IV to I.

This song has an atmosphere of fantasy, created in large part by its production. But the song itself shines through all the newly-discovered production techniques. Note the use of the 2/4 and 3/4 bars, and the erratic harmonic rhythm. At first Lennon holds the chords for two long bars each. Then at line 2, the chords begin to move quickly and then slow down again to one chord per bar.

Lennon's use of harmonic rhythm in the chorus is essential to achieving the resulting dreamy sound created by the fusion of the music and lyric.

▶ Melodic Phrasing
Lennon's long initial 4-bar statement sets a slow, dreamy tone for this psychedelic ballad:

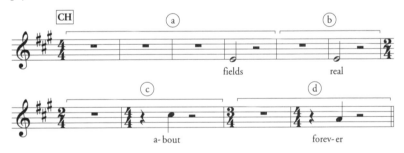

Fig. 5.18. Chorus melodic phrasing

The remaining six bars of the 10-bar section are divided up into *abcd* phrasing. It is a very unusual setup for such an overwhelmingly popular chorus. (It was the late 1960s, after all. The times were

becoming more experimental and Lennon was leading the charge.)
Each of the 2-bar phrases creates three totally different effects:

- The first phrases ⓐ and ⓑ utilize only 4/4 meter.
- The third phrase ⓒ utilizes both 2/4 and 4/4 meter.
- The fourth phrase ⓓ utilizes both 3/4 and 4/4 meter.

Verse

▶ *Harmonic Phrasing*

The verse moves directly into the sweet, heavenly key of E major.
(Music folklore attributes an aural connection between the key of E
major and heaven above.)

Fig. 5.19. Verse harmonic phrasing

The verse for "Strawberry Fields Forever" has two different keys.
Unlike the parallel keys of the chorus (A Mixolydian and A major),
the verse maintains E major for the first four bars and then modulates
back to A major for the last four bars. This works because the D triad
at bar 4 is heard as ♭VII in the key of E major. But the D triad in bar 5
is swept into a cadence back to A major at the sixth bar and is heard as
IV. The last two bars finish clearly in A major, ready to make another
entrance to the chorus.

Unlike other Lennon songs, *both* sections close down tight on the
tonic chord. Even though the song was very experimental in many
ways, Lennon retained an emphasis on tonic. The spotlighted tonic
acts as an anchor amid the myriad of sounds and keys.

▶ *Melodic Phrasing*

The phrasing in the verse section, *abab*, makes the verse actually
much more choruslike:

Fig. 5.20. Verse melodic phrasing

This simple phrasing provides a comfortable map for the adventurous road trip through Lennon's wandering melodies, lyrics, and modulations. The verses act as the journey, arriving back to the safe-at-home chorus as each comes to an end.

PROSODY

Chorus

The melody for this chorus begins simply, with a not-uncommon interplay between scale degrees 3 and 4. There is no hint whatsoever of the land of enchantment that Lennon has in store. The listener is nonetheless transported downward through the luscious Mixolydian G, finally coming to rest on the now-minor dominant, E–7. (Normally E7, with its bluesy tritone, would be the expected dominant. The E–7 has a more soft-pedaled effect.)

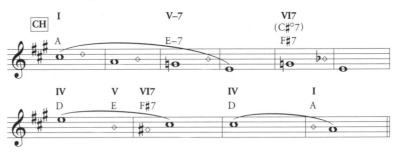

Fig. 5.21. Chorus structural tones

As Lennon then moves to reharmonize the gesture with the F♯7 chord, the melody sweeps the listener away by moving up an entire octave. But it's not a harsh movement, and as the chorus ends, the melody takes the promising lyric into a delicate landing on the tonic note and chord as we come to rest at Strawberry Fields:

...and nothing to get hung about,
Strawberry fields forever.

At the end of the chorus section, Lennon throws an interesting curve into the melodic rhythm. The harmony and form grind to a halt, while the lyric, the melody, and its melodic rhythm lurch forward to finish up on the second beat with the lyric "ever." Meanwhile, all the other instruments have stopped on beat 1.

This treatment helps create the dreamy, slip-sliding effect at the end of this section. The two downward shifts in the melody in line 1 moving to the dramatic upward shift in line 2 carry the listener along a rather rambunctious journey. But both the lyric and the music come together in perfect union to finish off this powerful verse.

Verse

The melody of the verse is a study in resolution and nonresolution:

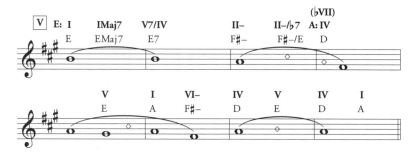

Fig. 5.22. Verse structural tones

Coming off the A chorus, the opening melody note B sounds as if it is the unstable 2nd degree Re over the E major triad, which sounds like the V chord. But the move to the Emaj7 chord at beat 3 establishes the key of E major, and the B takes on a stable character as its 5th degree. The A and F♯ in the second phrase now carry the motion and instability. In the third melodic phrase, the song begins to modulate back to A major and A begins to feel like tonic again.

This setup gives Lennon lots of room to use his musical and lyrical paintbrush. The B in the melody is enchantingly ambiguous: At first it is swallowed up in the stability of the opening E chord, but then the music and lyric relentlessly hammer the A until the verse ending finally delivers the requisite resolution.

Both musically and lyrically, each of the verses provides an inside view of three exquisite reveries from the mind of John Lennon. His choice to begin each of the verses on the dominant and modulate back to the tonic is an ingenious move. It works so well because he places the final tonic chord on beat 3 instead of beat 1 of the last bar. This treatment actually gives the ending an illusion of a meter shift to 2/4. The verse feels like it is literally spilling back into the contrasting chorus each time: dreamy internal images in the verses; dramatic external narratives in the chorus.

Backward Coda

"Strawberry Fields Forever" is the second song in which Lennon used the backward coda. This backward coda features tape loops of the rhythm section and vocals as in "Rain," but also features backward keyboard, horn, and string parts. It also includes the famous sloweddown Lennon quote, "cranberry sauce," at the very end. Later on, during the historic "Paul is dead" hoax of fall 1969, some fans interpreted the Lennon quote as "I buried Paul." Lennon, however, always confirmed that it was indeed "cranberry sauce." Lennon would include his signature backward coda for a third and final song, "I Am the Walrus," the following year.

SUMMARY

"Strawberry Fields Forever," together with Paul's "Penny Lane" A-side, was the Beatles' first single release for 1967. Lennon was on a roll with his newfound ideas for songwriting and record-making.

George Martin once described this song as a tone poem ballad reminiscent of the early impressionist composers Debussy and Ravel. He also compared the song with the art of Salvador Dali. The final recording of the song does indeed reflect both flavors. The music is an impressionistic pastiche of ambiguous tonality, while the lyric is a surreal, Dali-esque psychological journey. The A major/Mixolydian chorus, by now a classic Lennon compositional device, commands immediate attention with its compelling invitation to Strawberry Fields. Meanwhile the soft and lyrical E major verses take the listener on a floating, inside-out-view of the world and its psyche.

When interviewed by David Sheff for *Playboy* in 1980 (Dowdling, 1989), John said about the song: "It wasn't a new awakening. It was the fact that I was putting it down on paper. I was awake all my life." In other words Lennon was using the song to describe the way that his highly developed intuition about life and people made him feel so different from most people. He continues:

> *I was different than others. I was different all my life. My influences are tremendous, from Lewis Carroll to Oscar Wilde to tough little kids that*

used to live near me. I always was so psychic or intuitive and poetic, or whatever you want to call it, that I was always seeing things in a halluci-natory way that always saw beyond the mask. And it's very scary when you're a child, because there is nobody to relate to.

As you reflect upon the lyric and music for "Strawberry Fields Forever," realize that Lennon is trying to reveal his true inner self. Lennon's view is apparently one of inner isolation—but then isolation is something common to the human condition. We are all alone in the end. As Lennon sings about these complex issues in his own life, he sings about his listeners' lives as well, and his genuinely vulnerable lyric and music strike a chord.

CHAPTER 6   1967

The year 1967 was Lennon's most expansive one as a songwriter. The Beatles had given up touring, giving each member a chance to recharge and explore their music more deeply. Lennon was extremely interested in expanding the bounds of pop songs, and his songs from 1967 reflect that. With new technology came new possibilities in songwriting and record-making. By 1967 Lennon had full access to all the latest equipment at Abbey Road Studios—and to producer George Martin—in order to make his songs come alive.

This year saw Lennon's lowest output of songs: only six. He did cowrite with McCartney on three or four songs during this year, but he only contributed four songs of his own to the *Sgt. Pepper* album. Further, he only contributed *one* song, "I Am the Walrus" to the other 1967 album, *Magical Mystery Tour*. But while the number of songs may have been smaller, the depth of the songs was quite significant. The 1967 songs are much more complex than those of earlier years, both in terms of form and orchestration. The songs I will discuss represent the lion's share of his work for the year:

"A Day in the Life"
"Lucy in the Sky with Diamonds"
"All You Need Is Love"
"I Am the Walrus"

Lennon based "A Day in the Life" and "I Am the Walrus" on the standard AABA form, but with very unexpected transformations. He also conferred with producer George Martin in order to provide elaborate orchestrations for the songs.

In "Lucy in the Sky with Diamonds" Lennon explores the verse/transitional bridge/chorus form for the very first time. "All You Need Is Love" is treated to new compositional techniques, such as mixed meter and opposing bass lines between the verse and the chorus. Both songs are treated with studio and orchestral sweeteners of the composer's own design.

Lennon said in many interviews that he did not care much for production. In fact, his first solo album after leaving the Beatles, *John Lennon Plastic Ono Band*, was a stark-naked trio album. There was very little studio magic evident on that 1970 album. 1967, however, stands out as his year-long exploration into the myriad of studio possibilities.

All of the songs to be explored here are now classics. We will find as we continue to follow Lennon's journey in songwriting that, in the end, he would prefer the likes of the basic three-minute pop song, keeping the studio magic to a reasonable level. But right now, it's 1967 again. Let's take a detailed look at Lennon's offerings from the Summer of Love.

A Day in the Life

Words and Music by John Lennon and Paul McCartney

I read the news— to-day— oh,— boy a-bout— a lu-cky man— who made the grade.—

And though the news— was ra-ther sad, well, I just had to laugh— I saw the pho-to-graph.—

He blew his mind— out— in a car.— He did-n't no-tice that the lights had changed.

A crowd of peo-ple stood and stared. They'd seen his face be-fore.—

No-bod-y was real-ly sure if he was from the House of Lords.—

(Continued on following page)

Verse 3

> I saw a film today, oh boy,
>
> The English army had just won the war.
>
> A crowd of people turned away,
>
> But I just had to look,
>
> Having read the book.
>
> I'd love to turn you on.

Verse 4

> I read the news today, oh boy,
>
> Four thousand holes in Blackburn, Lancashire,
>
> And though the holes were rather small,
>
> They had to count them all.
>
> Now they know how many holes it takes to fill the Albert Hall.
>
> I'd love to turn you on.

Title	A Day in the Life
Recording Date	January 19, 1967
Meter	4/4 and 2/4
Key	G major and E major
Song Form	AAABCA
Phrasing	Verse 1: *aabcc*
	Verse 2: *abaca*
	Verse 3 and 4: *aabcbd*
	Primary Bridge 1: *abcd/abcc*
	Primary Bridge 2: *abac*
Recording	*Sgt. Pepper's Lonely Hearts Club Band*
	1967 EMD/CAPITOL

This song from the *Sgt. Pepper* album provides us with a good opportunity to compare Lennon and McCartney's songwriting styles. The verses of the song are Lennon's, while the connecting melody to the orchestral section and the primary bridge are McCartney contributions.

For John, this song began with his Uncle George, who taught him how to carefully read and enjoy a newspaper. The story goes that Lennon was reading the January 17, 1967 edition of the *Daily Mail* newspaper and began composing the song right from the day's news. Lennon appeared in the studio two days later to make the first recording of the song.

One of the news stories John encountered was the coroner's report on the death of twenty-one-year-old Tara Browne, heir to the Guinness fortune and friend of Lennon. Browne had fatally crashed his Lotus Elan into the back of a parked van on December 18, 1966. The other was a story of the four thousand potholes plaguing the streets of Blackburn, Lancashire. The subject of the third story was a film, *How I Won the War*, in which John had been an actor. The film was shot during fall 1966 and was released in fall 1967.

This song has received widespread praise, from inner-circle fan Julian Lennon to renowned composer Leonard Bernstein. McCartney credits the wild orchestral section between the verses and the bridge as being partially influenced by the music of twentieth-century avant garde composer Karlheinz Stockhausen.

The song's instrumentation was the most ambitious of the Lennon/McCartney repertoire. From the original January 19 2-track recording that consisted of guitar, piano, percussion, and vocals, the song kept evolving little by little until finally, a 40-piece orchestra was added on February 10. The song was released on the *Sgt. Pepper* album the following June.

chapter 6 · a day in the life

Song Form

Except for a couple of 2/4 bars that find their way into the bridge section, the whole song is set in 4/4 time. The form of the song is a slightly transformed AABA.

Both Lennon and McCartney had big plans for the two unfinished song sections that comprise this historic composition. John developed the A section, but after that it remained unfinished. Paul similarly had the genesis of something ready, but it also was unfinished. They decided to try to *push* them together to see if it would work. Usually, the team's cowriting efforts would involve one of them listening to the other's unfinished work and crafting new material based on that listening. Instead, they literally pieced the two unfinished parts together by scoring an orchestral section to both separate and connect the dreamy A section with the upbeat B section. After adding the orchestral coda, the final form becomes:

A	A	A	Interlude	B	C	A
10 bars	9 bars	11 bars	12 bars	9 1/2 bars	10 bars	11 bars

As you can see, there is not *one* standard 8-bar section in the entire song. The use of the sections containing an odd number of bars keeps things lurching forwards and jumping backwards, creating a slightly surreal backdrop for the song's otherwise squarish melodic phrasing.

Lyric Content

Of the four verses, the opening two are devoted to the aforementioned car accident, while the third verse is a sneaky film preview of *How I Won the War*. The final verse addresses the state of road conditions in Blackburn, Lancashire and their unexpected relationship to the Albert Hall.

The lyric weaves its magic for the most part without rhyme, except to punctuate the verse endings:

> "sad," "laugh," and "photograph" in verse 1
> "before" and "lords" in verse 2
> "look" and "book" in verse 3
> "small," "all," and "hall" in verse 4

It's interesting to note that Lennon used rhyme three times in both the opening and closing verses for acceleration purposes, but reverts to a standard of only two times each in the middle two verses. He uses a combination of deception and ambiguity—setting us up to expect a certain kind of rhyming structure, but then delivering a somewhat ambiguous structure instead. The addition of the third rhyme in verse 1 provides a bit of forward motion. By comparison, verse 2, with its two rhymes, seems to have more of a conclusion. This creates mild confusion for the listener: which is the true rhyme standard in the song, verse 1 or 2? Then verse 3, like verse 2, employs two rhymes—but they are in different locations. By verse 3, the listener realizes that there is no rhyme standard. Lennon brings the deception and ambiguity full circle as he fashions verse 4 to contain three rhymes—like verse 1.

The total effect of the ambiguity and deception is this:

Verse 1 sets the standard, rhyming the last three lyric lines.
(boy, grade, **sad**, **laugh**, **photograph**)
Verse 2 deviates from that standard. It is *deceptive.*
(car, changed, stared, **before**, **lords**)
Verse 3 further deviates from verses 1 and 2, and then leads the listener into the wild orchestral interlude and bridge. Its effect is both *deceptive* and *ambiguous.*
(boy, **war**, away, **before**, book)
Verse 4 returns to the standard set by verse 1. This is *deceptive*, but familiar.
(boy, Lancashire, **small**, **all**, **hall**)

Overall, the shifting rhyme patterns give the song a rather ambiguous, searching nature. Lennon's choice to align verses 1 and 4 with the same rhyme pattern gives a sense of closure to this rather unwieldy epic of a Beatles song.

PHRASING

Verses

▶ *Harmonic Phrasing*
The harmonic structure of "A Day in the Life" takes on several lives in the four verses and bridge. All of the verses are based on this simple 8-bar progression:

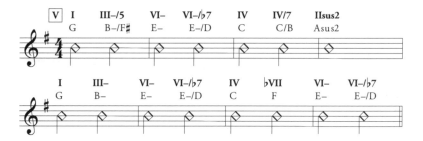

Fig. 6.1. Verse harmonic phrasing

The progression divides into two 4-bar sections. Each begins the same, but ends differently. In the first four bars, the bass line descends stepwise down an octave to cadence to A minor.

The second section drops a fifth down to F, and then continues stepwise down to E minor, then to E minor/D. Lennon employs three different endings for the four verses, utilizing the same ending for verses 3 and 4. In verse 1, he adds two extra bars to create a 10-bar verse. In verse 2, only one bar is added, creating a 9-bar verse. In verses 3 and 4, three extra bars are added, for two 11-bar verses.

In the first ending, Lennon simply repeats the last portion of the original 8-bar verse section and cadences back to G. Note the cadence does not move through the usual V7 chord but rather the more ambiguous C/D chord, which functions as V7sus4. The 3rd of the chord, or B, would normally lead strongly to the C. But because there is no B leading tone, this chord contributes ambiguity to the cadence, and supports a sense of **pandiatonicism** that permeates the song, as we shall examine in the melody section. (Pandiatonicism occurs when all seven notes of the diatonic scale are emphasized equally. In diatonic music, two notes dominate: the most stable note, Do, and the most unstable note, Ti. The resolution of Ti to Do defines a diatonic progression, and the suppression of that resolution often imparts a sense of pandiatonicism and allows space for other notes to "shine.")

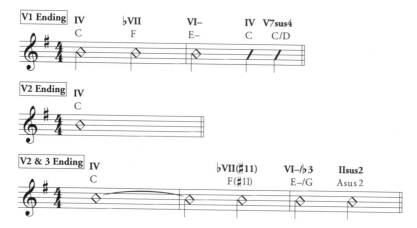

Fig. 6.2. Verse endings

In the second ending, Lennon has stopped short on the C chord and moved directly back to tonic.

By contrast, in endings 3 and 4, the bass line begins to move upwards from the F chord, which has been delayed a half bar, as illustrated in fig. 6.3.

This upward-moving bass against the static-sounding B (which is present in each of these chords) creates forward motion. As the bass moves up, the upper chord structures are either sustained or move back and forth. The changes are very subtle, so as not to confuse the listener—but rather to turn the listener on, as promised in the very dreamy lyric that goes with it.

Fig. 6.3. Bass line in ending for verses 3 and 4

▶ *Melodic Phrasing: Verse 1*

The lyric in verse 1 seems at first to divide up into four even 2-bar phrases. Four of them in a row imparts a sense of balance (2 + 2 balanced by 2 + 2). But Lennon's lyric for this verse is five lines long, not four. The fifth 2-bar phrase (echoing the fourth) appears to rhyme with the previous two, creating a 10-bar verse (2 + 2, imbalanced by 2 + 2 + 2).

This imbalance is excellent for verse writing, because it keeps the story moving in unexpected ways and keeps the listener's interest. The resulting phrase structure is *aabcc*. The illustration below shows that each of the first two phrases (*aa*) is two bars long and ends on beat 2. Lennon then creates motion in the verse by inserting the remaining three phrases to create the imbalance described above (*bcc*):

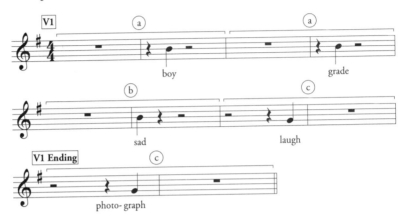

Fig. 6.4. Verse 1 melodic phrasing

The entire first line of the above example contains the opening *aa* phrases. The ⓐ phrase repetition creates symmetry and balance. What does the listener expect next, after hearing two ⓐ phrases? The answer is very simple: the same thing (ⓐ), or something new (ⓑ).

The next phrase is indeed new—ⓑ, ending on beat 1. Lennon's surprise, his subtle forward motion, is the introduction of the ⓒ phrases that end on beat 4. (Recall that beat 4 is the weakest beat of the bar and therefore has the most forward motion of all the beats.)

Taking a closer look at the closing six bars of the verse, one can also see more of Lennon's use of ambiguity and deception. The cumulative effect of the melodic and lyric phrasing helps this right along. For instance, rhyme creates a static thread that connects the ⓑ and ⓒ phrases ("sad," "laugh," and "photograph"). At the same time, Lennon uses two different melodic and two different rhythmic endings for these rhymes:

Mi (the note B) in the ⓑ phrase (beat 1)
Do (the note G) in the ⓒ phrases (beat 4)

With the melody, rhyme, and rhythmic ending of the ⓒ phrases exactly the same, deception and ambiguity rule the day. The emphasis in the verse shifts to the last two phrases. This further isolates the ⓑ phrase, leaving it to stand alone between two twin sections—*aabcc*. It is an excellent phrase structure for a motion-filled lyric. There is the deception and emphasis of the double ⓒ phrases, with the ⓑ emerging as its own focal point—simply because it is heard only once. The ⓑ is automatically elevated.

▶ Melodic Phrasing: Verse 2

The first eight bars of the second, third, and fourth verses are the same harmonically, rhythmically, and melodically. Verse 2, however, has one extra bar. Since the second verse is of a different length and has different phrase endings, the inner form is changed from *aabcc* to *abaca*. The initial rhythmic phrase ⓐ is repeated three times in this verse:

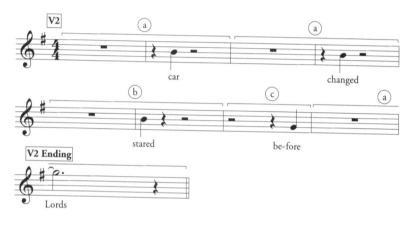

Fig. 6.5. Verse 2 melodic phrasing

Lennon uses an entirely different approach to the phrasing of verse 2, the most noticeable being the change in length from 10 bars to 9 bars. This is significant because he not only retained the five-line setup in the verse, and made the last line of verse 2 much longer than the last line of verse 1.

The *abaca* setup gives the ⓐ phrases the most repetition. A classic technique is to emphasize similar phrases by placing rhymes at the end. Lennon chose to disregard this technique by including no rhyme whatsoever. This dampens the emphasis of those ⓐ phrases. The lack of rhyme creates a more flowing, through-composed nature in the verse, despite the strong rhythmic appearance (three times) of ⓐ.

▶ Melodic Phrasing: Verses 3 and 4

Verses 3 and 4 both have three extra bars—creating an 11-bar section:

Fig. 6.6. Verses 3 and 4 melodic phrasing

Even though the beginning verses have a changing nature, the last two more or less solidify. We have observed how Lennon chose to align the rhyme patterns in verses 1 and 4. However, except for lyric, he chose to make verses 3 and 4 identical in *all* respects. While we will never know why Lennon did that, we can observe its effect: the similarity of verses 3 and 4 (harmonically, melodically, rhythmically, and phrasally) helps solidify their dominance in the song. This simple repetition makes verse 4 the strongest in the whole song, thereby emphasizing its lyric the most.

It is interesting to note that the "I'd love to turn you on" section that connects the melody to the orchestral section is the McCartney contribution to the evolution of the verses. All of the verse material is John's, except the lyric that connects the verses to the bridge. It is as if John hands off the song to Paul as the verses end and the bridges begin.

Orchestral Interlude

The "middle," as the Beatles called it, is a far cry from their 8-bar standard. In this case, after the vocal is complete in verse 3, there is a 12-bar avant-garde orchestral interlude.

There is really no score for the interlude, as orchestra members were directed to play out of tune and out of time. Each was given a starting and ending pitch and was told to simultaneously glissando (slide) and crescendo (get louder) upwards from the starting pitch. All at once, the orchestra arrives at its goal: an E major triad to set the harmonic tone for the next vocal section.

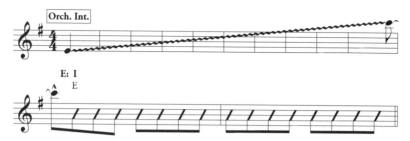

Fig. 6.7. Orchestral interlude

Primary Bridges

▶ *Harmonic Phrasing: Primary Bridge 1*
This section, written by McCartney, is basically in 4/4 time with a few bars of 2/4 peppered throughout. Normally, both Lennon and McCartney used a single primary bridge consisting of six to twelve bars. In this case, they used two vocal bridges. Let's examine the harmonic content of the first one:

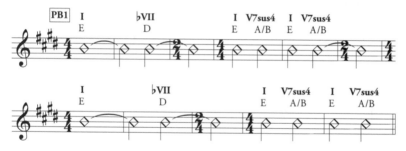

Fig. 6.8. PB1 harmonic phrasing

The first primary bridge is nine and a half bars long. It vacillates beautifully between E Mixolydian and E major, with the E–D–E progression setting up the Mixolydian tonality. With the addition of the ♭VII chord (D), the leading tone of the key (D♯) is lowered a half step to D♮. The use of the D softens the mode and contributes to the dreamlike character of the song. In fact, McCartney even uses the word "dream" toward the end of the bridge lyric.

▶ *Harmonic Phrasing: Primary Bridge 2*
This is followed by a second and different primary bridge, which also has vocals but no lyrics—only "ah's." The music seems to modulate back toward C major, but holds the E major firmly in its grip at bars 5 and 10 of this 10-bar section.

At last, in the tenth and final bar, a change in harmonic motion propels the section into the last verse, which is in the original key of G major. The entire section has moved along smoothly at one chord per bar until the tenth bar, when the chords disappear as the entire ensemble simply plays the notes E, D, C, D.

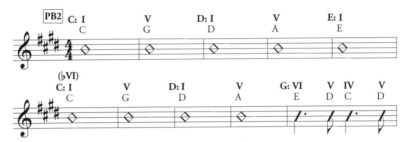

Fig. 6.9. PB2 harmonic phrasing

▶ *Melodic Phrasing: Primary Bridge 1*

The phrasing of the first primary bridge is an interesting mixture of balance and asymmetry. The bridge breaks up into four sections, but they are each five bars long—almost… Three of them actually are five bars long, but the second section is four and a half bars. The standard approach would be four 4-bar phrases. McCartney cleverly uses the extra bar for acceleration in the first two sections, but for deceleration in the third and fourth sections. (Recall that following any particular phrase with one that is shorter creates acceleration, and following any particular phrase with one that is longer creates deceleration. A section consisting of a series of phrases varying in length creates lots of motion: both speeding up and slowing down.)

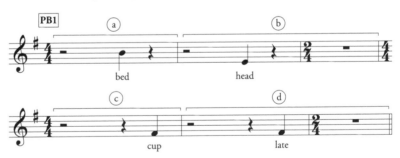

Fig. 6.10. PB1 melodic phrasing, part 1

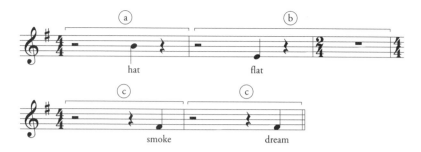

Fig. 6.11. PB1 melodic phrasing, part 2

This first section has very perky lyrics—wake up, gotta get ready, gotta go, off to work—while the answering section moves the protagonist into a daydream state. Refer to the lead sheet for this song and note that the rhythms used in PB1 are more erratic and less flowing than those used in the verses. One reason for this is that the tempo of this section is much faster than that of the verses. Also, the sixteenth-note rhythms created by McCartney utilize more unexpected anticipations and syncopation than Lennon's verse. This treatment makes this section more challenging to sing. As you can see, the resulting analysis for the first half of PB1 is *abcd*. There are no repeating rhythms, and this is made even more complex by the insertion of the 2/4 bar halfway through the section. This shifts the downbeat unexpectedly.

The second half of PB1 is reduced to four and a half bars. It also has been reduced from five lyric lines to four. This section is a bit easier to sing. The phrase analysis result here is: *abcc*.

▶ *Melodic Phrasing: Primary Bridge 2*

Next up is PB2, which consists of two more 5-bar sections with no lyrics at all—just dreamy, long "ah's." The longer notes make the perfect contrast to the funky sixteenth-note rhythms in the melody of PB1. The long notes, the steadier harmonic phrasing, and the slight melodic deceleration give a feeling of soaring and floating, as if in a dream state:

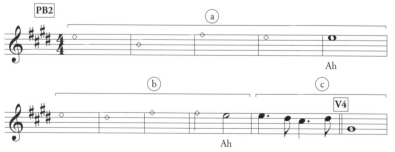

Fig. 6.12. PB2 melodic phrasing

McCartney treats the listener to the longest melodic line of the song: a full 5-bar phrase that soars up and down, finally settling on tonic E and creating the first melodic phrase, Ⓐ. As the melody begins again at bar 6, it seems that the second phrase will be a repeat of the first. But McCartney finishes the phrase one bar early, for a 4-bar Ⓑ phrase.

With the tenth and final bar, McCartney returns to the volatile atmosphere of PB1 by inserting a 2-bar phrase that overlaps back into verse 4. This last phrase is doubly accelerated because 1) it follows a longer 4-bar phrase, and 2) the rhythms used for the melody are faster-moving quarter notes and eighth notes. This active phrasing propels the bridge section back into the beginning of the final verse.

PROSODY

Verses

The melodic phrases have two interesting characteristics:

- There is no 7th in the melody. (This creates a six-note scale instead of the usual seven.)
- There is no dominant cadence in the harmony. (Lennon uses the blues-based plagal cadence, IV–I, or C–G in this key.)

The opening four bars in the verse move all the way down to the E in bar 4 before gliding up to the B that is prominent throughout the melody:

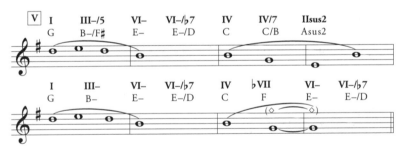

Fig. 6.13. Verse structural tones

The second four bars end on tonic G. This in and of itself should bring a sense of closure to the verse melody. But Lennon scores unstable chords (F, E minor, and E minor/D) for the harmonic under-pinning to give the verse a continued flow.

The harmonic progression consists mainly of the tonic chords from G major: G, B minor, and E minor. The only other chords are the strategically placed subdominant chords, C and Asus2, and the colorful modal interchange chord, ♭VII, or F in this key. The chord pattern begins simply with three static tonic chords, which gives the least movement to the phrase. It also ends on stable melody note B, Mi. By contrast, the next phrase starts and ends on the unstable C chord but still retains the B in the melody. The third phrase is nearly an exact repeat of the first. The fourth and fifth phrases provide the most motion of all. As before, the subtle B is still in the melody as the F major chord passes through, creating an exotic #11 tension in the melody, a tritone relationship to the root, F.

The critical ending melody note for all of the fourth and fifth phrases is G, the tonic note. But phrase endings are harmonized with either a C chord or an F chord. The G serves as a 5th of C and a 9th of F, which keeps the tonic G floating and maintains motion forward.

Primary Bridges

PB1 is set in a combination of E Mixolydian and E major. The melody is very rhythmic, making economical use of mostly three stable notes: Do, Mi, and Sol (E, G♯, and B).

McCartney divides the melodic phrase endings between Do and Re. The tonic is used to end the first and third phrases, but McCartney keeps the section open by ending the second and fourth phrases with the very unstable 2nd degree, F♯. The use of the D and the A/B chords at the end of each section combines with the aforementioned melodic endings to create a very unstable, and therefore forward-moving, section. These instabilities make for great bridge writing.

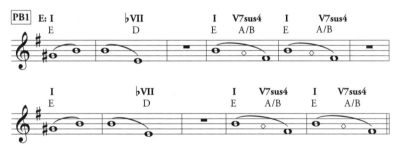

Fig. 6.14. PB1 structural tones

From PB2's start on a C major triad, the harmony progresses forward in perfect 5th motion until it arrives again at the E major triad at bar 5. This section is then repeated, except that upon arrival at the tenth bar, the tonic note E is transformed by modulation to La, the 6th degree. The horns then move down the G major scale as the primary bridge moves back to the verse—E, D, C, D, G (La, Sol, Fa, Sol, Do in G).

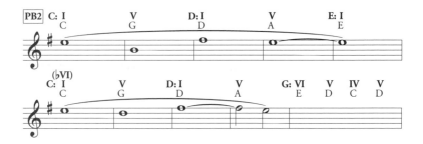

Fig. 6.15. PB2 structural tones

The presence of the F♯ and D♮ indicate that the melody itself has already moved back into the key of G. However, it is virtually impossible to know exactly where the harmonic progression is taking the song as it moves relentlessly in perfect 5th motion. It is difficult to guess whether it will return to the old tonic or establish a new one.

The final stepwise motion of the tenth bar (E to D to C), and then the final cadential melodic motion (D to G) at the beginning of the verse, resolves the question. The tonal ambiguity in the second primary bridge serves as a modulation device to get from the first primary bridge in the key of E, back to the final verse, which is in the key of G.

SUMMARY

Both composers show themselves to be at the height of their co-writing powers. Assisted by producer George Martin, the two song pieces that comprise the whole were developed into a recording that became a benchmark for future long forms in pop music.

Production indeed is a hallmark of the song. While the Lennon section lends itself to a simple acoustic guitar performance, the McCartney section needed to provide some sort of contrast with John's verses. The avant-garde orchestral section leading into Paul's playful bridge provided a subtle but effective contrast. In the verses, the production brought Lennon's acoustic guitar to the fore with the piano providing support. The opposite is true in the McCartney section: the lively piano is up front and the guitar is in the support role.

This big dramatic piece leaves the delighted listener pondering two mundane images: four thousand potholes in Blackburn, Lancashire, and the Royal Albert Hall. Merging them together creates a surreal image crackling with Lennon's typical wry wit.

Lucy in the Sky with Diamonds

Words and Music by John Lennon and Paul McCartney

(Continued on following page)

Lu - cy   in   the   sky —— with   dia ——— -monds.   Ah,

Verse 2

Follow her down to a bridge by a fountain,

Where rocking horse people eat marshmallow pies.

Ev'ryone smiles as you drift past the flowers,

That grow so incredibly high.

Newspaper taxis appear on the shore,

Waiting to take you away.

Climb in the back with your head in the clouds,

And you're gone.

Verse 3

Picture yourself on a train in a station,

With plasticine porters with looking-glass ties.

Suddenly someone is there at the turnstile,

The girl with kaleidoscope eyes.

Title	Lucy in the Sky with Diamonds
Recording Date	March 1, 1967
Meter	3/4 and 4/4
Key	A Mixolydian, F major, and G major
Song Form	Verse/Transitional Bridge/Chorus
Phrasing	Verse 1: *a/aab*
	Verse 2: *ab*
	Verse 3: *abc*
	Transitional Bridge: *ab*
	Chorus: *aab*
Recording	*Sgt. Pepper's Lonely Hearts Club Band*
	1967 EMD/CAPITOL

John Lennon's four-year-old son Julian was the inspiration for this song. Julian's schoolmate Lucy O'Donnell was the "real" Lucy. Early in 1967 Julian had brought home a painting from school and John asked what it was. Julian's reply was reportedly the very title of this song.

The phrase stuck with John and he was inspired to write. He combined it with influences from author Lewis Carroll (*Alice's Adventures in Wonderland*) and cowriter Paul McCartney. Within just a few weeks, he brought it in for the first recording by the group. The song was one of the quickest ever recorded. Recording began on Wednesday, March 1, 1967, and the song was completely wrapped and ready for mastering by the following Friday, March 3.

The instrumentation included John, Paul, and Ringo on the usual acoustic guitar, drums, and bass. George Harrison contributed the guitarlike Indian tambora, while McCartney played the captivating opening of the song on a Hammond organ using a special celeste stop.

The song was released on the landmark *Sgt. Pepper's Lonely Hearts Club Band* album on June 1, 1967 in England. America and the rest of the world got it the next day.

STRUCTURE

Song Form

This is yet another of Lennon's explorations of 3/4 time. It's a masterful undertaking, combining the simplicity of a child's lullaby with a modern psychedelic lyric. After a brief, 4-bar, single-line melody that serves as the introduction, a double verse ensues. The first is an unusual nine bars long and the second is ten bars long.

Lennon then explores a song section that he has only visited briefly in his songwriting past: the transitional bridge. He uses it twice in the course of the song to link the double verse with the chorus section. For this transitional bridge, Lennon has chosen to implement an uneven and unstable thirteen bars.

In the song "Please Please Me," Lennon used the verse/transitional bridge/**refrain** form. "Lucy in the Sky with Diamonds" marks the first time Lennon utilized the double-verse/transitional bridge/**chorus** form. Lennon was on the forefront of this now-standard pop song form:

Verse (V-a 1)	Verse (V-b 1)	Transitional Bridge	Chorus
9 bars	10 bars	13 bars	7 bars

Verse (V-a 2)	Verse (V-b 2)	Transitional Bridge	Chorus
9 bars	10 bars	13 bars	7 bars

Verse (V-a 3)	Verse (V-b 3)	Chorus
9 bars	10 bars	7 bars

Note that the first two verses lead into the transitional bridge, and then on to the chorus, creating two 39-bar song systems. However, the last verse omits the transitional bridge and is reduced to a final song system of 26 bars.

The chorus section is only seven bars long, quite short compared to the preceding sections. This suggests that the final section might be a refrain rather than a chorus. Usually a refrain is only three or four bars long. However, if the preceding section(s) are longer—say, sixteen to twenty-four bars—a refrain can be as long as eight bars. That is the situation here. The three relentless repetitions of the title, combined with a meter change from 3/4 to 4/4 and a dramatic change in dynamics, create a plausible case for the section being a real chorus.

Recalling that the traditional 8- and 16-bar sections provide stability in a section, we find that the odd numbers of bars in all three sections produce great forward motion and accentuate the sense of arrival with each new part.

Lennon sticks with the 3/4 meter in both the verse and the transitional bridge, but makes a dramatic shift to 4/4 time at the chorus. As the song goes from the 3/4 transitional bridge into the 4/4 chorus, the bass drum strikes the last three beats of a four-beat count-off, but in the space of two bars of 3/4 time. This metric exchange ($\downarrow$. = $\downarrow$) calls for two bars of 3/4 to be sandwiched into one bar of 4/4. In effect, it feels as if the beat slows down, putting an immense spotlight on the chorus lyric and title. The disciplined, marchlike 4/4 setting of this section is what the drifting verse and transitional bridge have been searching for as they spin their psychedelic story.

Lyric Content

John Lennon's story, as inspired by his son Julian's kindergarten painting, speaks of a typical childlike world. Real and surreal images like flowers of cellophane, porters of plasticine, and rocking horses dominate. But there is some familiar narrative order in the opening sections of this song of an ever-changing dream world. There is: instruction, action, description, and instruction

In the first of the double verses, Lennon instructs the listener to "picture yourself" or "follow her" in order to entice them into the song. The second of the double verses, by contrast, serves up action: "somebody calls you," "everyone smiles," and "someone is there."

The connecting transitional bridges are also split in two, in a similar narrative form (description, then instruction). The first half is a description: "cellophane flowers" and "newspaper taxis." In the second half, Lennon once again provides guidance to the listener by assisting with a second round of instruction: "look for the girl" and "climb in the back."

And even though we spend the duration of the song looking for "the girl with kaleidoscope eyes," it is we, the listeners, who get to view the world with kaleidoscope eyes—thanks to the creative genius of Mr. Lennon.

The arrival point of the lyric is at the three dramatic repetitions of the title setting. Each seems to have an exclamation point at the end of the line. The listener at last finds the missing girl alluded to in the verses.

PHRASING

Verses

▶ Harmonic Phrasing

The verse section is a double verse with two slightly different endings. They are labeled V-a and V-b. The harmonic progression for the verse establishes the key of A Mixolydian but adds the Aeolian modal interchange chords A/F and F.

Fig. 6.16. Verse harmonic phrasing

The first half of the verse section (V-a) is one long tonic chord (A) over a moving bass below that sets up the swirling atmosphere that supports this surreal lyric.

The V-b portion of the verse repeats the section, but stops short of the F major triad and sustains the A/F♯ (which is actually F♯–7) before moving on to the connecting D minor triad.

▶ *Melodic Phrasing*

The opening lyric is rather abstract. The somewhat nonsensical images and unusual descriptive juxtapositions put the song very much in the dream world.

The opening lyrical and musical phrase is *nine bars long!* This is the entire length of the first of the double verses. This long-lyric/long-melody setup is used for all three of the V-a sections:

Fig. 6.17. V-a melodic phrasing

With the absence of any stopping points along the way, the long phrase creates musical and lyrical space, suggesting, as the lyric says, "floating."

Lennon takes a different tack for all of the V-b sections. Here, he begins to add acceleration and motion by moving to shorter 2-bar phrases:

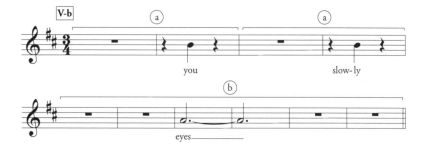

Fig. 6.18. V-b melodic phrasing

Only one image was presented in the previous section with the lone ⓐ phrase. Three images are presented in the V-b section: calling, responding, and seeing. This introduction of the three lyrical ideas, conjunct with the melodic support, creates a sense of acceleration in the song.

In the second and third verses, Lennon uses two completely different treatments:

V-b   Second Verse = *a* (one long 10-bar phrase)
V-b   Third Verse = *ab* (two 4-bar phrases)

These longer and shorter phrases are completely controlled by the lyric flow. Lennon's intrinsic sense of song prevails as he pilots the listener through a myriad of phantasmagorical images. His choice of phrasing allows him to present a single image or a series of images as he develops his story.

Transitional Bridge

▶ *Harmonic Phrasing*
As Lennon moves from the D minor triad at the end of the verse to the B♭ triad at the beginning of the transitional bridge, a new tonality is created: F major. The last chord is D major, which facilitates the move to the new key for the chorus, G major:

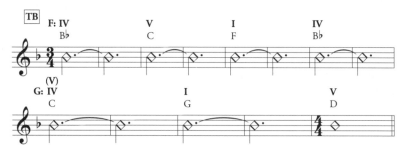

Fig. 6.19. Transitional bridge harmonic phrasing

▶ Melodic Phrasing

The 13-bar transitional bridge seems at first to promise some order to help us sort out this dream by delivering up the song's first square, 8-bar phrase:

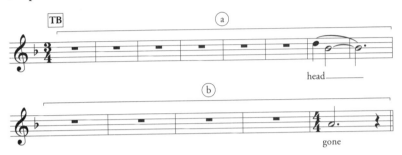

Fig. 6.20. Transitional bridge melodic phrasing

But Lennon quickly foils this by completing the transitional bridge with an uneven, unbalanced, forward-moving 5-bar phrase. It's just what the song needs to sustain its abstract nature. Are we going somewhere with all this, or will we drift for the whole song?

Chorus

▶ Harmonic Phrasing

Drift? Apparently not! The chorus is basic rock 'n' roll: I, IV, and V in G major. The refrainlike chorus is only seven bars long, but the melody and lyric are both so forceful and strident that they conjure a "feeling" of a classic chorus:

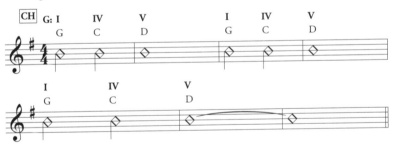

Fig. 6.21. Chorus harmonic phrasing

However, the chorus ends with elongated "ah's" and an open ending, while the band pounds out the dominant D major. A usual chorus has a stopping point before returning to the next verse. Instead "Lucy's" open chorus keeps the section rolling right back into the dreamland verses. (Note, however, that Lennon creates closure in the repeating chorus at the end of the song by transforming the chorus from seven to eight bars.)

▶ Melodic Phrasing

A quick statement of three ominous drum beats in the last bar of the transitional bridge deceives the listener. These beats occur not on beats 1, 2, and 3 from the well-established 3/4 time signature—but rather as 2, 3, and 4 from the *new* 4/4 time signature soon to take over in the chorus. This illustrates Lennon's ability to throw in a twist for the listener as he progresses to the title line:

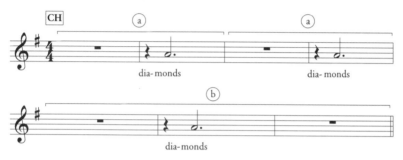

Fig. 6.22. Chorus melodic phrasing

We're off into a whole new world as the chorus gets underway. But in terms of melodic and lyric phrasing, what are Lennon's choices? First of all, there is an odd number of bars in the chorus. The accelerated 7-bar format propels the chorus deftly back into the verses. However, Lennon, with his phrase usage, secretly squeezes in the feeling of deceleration while not actually changing the tempo. The chorus begins with a standard repeating 2-bar phrase. The melodic and harmonic spotlighting with the repeating title lyric clearly demonstrate an arrival point. The 3-bar phrase that follows slows the motion slightly, spotlighting the last title repetition even more than the first two.

It is also interesting to note that upon arrival at the concluding, repeating chorus that leads to the fade-out, Lennon shifts—finally—to a standard 8-bar version of this section. It is made up of two 2-bar sections followed by a 4-bar section.

Lennon's use of a standard phrasing structure helps to impart a sense of order to what has been an abstract song of dreams up to this point. Its poetically abstract lyric leaves room for multiple interpretations—and thus, room for many ways to enjoy the song. Even when creating a somewhat adventurous-for-its-time psychedelic atmosphere, Lennon again reveals a song poised for widespread appeal.

Verse: Melody/Harmony

Now that the flow of the song is established—long, rolling, dreamy phrases in the verses and transitional bridges into the sharply executed, lyrical-repeating chorus—let's look at the music that supports all of this.

Lennon uses three different keys to set the three different sections. However, they remain connected as a cohesive whole. Despite the different harmonies, the verses and transitional bridges are connected by the persistent, plodding, quarter-note melody throughout.

The first section is set in A Mixolydian. Its continually descending bass line tends to promise resolution—perhaps the standard down-a-fifth movement to D major at some point in the future—but no plan is in the works. Where we might expect a D chord at bar 6, Lennon jumps back up to a G in the bass:

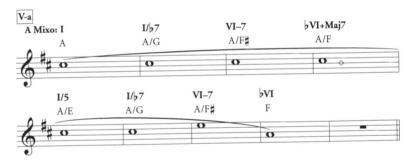

Fig. 6.23. V-a structural tones

The same effect happens in the second half of the verse. However, at the very end of the second of the double verses, there is a brief arrival at D minor (not the expected D major). But the bass line continues its descent as the transitional bridge takes over:

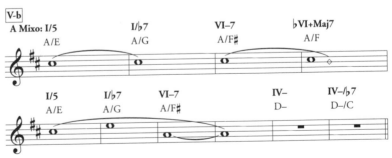

Fig. 6.24. V-b structural tones

The melody for all of the verses, both the 9-bar and the 10-bar ones, has an ever-so-brief pause in the fourth bar on the unstable Re (B in this key). This note is soon resolved to Do (A in this key) at the very end of the long verses. Even though the lyric lines go for the long haul, melodically there is a continuous inner Re–Do resolution at the end of each and every verse. This persistent return to tonic subtly provides the listener some stability in the dream world of the lyric.

As the transitional bridge takes over, the key shifts to F major, establishing the key with a standard IV–V–I cadence. Lennon's bridge melody shifts dramatically from the childlike Mi-Re-Do pattern of the verses. Here he uses a static melody—a continual repetition of the unstable D, which seemed to be promised from the harmonic implications of the verse:

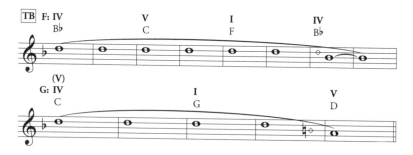

Fig. 6.25. Transitional bridge structural tones

Lennon uses an unstable/stable melodic setup in the bridge as well: the first phrase on a Bb, the unstable Fa or 4th degree in F major, which seeks resolution in the A. The transitional bridge ends on that very note.

At this point however, we have modulated again in preparation for the chorus, which will be in G major. The once-stable A is now heard over G major as an unstable note that wants to move to Re in the new key for the chorus.

The note A at the end of the bridge does indeed resolve with those hammering eighth-note Gs that begin the chorus and state the title. But, at the end of each 2-bar phrase is *another* A with no lyric, just sung vigorously on an "ah":

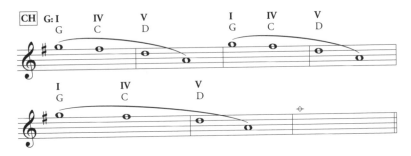

Fig. 6.26. Chorus structural tones

In fact all three of the chorus phrases and the chorus itself end on this unstable note, which creates movement forward to the returning verses. Note that because of the open and repeating nature of this section, Lennon wisely chose to end the song with a fade-out.

SUMMARY

Lennon's journey through the sky of diamonds captures a most child-like spirit while at the same time successfully providing a cutting-edge musical setting appropriate for those psychedelic times. His grasp of the simple and obvious are essential to great pop songwriting, and here in "Lucy," he manages to amalgamate a series of surreal story-book verses with a rocked-out chorus that finishes by fading out into the mist.

The music of the verse, with its static chords, static melody, and moving bass line provides the perfect canvas on which to paint Lennon's come-to-life daydream lyric. As the static transitional bridge melody takes over, the music begins to sway back and forth, pushing the lyric ever forward in search of the elusive Lucy. Finally as the chorus signals the arrival of the one for whom we have been searching, the listener knows they have found something special indeed.

Lennon's key choices are crucial in creating this effect. The song begins in the key of A, then abruptly moves down a third to F. The chorus then finishes up the song in G, only to move up once again to A as the verse begins again:

$$A \downarrow F \uparrow G \uparrow A \downarrow F \uparrow G, \text{etc.}$$

This downwards-then-upwards key movement helps create a fluid motion that supports the lyric and music.

The song will forever remain one of the most outstanding songs from the ever-popular *Sgt. Pepper* album. When one traces the song's development from humble beginnings to its final surrealistic presentation on the *Sgt. Pepper* album, it is apparent that Lennon once again managed to spin a moment of inspiration into pop writing gold. His weaving of melody with the nursery rhyme lyric perfectly captures the childlike spirit of the original inspiration—a moment in the life of his son.

All You Need Is Love

Words and Music by John Lennon and Paul McCartney

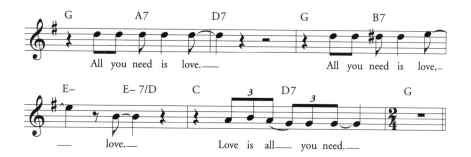

G   A7   D7   G   B7

All you need is love.—   All you need is love,-

E–   E– 7/D   C   D7   G

— love.—   Love is all— you need.—

Verse 2

There's nothing you can make that can't be made.

No one you can save that can't be saved.

Nothing you can do, but you can learn how to be you in time.

It's easy.

Verse 3

There's nothing you can know that isn't known.

Nothing you can see that isn't shown.

Nowhere you can be that isn't where you're meant to be.

It's easy.

BACKGROUND

Title	All You Need Is Love
Recording Date	June 14, 1967
Meter	4/4 and 3/4
Key	G major
Song Form	Verse/Chorus
Phrasing	Verse: *aabc*
	Chorus: *aabc*
Recording	*Yellow Submarine*
	1999 CDP 7243 521481 27/CAPITOL

This song was written during May 1967 in preparation for the upcoming first-ever worldwide satellite broadcast, "Our World," which was scheduled to occur the following month, on June 25. It featured the Fab Four playing all sorts of unusual instruments: John on harpsichord, George on violin, and Paul bowing a string bass with a violin bow. It also featured them on their regular instruments.

The Beatles were told they were going to be seen recording the song "live" via satellite, and an appropriate song was needed for the broadcast. John came up with "All You Need Is Love." The song was perfect, with its conversational and almost "unsing-along-able" verse juxtaposed with the infectious and very "sing-along-able" chorus section. Soon the whole world would be indeed singing along, in hopes of love and peace taking over from hate and war.

The main area of transformation in "All You Need Is Love" occurs in the multi-meter verse section, where Lennon utilized both 4/4 and 3/4 time signatures. The chorus, by contrast, has chromatic harmonic and melodic elements, which reflect the flavors of the influential songs of Lennon's youth.

"All You Need Is Love" was released as a single in England on July 7, 1967 and in America on July 17, 1967. The song appears on one album in England: *Yellow Submarine*, released January 17, 1969.

In America it appeared on two albums: *Magical Mystery Tour*, released November 27, 1967 and *Yellow Submarine*, released January 13, 1969. The song was re-released worldwide on the digitally remastered *Yellow Submarine* CD in 1999.

STRUCTURE

Song Form

The basic song form is very simple: verse/chorus, but adorned with an elaborate orchestral intro and conclusion. It is actually made up of three simple 4-line verses and a simple 4-line chorus.

With producer George Martin's help, the song was transformed with an elaborate orchestral introduction, as well as an even more elaborate conclusion or coda. The song begins with Martin's arrangement of the French national anthem, "Marseillaise." (The main melody is notated on the lead sheet included here to show how it intertwines with the Beatles' vocal entrance.) However, the repeat-and-fade coda is not notated and is not included in my detailed comments. The coda does contain some interesting explorations in twentieth century music. The last two bars of the chorus repeat over and over, and Martin overlaid several musical quotations, including a Bach two-part invention, a portion of a folk song called "Greensleeves," and a portion of a Glenn Miller song called "In the Mood." As a result the final performance form is:

Intro	Verse 1	Verse 2	Chorus	Verse (Solo)	Chorus	Verse 3	Chorus	Chorus	Coda
11 bars	8 bars	8 bars	8 bars	8 bars	8 bars	8 bars	8 bars	8 bars	8 bars, repeat and fade

Lyric Content

The lyric itself combines both the obtuse and the direct as it moves from verse to chorus. This is a characteristically Lennonesque lyrical device, and shows Lennon's increasing sophistication as a songwriter. The three verses create a rather conversational atmosphere woven with the thread of spiritual thought. This great writer of the romantic pop song asks the listener to consider a larger vision of love: love of oneself and love of humanity:

> There's nothing you can do that can be done.
> There's nothing you can sing that can be sung.
> Nothing you can say but you can learn how to play the game.
> It's easy.

His very first line tells us that life might seem purposeless at times when you compare yourself to others, but love yourself and you can love the world. A rather cerebral and utopian message for a pop song.

It is interesting to note that there are absolutely no rhymes in the chorus! This is very unusual for a pop chorus and very unusual for

Lennon, as well. In fact, the only parts of the song that do contain rhyme are the first two couplets of each verse, and even then, the first two verses don't contain exact rhymes: "sung" and "done," and "made" and "saved." It is not until the very last verse that Lennon gives the listener the song's only true rhyme: "known" and "shown."

Certainly when Lennon was "commissioned" to write a song for worldwide presentation, he rose to the occasion. This lyric represents the beginning of a number of song lyrics that became more common in his solo repertoire: songs dealing with very large topics like God, mother, peace, isolation, and truth.

PHRASING

Verse

▶ *Harmonic Phrasing*
This song contains both repetitive chord progressions and a through-composed progression:

Fig. 6.27. Verse harmonic phrasing

The meter is also of interest here—note the alternating use of 4/4 and 3/4 in the repeating sections (bars 1–4) with a sustained 4/4 meter during the bass line descent in the second half of the verse. The use of the 3/4 bar in the last bar of the verse helps propel the verse either back to the next verse or into the chorus. The alternating meter also supports the conversational tone achieved in the melodic setting for the verse.

▶ *Melodic Phrasing*
After a brief 3-bar orchestral snippet from the French national anthem, the boys themselves enter with an 8-bar introduction to the song, singing a tongue-in-cheek Beatles' version of "Three Blind Mice," or Mi-Re-Do in musical terms ("Love, love, love"). This little

melody is anchored with a sustained D in the vocal harmony. As we shall see, this D is both the dominant of the key and the main melody note of the upcoming chorus section.

The verse lyric and verse melody are perfectly aligned in four 2-bar phrases, but Lennon has taken this well-used form and created something quite startling:

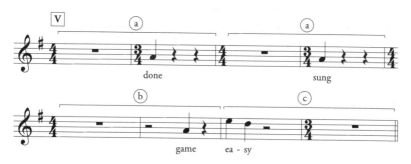

Fig. 6.28. Verse melodic phrasing

Despite the alternating bars of 3/4 and 4/4, the two repeating ⓐ phrases create some stability. Both of them end on beat 1 of the 3/4 bar. The appearance of the ⓑ phrase—the two "normal" bars of 4/4 time—destroys the illusion of stability. The verse now seems slightly off-kilter. Finally, the last phrase stops short melodically and lyrically, creating the most unexpected phrase of all: ⓒ. The final result: *aabc*.

The interplay between the bars of 4/4 and the bars of 3/4 create a stream-of-consciousness flow. In fact, not only is it unlike any melody Lennon has presented to date, it was unlike any melodic phrasing up to that point in pop music. Since this song was released as a single and got extensive airplay and publicity, its rather obtuse influence was felt worldwide. This increased Lennon's expansion as a writer and advanced new paths of exploration in the larger world of pop song.

Review the lead sheet for the verse section and note that it is peppered with triplets and sixteenths, as well as eighth- and quarter-note rhythms—a very unlikely combination for a pop melody. It makes this portion of the song very difficult to sing along with in just a few listenings.

Chorus

▶ *Harmonic Phrasing*

The chorus also begins with a repeating chord progression, but instead of using a descending bass line, the progression ascends upward to the dominant D7, providing an uplifting structure for the optimistic lyric:

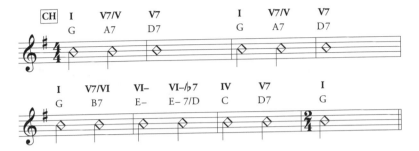

Fig. 6.29. Chorus harmonic phrasing

The second four bars are through-composed (no repeating chords) and move to the even more uplifting B7 that provides the climax of the chorus. The nondiatonic note D♯, which is contained both in the B7 chord and the melody at that point, provides the lift. From there, the B7 resolves down to E minor on its descent back down to the tonic G. The final 2/4 bar provides a playful skip-a-beat feel as it moves back to the top of the verse.

▶ *Melodic Phrasing*
The phrasing and rhythms for the chorus section are much more accessible:

Fig. 6.30. Chorus melodic phrasing

It is interesting to note that both sections form the same pattern, *aabc*, but while the form is the same, the rhythms are different. The complex rhythms for the verse and simpler rhythms for the chorus differentiate the sections and create two totally different atmospheres within the same *aabc* form. The rush of non sequitur images in the verse, along with the verse's complex melodic rhythms and changing time signatures, create the obtuse nature of the verses. With a simple repetitive lyric, "all you need is love," Lennon bundles the same form with an easy melody and simple phrasing to create a chorus that has a direct and clear message.

Verse

The verse melody opens with a variation on the Mi-Re-Do motif in the introduction. After making a rapid descent to the tonic G, the melodic phrase comes to rest on the unstable and forward-moving A, then drifts even further down to the also-unstable E.

This melodic progression occurs twice. Then the melody moves playfully between the B and the A (Mi–Re), increasing the instability and forward motion of the verse. This forward motion occurs because Lennon places the dominant notes in this phrase, Mi and Re (B and A), on the strong beats. (See bars 5 and 6 in the example below.) He heightens the unstable motion of the verse by leaving the Re's unresolved and ending the verses on D, instead of the tonic G.

Each verse concludes with a mini-resolution from the E to the D on the lyric "easy":

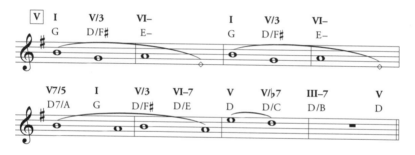

Fig. 6.31. Verse structural tones

The chorus, by contrast, sticks with a single D for the first four bars. The next four bars, starting with the same D, move chromatically upward, making a dramatic leap downward to B, then finally comes to rest on the tonic G.

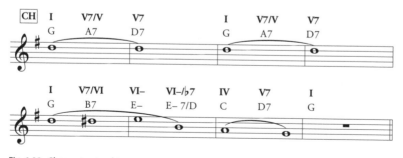

Fig. 6.32. Chorus structural tones

chapter 6 · all you need is love

Rather than presenting his message in a preachy tone, Lennon's concoction of uneven melody and rhythm in the verses seems more like a conversation than a sermon, as if someone were whispering the message in your ear rather than shouting it in your face.

The chorus lyric and music, by contrast, give more of a feeling of togetherness, as if we're all watching a parade and waving our flags. It's no wonder George Martin sweetened the chorus with those marching band–style horn arrangements. The chorus lyric and music both called for that sort of treatment to celebrate this brave idea: all we need is love.

SUMMARY

After looking over all the technical data, we find that the simple lyrical message is set with perfect prosody for the best impact. Alternating 4/4 and 3/4 meter gives an uneven, rather conversational feel to the flow of the song. Quickly moving triplet- and sixteenth-note rhythms give the verse melody the pace of everyday speech, and Lennon manages to spew out all of the ideals and concepts expressed into a single bar of 4/4. In doing so, he perfectly underscores the "it's easy" lyric, not with a proclamation, but rather with a sort of "conversational whisper" for the listener. The empty bar of 3/4 at the end of the verse barely gives the listener a chance to catch their breath—it is, after all, one beat short—when suddenly there is another bar of 4/4 with more information.

With a twinkle in his compositional eye, Lennon concludes each verse with advice that is a perfect summary: "it's easy." He reminds us that we all succeed along life's path even when we think we are confused or when we think we cannot see an answer. It's all been done before and you can do it, too.

The rambling, unstable nature of the verse lyric is echoed in the music perfectly as both careen back and forth up in the air. The "up-in-the-air" atmosphere is what composers of pop songs strive for in their verses. Reason? So they'll have somewhere to go—back down to an "arrival" point: the chorus!

The chorus melody makes a wonderful soft landing, using just a single melody note for "all you need…" while the chords move chromatically below. And then, that single note itself moves up chromatically with the music and an extended lyric with the repetition of the word "love." The *piece de resistance* is the final twisting around of the title, which unexpectedly leaves the song ending with the lyric "need."

"All You Need Is Love" will forever remain one of Lennon's outstanding contributions to the pop music genre. It was written, arranged, recorded, and performed with the whole world watching. (Who can write under *that* kind of pressure!?) The song is a milestone in pop history.

I Am the Walrus

Words and Music by John Lennon and Paul McCartney

(Continued on following page)

Verse 2 (V-b)

> Yellow matter custard dripping from a dead dog's eye,
> Crabalocker fishwife, pornographic priestess,
> Boy, you been a naughty girl, you let your knickers down.

Refrain 1

> I am the eggman, (ooh)
> They are the eggmen, (ooh)
> I am the walrus,
> Goo goo g'joob.

Verse 3 (V-a)

> Expert texpert choking smokers,
> Don't you think the joker laughs at you?
> See how they smile like pigs in a sty,
> See how they snide.
> I'm crying.

Verse 3 (V-b)

> Semolina pilchards climbing up the Eiffel Tower.
> Element'ry penguin singing Hare Krishna,
> Man, you should have seen them kicking Edgar Allan Poe.

Refrain 1

> I am the eggman, (ooh)
> They are the eggmen, (ooh)
> I am the walrus,
> Goo goo g'joob.

BACKGROUND

Title	I Am the Walrus
Recording Date	September 5, 1967
Meter	4/4
Key	A major (more or less)
Song Form	AAABA transformed
Phrasing	Verse V-a: *abc*
	Verse V-b/Refrain: *abbc/ddc*
	Verse V-a'/Refrain: *ab/cdcc*
	Primary Bridge/Refrain: *ab/ccd*
Recording	*Magical Mystery Tour*
	1967 EMD/CAPITOL

"I Am the Walrus" continued Lennon's journey into the world of the avant-garde. This is another song sparked by a chance moment. Lennon claims that the opening melody was inspired by an ambulance siren he heard while walking through Hyde Park in London. In addition to this ambulance melody, Lennon also had written the pastoral melody from the bridge section, as well as a short snippet of a third melody with fast-moving sixteenth notes.

The song began to crystallize after John received a letter from a schoolboy in Liverpool, who stated that his English class was analyzing Beatles songs. John was amused by this and immediately set upon finishing off the lyric, making it as indecipherable and disconnected as possible. The three melodies in search of a song fit perfectly into the "Walrus" scenario.

On September 5, 1967, John entered the studio to begin the first recording of the song. In England, the song was released as a single on November 23 and then again two weeks later on December 8 as a track on the *Magical Mystery Tour* double EP. In America, it was simultaneously released as a single and an album track on November 27, 1967.

STRUCTURE

Song Form

The form of "I Am the Walrus" is one of the most complex of all the Lennon Beatles songs. It is actually a massive transformation of the standard AABA format. The song contains four main areas within the verse sections, which I have designated as follows: V-a, V-b, Ref 1, and Ref 2. In addition, there is a primary bridge and three orchestral sections: the introduction, the interlude, and the coda.

The simplest view of the first A section reveals that it is really a double verse/refrain setup. The second A is designated as A' because it contains only one of the double verses. It is followed by a brand new refrain, designated Ref 2. The third A section can be called an A" because it contains the second half of the double verse (V-b) plus the original refrain (Ref 1). Lennon is taking the listener down a rather challenging road:

Intro	A			A'		A"		Orchestral Section	B		A			Coda
	V-a	V-b	Ref 1	V-a	Ref 2	V-b	Ref 1		Primary Bridge	Ref 1	V-a	V-b	Ref 1	
	6 bars	6 bars	3 bars	6 bars	5 bars	6 bars	5 bars	4 bars	5 bars	4 bars	6 bars	6 bars	6 bars	
	15 bars			11 bars		9 bars		4 bars	9 bars		18 bars			

After the three different statements of the A sections (A, A', A"), Lennon makes an unusual move. He inserts a brief orchestral interlude before the B section. Though he also used this technique in "A Day in the Life," it is something he rarely did in his songwriting.

The B section is also unusual, because it is made up of both the primary bridge *and* the original refrain. Most B sections consist of *only* the primary bridge. The final A section is an exact repeat of the first A section…almost. Lennon doubles the length of the final refrain (Ref 1) as the song goes into the coda, but other than that slight change at the very end, the listener is finally treated to a complete return to the originally stated A section. The ending coda section is a repeating 7-bar, avant-garde orchestral section à la the "Strawberry Fields Forever" coda, with a fade out.

Lyric Content

As much as many of us musicians tend to analyze lyrics for deeper meaning, this song offers us little in that way. The opening lyric line offers a rather deconstructionist description of the connection among humans—that we are all one within our individuality. But from that point on, it is one absurd image after another.

John must have chuckled about this as he proceeded to concoct "I Am the Walrus" from pieces of unfinished songs and non-sequitur–style lyric writing. One of the images is "semolina pilchard." Semolina is a type of gritty wheat used to make pasta, while pilchard is a rather low-grade sardine sometimes found in pet foods. Other portions of the lyric reveal the presence of elementary penguins, flying pigs, and a nod to a flying Lucy from the *Sgt. Pepper* album earlier that year. He even invented words for the last verse, such as "texpert" and "crabalocker."

Part of the lyric comes from an old childhood rhyme common in British playground parlance:

> *Yellow matter custard, green slop pie,*
> *All mixed together with a dead dog's eye,*
> *Slap it on a butty, ten foot thick,*
> *Then wash it all down with a cup of cold sick.*

Lennon seems to have two points of arrival in his song lyric: the well-known refrain, "I am the walrus, goo goo g'joob" and "I'm crying." The first is completely from the world of the absurd—one can only think, "What *does* that mean?"—while the other evokes a completely recognizable and melancholy image of someone sobbing.

Both of these lyrics are used four times each in the course of the song, with melodic development occurring in the middle of the song for the "I'm crying" lyric. Lennon gave the famous title/refrain lyric the signature oblivion coda treatment at the end of the song.

As in a dream, all sorts of images arrive and depart, playfully luring everyone into Lennon's made-up dream world.

PHRASING

Verses and Refrains

▶ Harmonic Phrasing

The harmonic progression contains only major and dominant 7th chords. Usually in establishing a major key, one might find the II minor, III minor, or VI minor chords among the choices. Here Lennon exploits only major triads from three different modes: I, IV, and V (A, D, and E from A major); ♭III, ♭VI, and ♭VII (C, F, and G from the parallel key of A minor); and II major (B, from A Lydian). The use of these triads brings the different modalities to bear on both melody and harmony, and thereby creates a starker landscape than just plain-Jane A major. This provides excellent harmonic support for the revolving images presented in the lyric and melody:

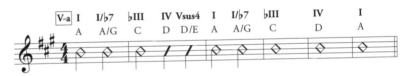

Fig. 6.33. V-a harmonic phrasing

In the first V-a section, we find that the harmony appears to be a combination of A major with one chord borrowed from A minor, the C triad. It's a little unexpected but not all that strange, compared with the upcoming V-b section:

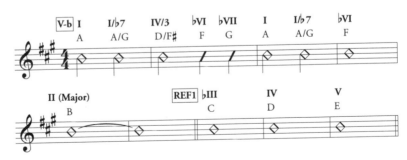

Fig. 6.34. V-b and refrain 1 harmonic phrasing

The V-b section seems at first to reflect the same A major/A minor combination, but this time the F and G triads are borrowed from A minor instead. The most unexpected chord is the B major triad, made even more unexpected by the angular tritone root approach to it from the preceding F major triad.

The refrain is attached to the V-b section. It begins with the now-familiar C triad from the V-a section as it moves up the scale to the open and unstable dominant chord, E major.

Upon repeating the V-a section, Lennon decides to attach an extra 5-bar section, creating a second and different refrain. This 5-bar section spotlights the other repeating lyric:

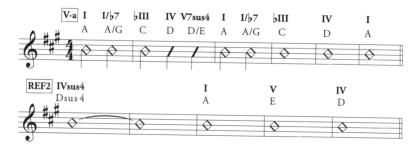

Fig. 6.35. V-a and refrain 2 harmonic phrasing

▶ *Melodic Phrasing*

The phrasing for the opening verse, V-a, is an excellent example of acceleration. The phrases get shorter and shorter as the section progresses:

Fig. 6.36. V-a melodic phrasing

Even though it is also six bars long, the V-b section introduces an entirely new phrasal pattern and the title-setting refrain made up of all 1-bar phrases:

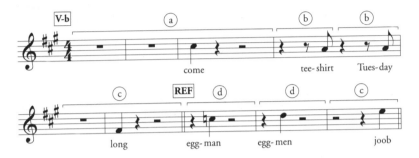

Fig. 6.37. V-b and refrain melodic phrasing

The returning V-a is followed by a refrain. The section should offer the listener some guidance, but the attachment of the unexpected second refrain, Ref 2, leaves the listener somewhat flummoxed. This, of course, is Lennon's ultimate goal:

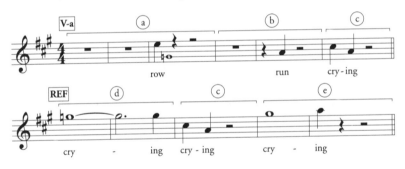

Fig. 6.38. V-a and refrain harmonic phrasing

We find a very odd series of phrases indeed:

V-a = *abc* (relatively simple, but no repeats)
V-b = *abbcdde* (complex, but with some repeats)
V-a' (V-a + Ref 2) = *abcdce* (very complex, only one repeat)

There is nothing classic or traditional about this phrase setup. This is unknown territory. But Lennon had hit upon a perfect formula: combine weird, wild music and the obtuse, disconnected lyric with extremely difficult-to-follow phrasing patterns, and voilà! His most avant-garde song yet.

Orchestral Sections

Before moving the verse/refrain A sections into the B section, Lennon decides to insert a brief 4-bar orchestral interlude. The first and fourth bars contain the swirling glissando, avant-garde effects, while the middle two bars contain melody, harmony, and orchestration:

Fig. 6.39. Orchestral interlude

Both the song's introduction and its coda are connected to the primary bridge chord progression, but with a variation or two in harmonic rhythm and chord placement:

Repeat and fade

Fig. 6.40. Intro and coda harmonic phrasing

The harmony for the interlude descends in whole-step major triads until it reaches the dominant E triad. This is the precursor to the B section, coming up.

Primary Bridge and Refrain

▶ *Harmonic Phrasing*

Fig. 6.41. Primary bridge and refrain harmonic phrasing

The primary bridge uses the same major triads from the orchestral interlude, except for the ending. There, Lennon makes that same tritone movement again from the V-b section (F major triad to B major triad).

The B major triad once again pushes upward to the C major triad as a 4-bar version of the original 3-bar refrain is introduced. The downward progression used in the primary bridge supports the lyric's resigned tone of sitting and waiting. By contrast, the upward movement of the refrain's harmonic progression is a perfect fit for the walrus's affirmation: "I am the eggman. I am the walrus!"

▶ *Melodic Phrasing*
As Lennon draws into the primary bridge, we note that it is in fact a primary bridge/refrain setup. This is very unusual, as refrains are usually attached to the verse only:

Fig. 6.42. Primary bridge and refrain melodic phrasing

Note the continuation of the unbalanced phrasing (3 + 2) for the bridge itself and then an extended 4-bar refrain that falls into a 1 + 1 + 2 phrasing pattern.

The alphabetical patterns used to label phrases in other songs are not quite as useful here. As mentioned above, the V-b verse forms an *abbcdde* pattern and the V-a' verse forms an *abcdce* pattern. The phrasing goes so far up the alphabet—all the way to "e"—that the song form becomes difficult for the listener to grasp on a single hearing.

All this random phrasing just shows how adept John had become as a songwriter. He knew nothing of the technical aspects of longer and shorter phrases, or of Roman numeral analysis, or of stable and unstable melody and harmony. He did, however, have an innate sense of what would produce a smoothly flowing phrase. In the case of "Walrus," he was not referring to his old rulebook, but rather was creating a new one.

PROSODY

Verses and Refrains

As noted previously in the discussion of phrasing, the V-a section is the most stable of the bunch. The melody stays on the static and stable E for the first two bars before coming to rest on the unstable G for the end of the first phrase. The section ends with its resolution of the G to the tonic A:

Fig. 6.43. V-a structural tones

In contrast, the V-b section is wildly unstable and forward moving:

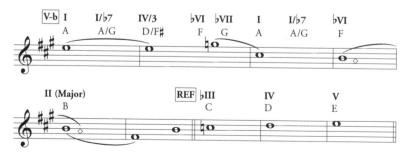

Fig. 6.44. V-b structural tones

This section begins exactly the same on that static E, but the G is no longer the ending note; it is located one octave higher now. Further, at the fourth bar, the extremely unstable and forward-moving 2nd degree, B, hammers right to the end of the section before it crashes down to end the section on the just-as-unstable F♯. The two verse halves couldn't be more like night and day.

The melody for the refrain is completely locked in with the chord progression and bass line as it marches right on up to the dominant E to end (C–D–E).

The final verse/refrain combination, V-a/Ref 2, takes the melody of the song to its highest point. It serves as the melodic climax:

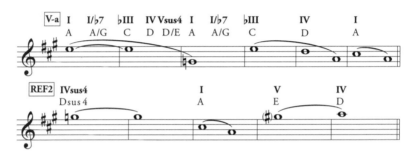

Fig. 6.45. V-a/refrain structural tones

This is an exact melodic repeat of its original appearance, except for a sustained high G that emphasizes the main lyric of Ref 2, "crying." The high G♯ in bar 4 of Ref 2 moves up to the high A, creating the most dramatic melodic motion and cadence of the entire song at the pleading lyric "crying." This lyric creates both action (someone is crying) and confusion (as most people cry over things out of their control). The G♯ in the melody cries out for tonic A to resolve this pain. Lennon, however, diverts the resolution harmonically by inserting the unstable D major triad where the G♯ moves to A. This creates a perfect blending of melody and harmony to support the refrain lyric.

Primary Bridge/Refrain

So far we see the use of a static melody against a lot of changing chords in the verses. This shifts the focus to the lyric. The tension-building repetitive melody acts as a megaphone for the lyric to ride above the fray. By contrast the refrain, with its lockstep melody/bass linkage, has a more concerted sound, as discussed just above.

For the primary bridge, Lennon skillfully devises even further contrast:

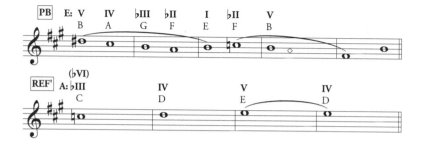

Fig. 6.46. Primary bridge/refrain structural tones

Note the melody here is simply utilizing the 3rd of the chord in the first two bars. This continues until the third bar, when the melody shifts to use the 5th of the chord. The section ends in exactly the same manner as the V-b section: a B melody note with a B major triad. The attached refrain here is exactly the same as before, except the melody continues to sustain the E with the final D chord.

SUMMARY

So what of "The Walrus" thirty-five years after its creation? With hindsight, we see that Lennon was having fun with fans and critics alike. Everyone was running around looking for the deeper meaning of "semolina pilchard" and "elementary penguin."

With "Rain," "Tomorrow Never Knows," "A Day in the Life," "She Said, She Said," and "Strawberry Fields Forever" under his belt, he certainly had mastered this new dream-state writing: composing the perfect musical environment for an obtuse, aleatory lyric like "I Am the Walrus." (By aleatory music, I mean music that uses or consists of sounds chosen by the performer or left to chance.)

The song at first promises to plumb the depths of the inner world and reveal the true meaning of life. The opening lyric line is actually the most accessible of the whole song. But as the listener is carried downwards to reflect on his being, he finds nothing to hang on to except the two haunting, lyrical refrains.

Like "Tomorrow Never Knows," this song gives a sense of the sea. But instead of a lovely wave washing over us as we set upon the shore, "Walrus" imparts a feeling of being adrift in 10-foot waves with no life jacket. With its constantly shifting lyrical and musical waters, the song carries us along like a cork on an ocean ride to who knows where.

It is indeed an amazing effect to achieve with words and music in a pop song. But "I Am the Walrus" is more than just a pop song. It remains one of the defining moments in the songwriting career of John Lennon. "Walrus" is really a sort of anti-pop song, breaking all the rules of lyric, melody, and harmony. Lennon was continuing the journey he began with "Rain" and "Strawberry Fields Forever." But with "I Am the Walrus," he finally walked through the door that "Rain" opened the previous year. His success would encourage him to further explore the expansion of the pop song idiom as he looked toward the next year, 1968.

CHAPTER 7   1968

By the beginning of 1968, John Lennon was ready for a change. He was still smarting from the death of manager Brian Epstein the year before, and from the lackluster reception of the Beatles new *Magical Mystery Tour* album. The year 1968 brought many changes in his personal life: a three-month visit to India; the end of his marriage to Cynthia Lennon; the beginning of his relationship with future wife Yoko Ono; his participation in political and social-based "happenings" with Yoko; and his famous drug bust from late 1968.

Musically, there were many changes as well. 1968 saw the release of the Beatles' only double album. In fact, it was the only album produced that year. It was called, ironically enough, *The Beatles*. (It is also known as the *White Album*.) I say "ironically" because the album was actually a series of songs from each of the individual Beatles. For this project, they prepared their own songs privately and brought the other Beatles in more or less as sidemen. Sometimes they even brought in outside musicians for assistance. This approach gave Lennon the freedom for which he was yearning.

I will review three of his songs from this historic year:

"Revolution 9"
"Revolution"
"Julia"

"Revolution 9" proved to be the most avant-garde of all of Lennon's offerings on any Beatles album. In fact, it is more of a modern twentieth-century sound collage by the likes of Berio and Stockhausen than a proper pop song from the Fab Four.

"Revolution" was extrapolated from the initial "Revolution 9" sessions. It provided Lennon with one of his greatest hits, despite its seemingly controversial provocative title and lyric. Because of the social turmoil during this period, most people expected the Beatles, or at least Lennon, to release a song that called for outright rioting in the streets. However, it was a song of personal revolution, from the inside out. Only Lennon could create a song like that and sell it to the public at large.

His musical persona was reaching a great dualistic peak during this year. The content of his songs show us that he was at once the most powerful man in pop music, while at the same time, just a regular guy innocently wondering why the world is so screwed up. John as regular guy surfaces with great tenderness in his lovely ballad, "Julia," composed at the end of the year. It is John's homage to his lost mother from his youth. Fittingly, it would be the last song he would record in 1968.

We start with his very avant-garde "Revolution 9." With a song like this, there really is no lead sheet. The following timeline of "Revolution 9" is offered as a general guide so we can explore it in more depth. This timeline represents mostly what is at the top of the mix, as it would be unwieldy and tedious to plow through every single sound submitted to tape. A dedicated fan of "Revolution 9" will find new sounds in every listening.

Revolution 9

Themes and Sounds

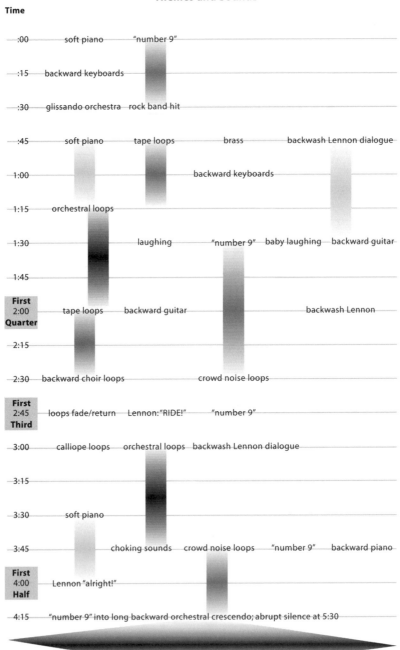

Time

:00 — soft piano — "number 9"

:15 — backward keyboards

:30 — glissando orchestra — rock band hit

:45 — soft piano — tape loops — brass — backwash Lennon dialogue

1:00 — backward keyboards

1:15 — orchestral loops

1:30 — laughing — "number 9" — baby laughing — backward guitar

1:45

First 2:00 Quarter — tape loops — backward guitar — backwash Lennon

2:15

2:30 — backward choir loops — crowd noise loops

First 2:45 Third — loops fade/return — Lennon: "RIDE!" — "number 9"

3:00 — calliope loops — orchestral loops — backwash Lennon dialogue

3:15

3:30 — soft piano

3:45 — choking sounds — crowd noise loops — "number 9" — backward piano

First 4:00 Half — Lennon "alright!"

4:15 — "number 9" into long backward orchestral crescendo; abrupt silence at 5:30

Themes and Sounds | *continued*

Time			
Second 5:30 **Third**	backward choir loops	Lennon: "clothes, etc."	crackling fire
5:45	voices	tape loop backwash	
Third 6:00 **Quarter**	backward choir loops	battle sounds	Lennon discusses a nightwatchman
6:15		tape loops	"number 9"
6:30	Lennon: "the watusi, the twist"	Harrison: "el dorado"	tape loop backwash
First 6:45 **Half**	Lennon: "take this, brother"		crashing piano sounds
7:00	Yoko dialogue	tape loops	radio backwash
7:15			
7:30			"Martha, My Dear" piano
7:45	Yoko: "become naked"	panning crowd noise	first football cheer: "hold that line!"
8:00			second football cheer: "block that kick!"

Title	Revolution 9
Recording Date	May 30, 1968
Meter	None
Key	None
Song Form	Collage
Recording	*The Beatles (White Album)*
	1968 EMD/CAPITOL

There is no doubt that this is the strangest "song" Lennon ever offered for release on a Beatles album. It was one of the first recorded for the *White Album*. The first song recorded for that album became known as "Revolution 1"—or the "slow" version of "Revolution" from the *White Album*.

Having three songs in one's repertoire entitled "Revolution," "Revolution 1," and "Revolution 9" would be enough to confuse anyone. Of the three songs I will discuss only two in detail: "Revolution" and "Revolution 9." Both of these songs are offshoots of the original song, "Revolution 1."

On May 30, 1968, Lennon entered Abbey Road Studios to record "Revolution 1," which at the time was called simply "Revolution." Take 18 of the song proved to be ten minutes long, with the last six minutes getting further and further away from blues and heading closer and closer to the aleatory and avant-garde. "Revolution 9" is Lennon's venture into these areas. The song broke down tonality, form, rhythm, and lyric into a collage of sounds for the listener's entertainment.

The first portion of the take became the four-minute album track, which was retitled "Revolution 1." The rest of it would undergo a transformation similar to the avant-garde treatments found in "Tomorrow Never Knows," "Strawberry Fields Forever," and "I Am the Walrus."

That accounts for "Revolution 1" and "Revolution 9." But what of "Revolution"? The song simply titled "Revolution" is the "fast" version of the song and will be discussed in detail later on in this book.

Lennon began compiling tape loops and sound effects for the seemingly unstructured sound collage that was to become "Revolution 9" in early June 1968. On June 21 he completed most of the final recording. According to writer Mark Lewisohn (in *The Beatles: Recording Sessions*, 1988):

> *John Lennon commandeered the use of all three studios at Abbey Road for the spinning in and recording of the myriad tape loops. Just like the 7 April 1966 "Tomorrow Never Knows" sessions, there were people all over EMI studios spooling loops onto tape machines with pencils. But instead*

of Geoff Emerick sitting at the console fading them in and out in a live mix, it was John Lennon, with Yoko closely by his side.

The original tape does indeed show that John and George went out on the studio floor to read out bizarre lines of prose—in voices sometimes equally bizarre—into a couple of microphones, abetted by Yoko Ono humming at a very high pitch. These ran for the duration of "Revolution 9," being faded in and out of the master at John's whim. Among John's random pieces were "personality complex," "onion soup," "economically viable," "industrial output," "financial imbalance," "the watusi," "the twist," and "take this brother, may it serve you well." George's contributions included "El Dorado" and, shared with John Lennon and whispered six times over, "There ain't no rule for the company freaks!"

Second engineer Richard Lush has a detailed memory of the session and the discovery of the most famous of all the "Revolution 9" sound effects—the repeating "number 9, number 9, number 9..." According to Lewisohn (1988):

Lush recalls, "Lennon was trying to do really different things...we had to get a whole load of tapes out of the library and the 'number nine' voice came off an examination tape. John thought it was a real hoot! He made a loop of just that bit and had it playing constantly on one machine, fading it in or out when he wanted it, along with the backwards orchestral stuff and everything else."

Four days later on June 25, the song was completed as it was edited from 9:05 down to the final 8:12 final version heard on the *White Album*.

STRUCTURE

It is very hard to assign a structure to a composition of this nature. It is hardly a verse/chorus or verse/refrain song. I will use a technique that is often used to analyze avant-garde or contemporary art music composition. That is, I will divide the song into thirds and then further divide it into quarters. This will provide at least a mathematical lens through which to view the composition. We can then assess whether or not a structure does surface amid the apparent random nature of the piece. (This method is common among music academics. I first used this method for an indepth study of the music of Karlheinz Stockhausen, along with other composers of aleatory music, while I was at graduate school at Florida State University during the 1970s.)

As you read, refer to the timeline at the beginning of this chapter. It subdivides the song into 15-second segments, with descriptive detail added. It shows more clearly the changes in textures as the collage progresses from beginning to end. In a piece like this, each listener will hear something entirely different. What one takes away from a random aleatory composition depends entirely on how closely one is listening. The analysis of the demarcation points (thirds and quarters) will serve as guideposts for the listener.

THIRDS

Dividing a song into thirds gives a very clear concept of the beginning, middle, and end of the song, as discussed in chapter 1. For comparative purposes, one can find the "beginning, middle, and end" paradigm throughout Western music. For instance, it is evident particularly in the sonata forms of Mozart and Beethoven, which consistently include an exposition, development, and recapitulation. A musical idea, or theme, is presented in the **exposition**, which is the first major part of the sonata. The theme is transformed and varied in the **development section**. In the **recapitulation**, the theme is revisited. This music helped to set a three-part convention that stands today: Several of John Lennon's employ a classic three-verse structure. "Day Tripper" and "Revolution" are two good examples.

"Revolution 9" is exactly 8 minutes and 12 seconds long. When 8:12 is divided into thirds, the result is three equal segments of 2:44 each. This divides the song as follows:

2:44 = End of section 1/Beginning of section 2
5:28 = End of section 2/Beginning of section 3

Does anything significant happen at those two points in the song? Let's review at the dividing points and decide.

At 2:44 into "Revolution 9" three events happen at once:

- The backward tape loops that have dominated the previous 30 seconds begin to fade.
- Another tape loop of Lennon's voice, which has previously been percolating in the background of the tape, begins to surface. It culminates in a classic Lennon scream of the word "ride"… more like "Rrriiiiiiiiiiiiiiiiiiiiiiiiidde!"
- There is a recapitulation (or return) of the "number 9" theme that opens the song.

All three of these events demarcate the transition from the first third of the sound collage to the second third. At this point, while the tape loops fade, Lennon uses a combination of old material ("number 9") and new material ("ride").

At 5:28, at the transition point from the second third to the final third, there are two significant events:

- A tape loop crescendo (getting louder) that has been building over the last minute of the song begins a rapid decrescendo (getting softer).
- This reveals a voice sounding rather like the composer himself saying:

  ...my broken chair. My strings are broken and my chair is broken. I'm not in the mood for wearing clothes...

Lennon's speaking voice serves as a dividing line for the three sections of the sound collage. Though his speaking voice is present throughout the piece, it is at these intervals that it rises to the surface of the mix.

FOURTHS

As we have discussed (ad nauseum?) up to this point in the book, dividing a song into four parts was not a foreign concept to Lennon. Recall his extensive use of the four-part AABA form in songs like "I Call Your Name," "If I Fell," and "You Can't Do That." Dividing this song accordingly, the result is four equal segments, lasting 2:03 each:

> 2:03 = End of section 1/Beginning of section 2
> 4:06 = End of section 2/Beginning of section 3
> 6:09 = End of section 3/Beginning of section 4

Lennon's voice again demarcates the four sections. At 2:03 into "Revolution 9" the following three events occur:

- Just before the 2:03 point, the listener is treated to lovely backward guitar work reminiscent of guitarist George Harrison's contribution to "Rain" and "Tomorrow Never Knows."
- Right at 2:03 is the recurrence of that famous "number 9" repetition that begins the piece.
- Lennon's voice is buried below the main mix but floats on top of a background of sounds and tape loops.

At 4:06, the following two events occur:

- There is a reappearance of the same backward piano from the opening seconds of the song.
- Lennon shouts: "Alright!"

At 6:09, the following three events occur:

- The sounds of war and battle that began at exactly at 6:00 begin to fade out.
- Lennon's voice is heard once again, this time discussing a "night watchman."
- The backward-tape choir heard during the first two minutes of the piece reappears.

8:12

Like any song, "Revolution 9" is headed for the ending, no matter how you cut it. But really, there is no indication to the listener that the end is near. Lennon concludes the song in this manner:

7:44–7:47	For three seconds the entire composition stops while Yoko Ono says: "If…you become naked."
7:47–7:57	For the next ten seconds, a football cheer is heard over the noise of a crowd: "Hold that line! Hold that line!" etc.
7:57–8:12	For the final fifteen seconds a second football cheer is heard, also amid crowd noises, until the song finally fades out: "Block that kick! Block that kick!"

In the final coda, Lennon takes an atypical songwriting approach. Rather than revisiting the song's musical or lyrical refrain to end the song, he introduces three new items: a dramatic pause, followed by Yoko's voice and two different football cheers. Here, even the perpetual title setting "number 9, number 9, number 9" is absent.

AN AERIAL VIEW

The mathematical analysis of "Revolution 9"—dividing the piece into thirds and fourths—does indeed give a detailed view of Lennon's most complex offering while with the Beatles. However, there is a somewhat simpler view that also fits the beginning/middle/end paradigm—a big-picture, aerial view.

Another way to view "Revolution 9" is as a three-part, through-composed composition:

- Beginning section: Introduction of sounds and themes
- Middle section: Development of sounds and themes
- Concluding section: Introduction of new sounds and themes

Just over halfway through the piece, there is a long, 75-second developmental section that comprises the most complex portion of "Revolution 9." It occurs at about 4:15 and lasts until approximately 5:30. This section is wild and frenzied compared to what comes before and after it. It also contains the thickest, most complex layerings of sounds in the whole piece, with all kinds of material, old and new. It serves as a development of the sounds and themes of the beginning section. What comes before it serves as an exposition and what comes after it serves as a recapitulation, but with variations and additions of new material.

Like the standard sonata form discussed earlier, there are several themes introduced in the beginning section that *do* reoccur in the concluding section: number 9, general tape loops, crowd noise loops, and Lennon background dialog. In this way, the song seems to loosely conform to the standard three-part, sonata-like structure. But there are variations. The beginning section contains specific sounds that *do not* reoccur in the final section: soft piano, backward keys, backward guitars, the sound of a baby laughing, orchestral loops, and calliope loops. Further, the concluding section, normally used to recap themes, here introduces *new* material: backward choir loops, sounds of crackling fire, sounds of battle, featured dialog from John Lennon, Yoko Ono, and George Harrison, as well as the well-known football cheers that punctuate the song's ending.

Despite its seemingly disordered barrage of themes, it may in fact be true that "Revolution 9" is underscored with traces of narrative order. It certainly does demonstrate an intrinsic use of the exposition/development/recapitulation structure found in many types of music. Lennon's mastery of the standard song forms likely played some part in the intuitive direction behind the spontaneous fashioning of this avant-garde exploration.

SUMMARY

How does one even begin to summarize this song? Is it actually a song? Though it may not be considered a song in the time period in which it was written, Lennon proved himself once again to be ahead of his time. To classify "Revolution 9," we must draw from the terminology of the avant-garde: It is a twentieth-century sound collage.

But how does Lennon's creation of a sound collage relate to his earlier songwriting endeavors? Is there any connection at all? Certainly, the use of contrast is present throughout. In writing songs, any composer looks for contrast and variety, and Lennon had developed that technique thoroughly as a songwriter: contrast in rhythm, contrast in pitch, contrast in harmony, contrast in lyric. In "Revolution 9," contrast is manifest in the many textures, dynamics, and flow of the song. It provides spotlights along the way to emphasize certain musical and lyrical points. In that sense, the song demonstrates contrast as its main compositional technique.

The song has no coherent melody, harmony, rhythm, pitch, or lyric, and therefore cannot create any memorable themes the way a "normal" song would. There is one theme, however, that does get the pop-song repetition treatment: the endlessly repeating "number 9...number 9...number 9...."

By this time, Lennon had already demonstrated that he could compose mainstream pop with the best of them. But in "Revolution 9," he was pushing the envelope of pop music to the limit. Despite Lennon's exploration of new songwriting territories, "Revolution 9" remains one of the least popular of all the Beatles songs. Lewisohn (1988) writes:

> *"Revolution 9" was to have a divided effect on its audience when released on* The Beatles, *most listeners loathing it outright, the dedicated fans trying to understand it.*

"Revolution 9" is the penultimate song on the *White Album*. And what is the album's ultimate song—the very last song heard? Another Lennon song, "Good Night." After all the netherworldly sounds of "Revolution 9" have bombarded the listener's senses for a full 8:12, the song "Good Night" makes a timid entrance with its luscious Hollywood-style orchestration. Lennon turned this schmaltzy little lullaby over to George Martin for orchestration and musical performance, while Ringo provided the vulnerable daddy's vocal that gives the song its credibility. Though "Good Night" is not included for full analysis in this book, it is noteworthy that Lennon claimed the last two spots on the *White Album* for himself.

With the juxtaposition of these two songs as the ending for this landmark album, one can easily see the breadth of Lennon's interest in song composition. The proximity of these songs at the end of the album show Lennon's writing at its extremes. "Good night, number 9."

Revolution

Words and Music by John Lennon and Paul McCartney

(Continued on following page)

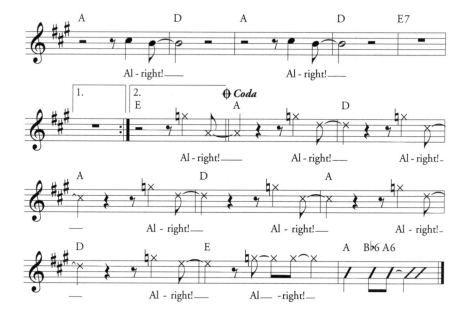

Verse 2

You say you got a real solution,

Well, you know, we'd all love to see the plan.

You ask me for a contribution,

Well, you know, we're all doing what we can.

But if you want money for people with minds that hate,

All I can tell you is, "Brother, you have to wait."

Verse 3

You say you'll change the constitution,

Well, you know, we all want to change your head.

You tell me it's the institution,

Well, you know, you better free your mind instead.

But if you go carrying pictures of Chairman Mao,

You ain't gonna make with anyone anyhow.

Title:	Revolution
Recording Date:	July 10, 1968
Meter:	4/4 and 2/4
Key:	A major (speeded up to B♭ major)
Song Form:	Verse/Transitional Bridge/Chorus
Phrasing:	Verse: *abab*
	Transitional Bridge: *ab*
	Chorus: *abc*
Recording:	*Beatles: Past Masters, Vol ume 2*
	1988 EMD/CAPITOL

"Revolution" is the fast version of "Revolution 1," which appeared on *The Beatles (White Album)*. John has also referred to the fast version as "Revolution 2."

John wanted to release the slow version as the first single on the Beatles' new Apple label. Producer Martin and band member McCartney, however, overruled this version as unacceptable for the single precisely *because* of the slow tempo.

Lennon quickly arranged the fast version of the song and recorded it with the Beatles on July 10, 1968. Released on August 26, 1968 in America, and on August 30 in England, it was the very first single on the new Apple Records label. It was a return-to-his-roots, tour-de-force Lennon rocker.

Both the music and lyric are passionate. Lennon and George Martin's decision to overdrive the control board preamps on the guitar tracks gave the record a hard-edged sound that gave even the Stones a run for their money. The song is the Beatles' very first to address political issues directly. However, upon a closer listening, the lyric is both confounding and delightful. It is accessible yet vague in a characteristically Lennon sort of way.

STRUCTURE

Song Form

In "Revolution" Lennon once again embraces the verse/transitional bridge/chorus form, as he did in "Lucy in the Sky with Diamonds:"

Verse	Transitional Bridge	Chorus
14 bars	5 1/2 bars	8 bars

Lennon's approach in "Revolution" is much more direct than his dreamy and wandering one in "Lucy," which involved surreal lyrics and evolving key signatures. As we will find in our exploration ahead, his direct presentation of the form totally supports the music and lyric.

Lennon is still in an embryonic stage of discovery with this three-part form. Just as in "Lucy," Lennon's chorus lyric is short and repetitive. This lyric is so short and succinct that it too could be set in just a few bars, like a refrain. But Lennon has chosen a square, standard 8-bar form for the transmission of these summary lyrics:

> Don't you know it gonna be alright.
> Alright.
> Alright.
> Alright.

This leaves room for the distorted, hammering low-voiced guitar work that adds to the song's gritty rock 'n' roll feel.

The lyrics make for a great chorus. Lennon was perhaps taking a cue from the embryonic choruses found in earlier folk music of the decade. Lennon's chorus was much like Bob Dylan's in "It's a Hard Rain's Gonna Fall"—only backwards:

> It's a hard,
> It's a hard,
> It's a hard,
> It's a hard,
> It's a hard rain's gonna fall

Thirty years later, we find that chorus lyric content tends to be more complex. Lennon was at the cutting edge in the late 1960s in developing this chorus form into the standard that it is today.

Regarding meter, the verse is a 14-bar blues made up of twelve bars of 4/4 and two bars of 2/4. If one added the two 2/4 bars together, what is actually heard is a *13-bar blues!* In the transitional bridge, an inserted 2/4 bar creates a 5 1/2-bar section. In both the verse and the transitional bridge, Lennon is creating his own revolution in terms of form.

The addition of these extra bars of 2/4 gives both of these sections a pleasantly out-of-control feel. The extra 2/4 bar moves the downbeat forwards and backwards, causing a momentary but pleasant confusion—great prosody for the "revolutionary" lyric. Lennon, however, did not lose his listeners with these wildly changing meter patterns, but rather enticed them with a musical version of a pleasantly careening carnival ride.

In contrast to the verse, the chorus is straight-ahead: eight bars long and 4/4 time all the way. This gives a respite from the very forward-moving verses and transitional bridges, and a perfect arrival point for all the song's lyrics.

Lennon's innate concept of form and meter is both shrewd and astute: In this song of "Revolution," he stirs things up in the initial sections, but gives a safe harbor in the choruses. It is a meaningful revolution but not outright anarchy.

Lyric Content

The lyric is a very interesting contrast to the title. The title implies maybe we're all going to go mad in the streets with a violent overthrow of whatever or whoever we don't like. This lyric gave Lennon a vehicle to discuss several things at once. On the surface it seems to be a political statement on the times. Through the Beatles, he could make a dramatic statement on the Vietnam War, world politics, and the like. This was the first of his songs that crossed the political line lyrically. It also gave Lennon a platform to send a message to all of his fans and followers: Revolutionize yourself; "change your head."

Lennon's lyric is more restrained and introspective, calling for revolution from within before any true social change is possible. The song was a message to those who sought his support for their political causes. In the first verse, Lennon mentions destruction, then says to count him *out*. However, in the slow version he said to count him *in*. And in the video for the fast version, taped specifically for *The Smothers Brothers* television show (September 1968), he says *both*. This lyric received great criticism from the left-wing fringe groups that were hoping for his direct support. Lennon made it very clear in subsequent interviews that he would only support those who would demonstrate their dissent with flowers—not bullets.

PHRASING

Verse

▶ Harmonic Phrasing

The verses, as mentioned briefly above, are set in 14-bar blues. While I have set the song in A major for this analysis, the song is actually closer to B♭ blues on the single. However, in the video for the single, one can easily see that they are "synch-playing" in key of A blues, since the instruments are not live. Since the slow version is in the key of A blues—and it is, in fact, the original—I analyze it in the great guitar key of A blues instead of the piano key of B♭ blues:

Fig. 7.1. Verse harmonic phrasing

Note the use of the classic I, IV, and V7 chords (A, D, and E7) to establish the A blues tonality. The potent 2/4 bars give a more conversational setting to underscore the colloquial "well, you know" lyric line at each of the 2/4 bars. Inserting the 2/4 bar at the beginning of the line creates an odd line length, making the line flow more freely than a lyric bound to a more square, structured framework.

▶ *Melodic Phrasing*

The phrasing for the verse is the most classic and accessible of the three sections. It is the common *abab* form:

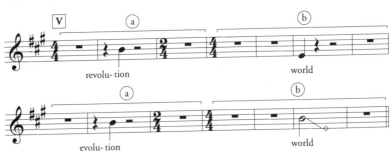

Fig. 7.2. Verse melodic phrasing

Note each line starts with a slightly disjointed 2-1/2-bar phrase and is followed by a standard 4-bar unit. The "Well, you know" lyric in the 2/4 bar plugs in as a pickup to the answering 4-bar phrase.

Transitional Bridge

▶ *Harmonic Phrasing*

The appearance of the transitional bridge is both unexpected and effective. The band arrangement for the bridge is basically just drums and vocals. Suddenly reducing the whole band down to just one screaming vocal with beating drums (tomtoms, no less!) creates a downright Neanderthal sound that makes the hair stand up on the back of your neck:

Fig. 7.3. Transitional bridge harmonic phrasing

The harmony for the bridge is a continuation of the II–V cadence that concluded the verse. The band reappears at the 2/4 bar, which ends on the uplifting VI major (F♯ major)—the same exhilarating chord found in the chorus of "Strawberry Fields Forever." The F♯ chord, containing A♯ as its third, emphasizes a note that is a half step above the tonic. This gives the chord an uplifting feeling. This transitional section then moves down to the dominant to move to the chorus.

❱ Melodic Phrasing

The transitional bridge, only 5 1/2 bars long, has only two phrases, *ab*:

Fig. 7.4. Transitional bridge melodic phrasing

Lennon maintains the conversational tone that irregular meter established in the verse. Its effect is somewhat different, however. In the verse, the 2/4 bar acts as a pickup bar to the next phrase. Here, it is used in the middle of the phrase to accent that "count me out" lyric. The ultimate effect of this treatment is that it makes the section feel quite frenzied and sends it barreling forward into the refrain.

Chorus

❱ Harmonic Phrasing

Lennon keeps the harmony for the chorus very simple, a series of bluesy plagal cadences before ending, like all the other sections, on the forward-moving dominant E7:

Fig. 7.5. Chorus harmonic phrasing

The melodic phrasing for the song's 8-bar chorus is unique in the sense that it has the most space and the least amount of lyric in the whole song:

Fig. 7.6. Chorus melodic phrasing

It would be quite common to expect four 2-bar phrases for an 8-bar section. However, the phrasing here is much more interesting and emphatic: a 3-bar phrase, a 2-bar phrase, and a 3-bar phrase. To create a further sense of revolution in this otherwise square 8-bar chorus, Lennon inserts a distortion-laden guitar lick in the last two bars, instead of repeating the "alright" lyric for a fourth time, as might be expected.

PROSODY

Verse

The melody for the verse includes great movement and very little resolution, spanning an octave but settling more or less on the unstable 2nd degree, which remains unresolved throughout the entire verse:

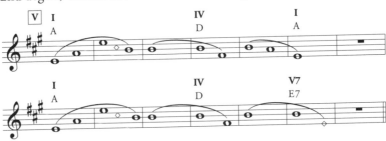

Fig. 7.7. Verse structural tones

There are only two melodic resolutions in the verse. The first occurs when the B (Re) in bar 5 moves briefly to the tonic note A. However, the unstable F♯ from bar 4 has the strongest resolution to the E in bar 6, putting a musical period halfway through the verse.

Overall, the melody remains in motion, leading right into the bridge and refrain.

Lennon thus creates a standard open verse setup with the unfinished lyric, the use of the dominant chord E7, and the focus on the unstable Re as the melody note for the concluding lyric.

Transitional Bridge

Again, the note B introduced in the verse continues its playful nonresolution in the transitional bridge:

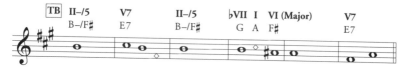

Fig. 7.8. Transitional bridge structural tones

The B (Re) is looking, of course, for the tonic A to come to resolution. And what does Mr. Lennon deliver up melodically for the end of this section? A♯! The B is *almost* resolved. In fact, it could not be more unresolved: The A♯ sits one half step above tonic, so close, yet so far from resolution. Lennon successfully uses it to accomplish transition and a sense of spilling over into the arrival point, the chorus.

The tonic A does exist in the very last bar. This theoretically would give some resolution, but since it is coupled with the unstable E7 chord, the movement of the bridge remains unstoppable.

Chorus

At the outset of the chorus, we find once again the unstable melody note B at the end of each phrase (bars 2, 4, and 6):

Fig. 7.9. Chorus structural tones

Lennon loved the note so much that he decided to leave the song unresolved with it. It's quite an ironic setting. The lyric implies that everything will be alright—a feet-planted-firmly-on-the-ground kind of thing. But meanwhile, the harmonic cadence is left open. The melody keeps ending on the unstable IV chord (D). Further, the whole section ends on E7, with that guitar lick that has a forward-moving instability of its own. A song with such unstable and forward-moving sections definitely needs an ending. And what an ending Lennon delivers:

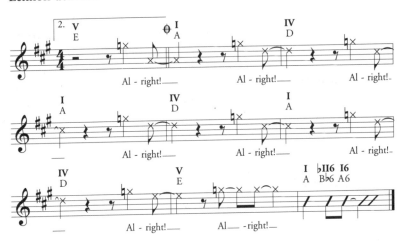

Fig. 7.10. Song ending, "Revolution"

Finally, the listener is treated to the "really big" showbiz ending: a chromatic and syncopated movement of the B♭6 to the A6, to bring this driving rocker to a raucous conclusion. The B♭6 chord is a substitute dominant, often used in Hollywood-style orchestral settings. However, in this song, the amps are so loud and overdriving that the song ending is raucous and distorted—not a Hollywood ending at all.

SUMMARY

"Revolution" goes straight for the gut. When DJs first received the single in August 1968, many sent it back, thinking they had received a distorted version. But John had wanted that sound. In his book, Mark Lewisohn (1988) records tape operator Phil MacDonald's firsthand account:

> *John wanted that sound, that distorted sound. The guitars were put through the recording console, which was technically not the thing to do. It completely overloaded the channel and produced the fuzz sound. Fortunately, the technical people didn't find out. They didn't approve of "abuse of equipment."*

No one, not even those involved directly in the music business, was ready for the likes of a song like "Revolution." But today, some thirty-three years later, it still stands.

The original slow version was no doubt meant to be a revolution "whispered in your ear." The fast version by contrast is totally "in yer face," as Lennon might say, with its distortion, beating tomtoms, and the relentless, unstoppable, repeating chorus of "alright's" that conclude each verse.

The lyric is of course somewhat dated, with its reference to Chinese Chairman Mao. John said in an interview that he wished he had not included Mao in the lyric. Overall, however, the lyric will excite listeners for years to come. The upbeat, bluesy rock setting is perfect prosody for his raucous message. The song's easy transition from a fast to a slow version is not unlike the successful transformation of another one of rock's more recent anthems: "Smells Like Teen Spirit" by Nirvana. Tori Amos also recorded a delicate, slow version of that grunge hit. It goes to show that a great song is a great song and can be done in many styles.

"Revolution" will continue to enjoy an honored place in the annals of political rock. Lennon realized he was pushing the envelope of the Beatles' format by releasing such a potentially controversial song. He told *Playboy* magazine, "I wanted it out as a single, as a statement of the Beatles' position on Vietnam and the Beatles' position on revolution." (Dowdling, 1989) After ten years of being one half of the greatest songwriting teams in pop music, he decided the time was right for him to make a statement, to express an opinion, with the solid backing of his own band, the Beatles.

Julia

Words and Music by John Lennon and Paul McCartney

So I sing a song— of love.— Ju——— - li— - a.

Verse 2
Julia, seashell eyes,
Windy smile calls me,
So I sing a song of love, Julia.

Intro 2
When I cannot sing my heart,
I can only speak my mind, Julia.

Verse 4
Julia, sleeping sand,
Silent cloud touch me,
So I sing a song of love, Julia.

Coda
…calls me,
So I sing a song of love, Julia,
Julia,
Julia.

BACKGROUND

Title:	Julia
Recording Date:	October 13, 1968
Meter:	2/2
Key:	D major
Song Form:	Verse/Chorus w/Primary Bridge
Phrasing:	AABA w/variations
	Intro Verse: *ab*
	Verse: *aabc*
	Primary Bridge: *ab*
Recording:	*The Beatles (White Album)*
	1968 EMD/CAPITOL

"Julia" is one of Lennon's acoustic offerings, created near the end of his Beatles career. It is a very introspective and impressionistic song about his mother, Julia. The song also includes lyrical references to Yoko. It was the 32nd and final song composed for the *White Album*.

In interviews, John has credited the authorship of this tender ballad as a "Lennon/Ono/Gibran" song. Yoko helped with some of the lyric, and the first two lines of the song were inspired directly from the mystic Lebanese poet Khalil Gibran. Gibran had published a book of proverbs in 1927 called *Sand and Foam*, which Lennon was reading at the time. The finger picking–style guitar work had less cosmic influences: John said that he was influenced directly by the singer Donovan, who taught him the intricate picking pattern that we hear on the final recording.

This song marks the first and only time John recorded an entirely solo piece for a Beatles album. The *White Album* also marks the first appearances of Yoko Ono on a Beatles album: as backup singer on "The Continuing Story of Bungalow Bill"; as cowriter and coproducer of "Revolution 9"; and as cowriter on this song.

Recording for the *White Album* began on May 30, 1968 with "Revolution" and "Revolution 9." "Julia," as mentioned above, was the very last song, recorded on October 13, 1968. Spanning approximately four and a half months, it was the longest recording process of any Beatles album.

The album was released on November 22, 1968, exactly five years to the day after the Beatles' second album, *With the Beatles*, and the same day that President Kennedy was assassinated.

STRUCTURE

Song Form

The form is a clever old-and-new variation on the standard AABA. The song begins with an old-style intro verse for a total of eight bars. We then hear the standard AABA format. But then Lennon brings back the intro verse again. Following that, he moves to one last A section. The final coda section is basically an A section:

Introductory Verse	A	A	B	A	Introductory Verse	A	Coda
8 bars	12 bars	14 bars	10 bars	14 bars	8 bars	12 bars	17 bars

One unusual thing occurs in this song and no other. The melody for the intro verse, after sustaining the static A for the duration, suddenly cadences down to D, the tonic. That in and of itself is not so unusual. What is unusual is that at the same moment that Lennon is singing the D, we also hear him, from out of nowhere, singing the title of the song on one of those now-familiar A's. Then of course we realize that the verse has begun.

If this were one of the famous Lennon and McCartney vocal duets, we wouldn't be surprised to hear two voices. Nor would we be surprised to hear that John had double-tracked his own vocal. But this taped overlap of the last syllable in the intro verse and the first syllable of the verse proper makes a solo live performance totally impossible. If you resolve down to the D, you are late for the A, or vice versa.

Lennon uses this device to connect verses 1 and 2. The form allows for four hearings of the verses, but there are two different lengths: one is twelve bars long, the other is fourteen. Lennon uses the overlap at the end of the 12-bar verses, so there are two other overlaps: 1) connecting the first and second A sections, and 2) connecting the second intro verse with the final A section.

Lyric Content

The verse lyric again reveals Lennon in his simplest mode. He calls out his mother's name, then attaches several two-word descriptions: "seashell eyes," "sleeping sand," and "windy smile," all of which continue to the same refrain, rejoicing in the song of love to his mum. There are some references to his wife Yoko, as well: "ocean child" (the English translation of the name "Yoko") and "silent cloud." (While John was in India, Yoko wrote in a letter to him, "I'm a cloud. Look for me in the sky." [Coleman, 1984.]) The verse has many short phrases, but the ethereal bridge lyric is just the opposite. Rather, it is one long lyrical line that describes her hair as sky that is "shimmering" and "glimmering" in the sunlight.

After the bridge, a single verse returns. Astoundingly, Lennon brings the intro melody back at this point with another expansion of the Gibran lyric:

> *When I cannot sing my heart,*
> *I can only speak my mind, Julia.*

The fourth and final verse falls into place and leads to a humming verse-based coda which takes the lyric out, repeating his mother's name as the refrain. The lyric phrasing alternates throughout the song, like a woven tapestry. The whole lyric, taken altogether, reveals this picture.

Intro:	Long, lyrical
Verses:	Short, minimal
Bridge:	Long, lyrical
Verse:	Short, minimal
Intro:	Long, lyrical
Verse:	Short, minimal
Coda:	Long, lyrical

PHRASING

Intro Verse and Verses

▶ Harmonic Phrasing

In the intro verse, the harmony is totally still, helping to set up an ethereal atmosphere. Set in the key of D major, the song only uses the stable tonic chords D, B–7, and F♯ minor:

Fig. 7.11. Intro verse harmonic phrasing

Lennon finally introduces the dominant A chord at the last bar to set up the verse. As the verse opens, it appears to be a repeat of the introductory verse, but Lennon then introduces the delectable A minor triad, with its dreamy, out-of-the-key C♮ in the harmony. (Recall that using a V minor chord had a similar effect in "Strawberry Fields.")

Fig. 7.12. Verse harmonic phrasing

Lennon then inserts even more intoxicating harmony with the introduction of the B7, G7(9), and G–7 chords. The intricate chromatic lines illustrated in bars 3 through 8 of fig. 7.12 support the harmonic progression as it drifts smoothly through the chromatic B7, coming to the final cadence point at the G7(9) and G–7 chords. The progression finishes up by simply repeating the last few bars of the introductory verse.

▌ *Melodic Phrasing*

Lennon opens the song with an imbalance in the intro verse:

Fig. 7.13. Intro verse melodic phrasing

As soon as the first verse enters, the lyric and phrasing shift to four consecutive 2-bar phrases culminating with that wonderful G7(9)-to-G–7 phrase:

Fig. 7.14. Verse melodic phrasing

Those shorter phrases give the verse a lightness that the intro verse doesn't have. As you can see, the 12-bar verses really turn out to become 13-bar verses with the overlap. The result is *aabc*. The 14-bar verses are exactly the same as the 13-bar ones, except the ⓒ phrase is six bars instead of five.

Primary Bridge

▶ *Harmonic Phrasing*

As Lennon moves into the bridge, the chord progression leads the listener into a harmonic hinterland. The whole notes refer to the inner harmonic line—which is the subtle descending line one hears as the chords change:

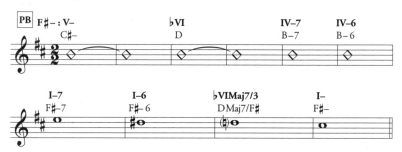

Fig. 7.15. Primary bridge harmonic phrasing

The C♯ minor chord that begins the bridge introduces a G♯ into the mix. This nondiatonic note signals that something new is afoot. But the song suddenly returns to the familiar D and B–7 chords heard earlier. Then, with the return of the F♯ minor chord, Lennon introduces a chromatic descending inner line, illustrated in the example above in whole notes. Because this kind of "James Bond"-style chromatic line over a sustained chord normally occurs over a tonic, this line has a tendency to turn the F♯ minor into the new tonic chord briefly.

The bridge ends, and we wonder if we have arrived at a new tonic. Just as we get used to that possibility, the verse returns with the tonic D and the bridge becomes a distant memory.

▶ *Melodic Phrasing*

The melodic phrasing in the primary bridge is a 180-degree departure from that of the verse:

Fig. 7.16. Primary bridge melodic phrasing

The phrasing is divided into two phrases: 4 bars + 6 bars. However, examination of the lyric line reveals that it may also be heard as one long 10-bar phrase encompassing the entire section. The lyric line, "Her hair of floating sky is shimmering, glimmering in the sun," can be read as one long sentence, as indicated with the comma. When divided into two phrases (4 + 6), the lyric at the end of the first phrase ("shimmering") doesn't rhyme with lyric at the end of the second phrase ("sun"). Instead "shimmering" rhymes with the first word in the second phrase. This provides some unexpected motion for the bridge. A listener may hear it one way or the other, or both at the same time. When viewed in this manner, the lyric connects all the melodic pauses to achieve an incredibly long melodic statement.

PROSODY

Intro Verse and Verses

The melody immediately drenches the listener with a strident A. That outstanding melody note just goes on forever! By this point, Lennon had proved his mettle at creating a song with a static, one-note melody. He often used this compositional device to spotlight lyrics, as in "All You Need Is Love," "A Hard Day's Night," and "Girl." In "Julia," the device plays out like this:

Fig. 7.17. Intro verse structural tones

Though the A is sustained throughout, its function changes as the chords move beneath it: starting as the 5th of D, the ♭7 of B–7, the ♭3 of F♯–7, and finally, as the root of the A major triad that ends the intro verse and resolves into the first verse proper.

As the melody continues in the verse, that same A dominates the first three bars. Lennon's choice of harmony brings dramatic contrast to the diatonic opening. At bar 3 he inserts an A–7 that is not from D major, but rather D Mixolydian:

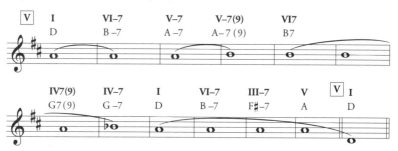

Fig. 7.18. Verse structural tones

The drama created by the repeated A continues as the harmony moves to B7. This leads us to expect the II–7 chord, E–7. But Lennon sidesteps the expectation, and instead moves headlong into yet-unexplored territory. He moves to the bluesy G7(9) chord and puts the luscious 9th in the melody—and that 9th is that A again! As if that weren't enough, he then moves to the minor. The melody moves up a half step to B♭, a welcome relief from the A. These two bars are the high point of the song. This is because:

- The melody moves to much longer whole notes in both bars.
- Neither chord is diatonic to D major, creating a contrast to the prior section.
- The repetition of "call" and "touch" create a lyrical arrival point.
- The following bar returns to tonic, which provides a true reference for the chromatic chords.
- The juxtaposition of the A and the B♭ provide both the familiar and the unexpected, melodically.

Primary Bridge

Without a doubt the most unusual part of the song is the primary bridge. After hearing D major clearly established as tonic, we are startled to hear the C♯ minor chord at the bridge's outset, because it contains a G♯, which is not associated with D major. This indicates a new tonal direction.

The song moves dead ahead into a delightfully ambiguous combination of the F♯ Aeolian and F♯ Dorian modes. Combining the two is not that strange; they are well-known cousins. The startling part is the modulation up a major third from D major to F♯ minor in the first place:

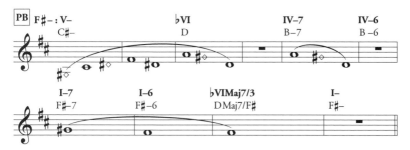

Fig. 7.19. Primary bridge structural tones

D♯ is added to the melody in the bridge, but the quick return back to D♮ marks the Dorian/Aeolian interplay. The harmony probably wouldn't have sounded so ambiguous if the F♯ minor chord had begun the progression, but the bridge begins with a C♯ minor chord, which is V minor in this key. Lennon then moves back to the familiar D and B–7 chords used earlier. However, in the new key they have different functions:

- D was I, but is now ♭VI in F♯ minor.
- B–7 was VI–7, but is now IV–7 and IV–6 in the new key.

It's a very clever modulation. The true key is hidden and is not revealed until the very end of the bridge.

SUMMARY

"Julia" is a most charming tribute of a son to his mother. It is a very personal introspective account that is spiritual and poetic in nature, both musically and lyrically. The song, written ten years after Julia's death, is a reverent homage to her life. The sustained A serves as a descant (ornamental) sustained voice one might expect to hear in a choral setting. The jazzy harmonies (G7(9) and G–7) and the unusual harmonic move to III minor in the bridge gives the song a feeling of floating, also associated with a spiritual journey.

Lennon wrote another song about Julia, called "Mother," two years later on his 1970 solo album *John Lennon/Plastic Ono Band*. When "Julia's" uplifting remembrance is juxtaposed with the portrait of primitive longing and despair illustrated in the lyrics of "Mother," it is clear that "Julia" paints the lighter side of the picture of John's free-spirited mother.

CHAPTER 8 1969

January 1969 was a very full month. The Beatles gathered at three different locations for the filming of their last movie, *Let It Be*. During this period, all the songs for the *Let It Be* album were recorded, as well. Both projects proved to be somewhat a disaster. Neither the movie nor the album were released for another eighteen months.

The recording process proved difficult. Tensions were rising among the band members due to changing musical directions and emotional stress brought on by John's insistence on having Yoko at the sessions. Further, George Martin, who was present at the *Let It Be* recording sessions, found his role as producer slipping away as the band members fought amongst themselves.

Some good did come from the chaos. Lennon composed "Across the Universe" for the album, and considered it one of his best songs. Lennon offered only two more songs for these controversial sessions: an older song from his repertoire ("One After 909") and one he didn't like very much ("I Dig a Pony").

The Beatles went their separate ways for the spring and early summer of 1969. Paul married Linda on March 12. John and Yoko were married eight days later, on March 20.

When the Beatles returned to the studio in July 1969 to record the songs for their last album, *Abbey Road*, much of the acrimony from the previous *Let It Be* sessions was put to rest. George Martin appeared in his usual role as producer for *Abbey Road*, a role that was delegated to Glyn Johns and Phil Spector for the *Let It Be* album.

John's offerings for this album—the last one recorded by the Beatles—totaled six. Three were lighter songs, both melodically and lyrically: "Sun King," "Mean Mr. Mustard," and "Polythene Pam." Two were much more classic Lennon rockers: "I Want You (She's So Heavy)" and "Come Together." The sixth, "Because," brought out the classic John, Paul, and George Beatles-harmony vocal performance.

For this chapter, I have selected the one song that truly represents peak writing for John Lennon. The song

"Come Together" shows Lennon at his simplest and yet richest. It is no wonder that it is the opening track for this very popular Beatles album.

As we will soon see, John Lennon's recording days with the most famous band in the world came to an end by August of this very year. The year's output matched those early hectic years of 1964 and 1965: two albums, several singles, and a movie. However, unlike 1964 and 1965, the year 1969 included *no* touring. There was a one-stop "World Tour" filmed atop Abbey Road Studios at 3 Saville Row in downtown London on January 30. That January rooftop concert was the last performance by Lennon and the Fab Four in front of a live audience. The Sixties were about to end...for real.

Come Together

Words and Music by John Lennon and Paul McCartney

272

Verse 3

He bag production,
He got walrus gumboot,
He got Ono sideboard,
He one spinal cracker.
He got feet down below his knee.
Hold you in his armchair,
You can feel his disease.
Come together, right now, over me.

Verse 4

He roller coaster,
He got early warning,
He got Muddy Water,
He one Mojo filter,
He say, "One and one and one is three."
Got to be good-looking,
'Cause he's so hard to see.
Come together, right now, over me.

BACKGROUND

Title:	Come Together
Recording Date:	July 21, 1969
Meter:	4/4
Key:	D minor
Song Form:	Verse/Refrain
Phrasing:	Verse/Refrain: aaaabbc
Recording:	*Abbey Road*
	1969 EMD/CAPITOL

"Come Together" is a classic 1960s rock anthem. Lennon claimed it was one of his favorite songs from his Beatles period. However, the song has quite a controversial history.

Originally it started off as a campaign song written for Timothy Leary, the ex-Harvard professor and "LSD guru" who became a voice for youth during the late 1960s. At the time, Leary was considering a run for political office. But Leary's campaign ended unexpectedly and Lennon decided to record a version of the song with the Beatles for the upcoming *Abbey Road* album.

Two important figures raised objections to the song: Timothy Leary and Chuck Berry. Leary objected because he was under the impression that John had written the song for him personally, whether or not Leary used it for campaign purposes. He wrote to Lennon with a mild objection, but by this time it had already been released both as a single and an album track. So Leary did not pursue his objections any further.

Chuck Berry, on the other hand, cited a copyright violation. Lennon's opening lyric line about the flat-top was a direct quote from Berry's song "You Can't Catch Me." Lennon regarded it merely as a musical "tip-of-the-hat" to one of his songwriting heroes from the 1950s. Other than the quote of the one single line, "Come Together" has virtually nothing in common with "You Can't Catch Me." Lennon finally agreed to record three songs that were held by the copyright owner of "You Can't Catch Me" as a way to resolve the issue. In the mid-1970s, John recorded "You Can't Catch Me" and "Sweet Little Sixteen" on his 1975 *Rock 'n' Roll* album, and "Ya Ya" on his 1974 *Walls and Bridges* album.

Recording on "Come Together" began on July 21, 1969. It finished up nine days later. Mixing was on August 7. This song has four different release dates. In order, they are: September 26, 1969 as an album track on the English *Abbey Road* LP; October 1, 1969 as an album track on the American *Abbey Road* LP; October 6, 1969 as a single in America; and finally, October 31, 1969 as a single in England.

"Come Together" was the B-side of George Harrison's single "Something," Harrison's first-ever A-side with the Beatles.

STRUCTURE

Song Form

It is significant that this song is a *tour de force* in songwriting because "Come Together" has only one section: a verse/refrain. There are no bridges or choruses in a verse/refrain format. There is, in effect, nowhere to go. Therefore, the lyric and music must be strong enough to stand on their own, verse after verse, straight through to the end. In addition, if the song is to endure, it must be strong enough to withstand multiple playings. This song certainly could; it has a sacred place in the hearts of Beatles fans everywhere and still holds up after more than thirty years.

The song form heard on *Abbey Road* is as follows:

Intro	Verse	Verse/Refrain	Verse/Refrain	Guitar Solo (Verse/Refrain)	Verse/Refrain
4 bars	8 bars	8 + 2 bars	8 + 2 bars	10 bars	10 bars

Lyric Content

The spirit of the lyric is really located in the refrain and title "Come Together." The title is inspired by one of the readings from the *I-Ching*, the Chinese book of changes. The accompanying lyrics for the verses are comprised of a series of short, 1-bar non-sequiturs, which are very visual as they make their aural impact:

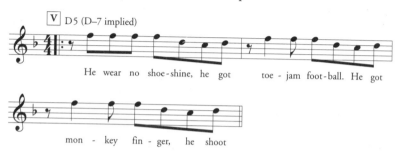

Fig. 8.1. Verse 1 lyrics are a series of 1-bar phrases.

The lyric is totally supported by the smoky, swampy New Orleans blues–style musical setting. The short lyrical statements seem to reach out of the mist and then recede as they drift freely in the musical mix, all leading up to the final lyrical cadence, "Come Together."

PHRASING

Verse

▶ Harmonic Phrasing

The tonic D sustains its hold on the verse for half of the 8-bar verse, then continues with the most logical chords for this blues-based song: the V chord and the IV chord:

Fig. 8.2. Verse harmonic phrasing

In the very first verse, Lennon withholds the 2-bar "come together…" refrain that is attached to each of the other verses.

Refrain

▶ *Harmonic Phrasing*

In setting up the refrain, Lennon chooses the unexpected and electrifying B minor triad. The presence of the note F♯ as the 5th of the triad is what makes it so exhilarating, because most of the melody up to this point has been composed of F♮:

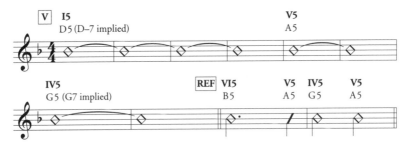

Fig. 8.3. Refrain harmonic phrasing

This move from the IV chord to the VI minor chord, though quite rare, can also be heard in the famous song "I Heard It through the Grapevine."

The refrain appears to be only two bars long, but is actually *three* bars, because the melody and lyric continue beyond the last A5 chord in bar 10 and conclude on the D5 chord that follows. There is a 4-bar interlude—which is actually the song's introduction—between each verse, sustaining the tonic D. This interlude very effectively sets up the next section, as we shall see in the discussion on melodic phrasing coming up next.

Verse

▶ *Melodic Phrasing*

Lennon begins his setting of the aforementioned non-sequiturs with four 1-bar structures. Each lyric ends on the punchy and forward-moving beat 4. This creates an *aaaa* phrasing structure:

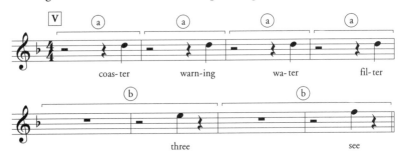

Fig. 8.4. Verse melodic phrasing

Then, Lennon moves into 2-bar phrases. So far Lennon has created an *aaaa/bb* form. But what of the refrain and title setting?

Refrain

▶ *Melodic Phrasing*

The last two bars complete the verse/refrain setting. The refrain line actually ends with the word "me." That word is tied over rhythmically into the guitar/bass-riff interlude that separates each verse:

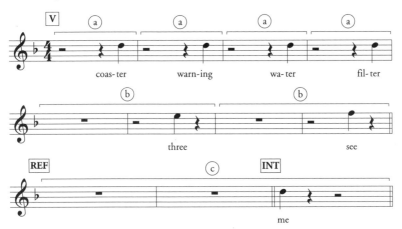

Fig. 8.5. Refrain melodic phrasing

In this illustration, we see the full impact of the phrasing upon the form for the first time:

- Line 1 contains the 1-bar phrases (*aaaa*).
- Line 2 contains the 2-bar phrases (*bb*).
- Line 3 shows the 3-bar refrain that comprises the last two bars of the 10-bar verse and the first bar of the interlude, creating the ⓒ phrase.

The result is *aaaa/bbc*.

The last overlapping phrase makes an 11-bar verse/refrain from a 10-bar form. The use of 1-bar phrases decelerating into 2-bar phrases signals the approach of the title setting. The final 3-bar overlap phrase creates the most deceleration of all. It also creates the biggest spotlight for the title itself.

Melody: Verse

The melody for the first four bars of the verse moves within the range of a perfect 4th and consists of literally just three notes: the tonic note D and the two potent "blues notes," F (♭3) and C (♭7). These rich notes help to define the melody and reveal its allegiance to both the blues and minor modes:

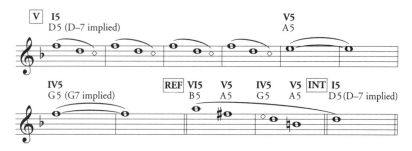

Fig. 8.6. Verse structural tones

After so much repetition of the D and F notes, Lennon strategically provides melodic contrast in bar 5 by moving to the note located between them, the unstable 2nd scale degree, E. For further contrast, he stays on the note for a full two bars. Then, an answering 2-bar phrase, also featuring only the now-familiar F, concludes the 8-bar verse. Using only three notes, Lennon shows amazing agility in fashioning a powerful melody—a rocking pop masterpiece!

Melody: Refrain

Lennon saves up all his melodic action up for the exciting 2-bar refrain section. We have already seen how the B minor triad plays such an important part in the impact of the refrain.

In fig. 8.6, you can see that Lennon moves to the highest note of the song, A, and then down to the contrasting and electrifying F♯. From there, the melody moves right down to the tonic D with the lyric "right now." One might think that it would end there, but the lyric continues with "over me," utilizing another *very* unexpected melody note: B♮. The key of the song, D minor, has the notes F♮ and B♭; the parallel key of D major has the notes used in the refrain, F♯ and B♮. It seems that the refrain setting for this song, composed in the key of D minor, is actually borrowed from the parallel key of D major.

The final lyric needed some drastic contrast after all the repetitive patterns established in the verse. Lennon's choice of modal interchange for the refrain, both in terms of melody and harmony, was the perfect solution. It gives the title lyric its powerful impact.

SUMMARY

"Come Together." We see the title on the album cover. We hear the first verse come and go. We think, where is this song going? A description of some joker who has both a flat-top *and* hair down to his knees? No title?

The second verse seems to be more of the same, but it is actually a covert description of Lennon himself. After the glorious imagery of verse 2, the listener is treated to the title setting in the familiar but contrasting parallel key. The move is a stroke of genius. The decision to move out of the minor into the major to spotlight the title gives a bright uplift and a consummate move away from the bluesy, minor verses.

With these two devices in place, the song needs nothing else. The song stands beautifully on its own. Lennon, as the shrewd artist, knew exactly when to put down the paintbrush and declare the canvas finished.

CHAPTER 9 august 20, 1969

At 2:30 p.m. on August 20, 1969, John Lennon began a three-hour session at Abbey Road studios for the final mixing of "I Want You (She's So Heavy)." It was the last song to be mixed for the *Abbey Road* album. If I could have included one more song in this book, it would have been this great Lennon creation. I encourage you to get the music to this song and dig in.

"I Want You (She's So Heavy)" was actually the first song to be recorded for the album back in February 1969. John had two recordings of the song in progress: one at Abbey Road Studios and the other at Trident Studios. He was determined to include both in the final mix. He ended up combining the two using mixing techniques that were quite sophisticated for their time. The first 4:37 of the song is from the Abbey Road sessions, while the remaining 3:07 is from the Trident sessions. The transition occurs right where Lennon sings "she's so..."

There is much to be explored in "I Want You (She's So Heavy)," but the reader should note that the song does contain one key feature. Its introduction—which becomes the chorus later on—is in the key of D minor. The song itself, however, is in the key of A minor. It marks the use of one of his signature techniques: composing a dramatic, forward-moving introduction and then surprising the listener with an unexpected harmonic arrival.

August 20, 1969 was an important date for the Beatles. It was the last day that John Lennon worked on Beatles songs together with the other three Beatles at Abbey Road. At 6:00 p.m., the four gathered to make decisions regarding the sequential master for *Abbey Road*. The session ran from 6:00 p.m. to 1:15 a.m. Deciding on the final order for the seventeen songs was the last task for Lennon and the other Beatles. It marked the end of an era that Lennon had spawned with his cutting edge band, the Beatles.

The whole of 1969 was a deceptive year for Beatles and

Lennon fans. What was up with the Beatles? What was up with John? John's musical work was coming to the public from two sources, the Plastic Ono Band and the Beatles. Lennon had begun to pursue other musical endeavors outside the Beatles. During that summer he formed a new group called the Plastic Ono Band, consisting of himself, Yoko Ono, Ringo Starr, and Klaus Voorman. The group also included other drop-in personnel such as Eric Clapton and Tommy Smothers. In July 1969, the group released its first single, the anti-war anthem called "Give Peace a Chance." Yet another Plastic Ono Band single, "Cold Turkey," followed in September. Rumors abounded all summer of John's impending departure from the group.

It was no longer a couple of singles and a couple of albums a year from the Fab Four. The output turned torrential in 1969. Literally every month there was something new, different, and unexpected. Take a brief look at what the fans were receiving that year in terms of record releases:

- April 1969: Beatles' single release of "Get Back" (McCartney) and "Don't Let Me Down" (Lennon)
- May 1969: John and Yoko album release of *Unfinished Music No. 2: Life With the Lions*
- June 1969: Beatles' single release of "The Ballad of John and Yoko" (Lennon) and "Old Brown Shoe" (Harrison)
- July 1969: Plastic Ono Band's single release of "Give Peace a Chance" (Lennon) and "Remember Love" (Ono)
- September 1969: Beatles' album release of *Abbey Road*
- October 1969: Beatles' single release of "Something" (Harrison) and "Come Together" (Lennon)
- October 1969: Plastic Ono Band's single release of "Cold Turkey" (Lennon) and "Don't Worry, Kyoko" (Ono)
- November 1969: John and Yoko's album release of the *Wedding Album*
- December 1969: Plastic Ono Band's album release of the *Live Peace in Toronto*

Despite the rumors of fighting and arguing among the Beatles, fans enthusiastically received the new April single—McCartney's "Get Back" and Lennon's "Don't Let Me Down"—and believed that the rumors were false.

But the very next month, fans were presented with another avant-garde offering from John and Yoko called *Unfinished Music No. 2: Life With the Lions*. The revolving litany continued to year's end with another Beatles single in June and a Plastic Ono Band single in July. These were followed in the fall of 1969 with a new Beatles album and single, along with yet another Plastic Ono Band single and album. It is no wonder everyone was confused. Something was changing, but nobody was talking about it.

Amid all the conflicting rumors about the Beatles demise, amid all the flood of Beatles and solo Lennon music coming at the listeners, amid all the chaos about the apparent dissolution of Apple... amid all this, August 20 marked the manifestation of Beatles fans' worst fear throughout the turmoil of 1969: It was the last day the four Beatles would ever be as one.

Lennon would be the first to return to Abbey Road a month later to record "Cold Turkey" for his newly-formed Plastic Ono Band. So began John's solo period—but that's another book.

Though Lennon had threatened to leave the group during the summer of 1969, the Beatles did not officially break up until April 10, 1970. Between 1957 and 1969, John Lennon's musical journey had taken him all the way from Elvis and Chuck Berry to Pepperland and primitive musicscapes. Having listened closely and avidly to the songs of John Lennon over the past thirty-eight years, I count myself lucky to have experienced the musical and lyrical offerings of one of the twentieth century's greatest pop composers. His natural sense of song and his acumen in expanding pop song style and presentation is without peer. Well, except of course, for the equally talented Mr. McCartney.

I hope this book has illuminated some of the mysteries behind the songs of John Lennon. Since there are approximately eighty-five songs from the Beatles period that contain Lennon's fingerprints, I encourage you to explore them all using your enhanced insight into the prodigious talents of this visionary songwriter.

With no musical training to speak of, John Lennon managed to take the rock 'n' roll world by storm. He skillfully wielded his musical vision, his art, his writings, and his wit to transform the world of songwriting in ways that are still evident today. His songs broke the bonds of the conservative area of mainstream pop song form. Though he relied heavily on the refrain for many of his songs, it was his experimentation with the chorus that helped establish it as the entity we know today. In this same regard, the use of the now-commonplace transitional bridge is evident on his very first hit, "Please Please Me." His exploration of unprecedented musical alternatives—from the fuzz tone beginning of "I Feel Fine," to the spliced and slowed-down "Strawberry Fields," to the outrageously avant-garde "Revolution 9"—opened the door for others to go even further.

With the Beatles, John Lennon wielded a toolbox of musical tools, whether consciously or subconsciously, to artistic perfection. His ability to work within musical convention—but also to expand and even define its outer limits—characterizes his music during the Beatles period. His mastery of language, his use of word play, his ability to craft the perfect piece of music using lyric, melody, and harmony, and combining them into poetry, is what warrants the writing of this book. It is what made John Lennon's music ageless and timeless.

John Lennon plumbed the depths of many areas of life to see what he could discover. His were not only musical explorations, but also political, social, spiritual, and even utopian. Lennon freely shares all of these different explorations with us in his songs, looking us squarely in the eye, unafraid.

References

Coleman, Ray. *Lennon*. New York: McGraw-Hill Book Company, 1984.

Dowdling, William. *Beatlesongs*. New York: Fireside Books, 1989.

Lewisohn, Mark. *The Beatles: Recording Sessions*. New York: Harmony Books, 1988.

Turner, Steve. *A Hard Day's Write*. New York: Harper Collins Publishers, 1994.

Copyright Notices

ABOUT THE AUTHOR

John L. Stevens, Jr. was born and raised in Georgetown, on the Grand Strand, in South Carolina. After finishing high school in Natchez, Mississippi, he went on to graduate from the University of Mississippi with a Bachelor's degree in Music Theory and Composition. He completed a Master's degree in Music History and Literature at Florida State University in Tallahassee. His thesis title was "Jazz Influences in the Music of Karlheinz Stockhausen."

In 1976, Mr. Stevens joined the faculty of Berklee College of Music in Boston, Massachusetts. He teaches songwriting, jazz and pop music theory, voice, and guitar/vocal accompaniment classes. Since 1981 he has taught a class that he developed himself, called  "The Music of John Lennon." He is the director of Berklee's annual Performer/ Songwriter Showcase, and co-director of the annual Songwriters' Competition.

Since 1964 Stevens has been in a multitude of performing and recording situations. Currently he has an all-Beatles band called "The Blue Meanies," in which he sings all the Lennon vocals and plays all the Lennon guitar work. He also performs his own original songs with various band line-ups, both at Berklee College of Music and throughout the New England area. His two current CDs, *Mars In Scorpio* and *Low Profile,* are available through <singingink@aol.com>.

INDEX

More Fine Publications from Berklee Press

As Serious About Music As You Are.

Music Business and Reference Books
from Berklee Press

As Serious About Music As You Are.

COMPLETE GUIDE TO FILM SCORING
▸ by Richard Davis
Learn the art and business of writing music for films and TV. Topics include: the film-making process, preparing and recording a score, contracts and fees, publishing, royalties, and copyrights. Features interviews with 19 film-scoring professionals.
50449417 Book $24.95

THE CONTEMPORARY SINGER ▸ by Anne Peckham
Maximize your vocal potential by learning how to use and protect your voice properly. Develop stage presence, microphone technique, stamina, range, and sound with exercises for all voice ranges and types on the accompanying CD. Includes lead sheets for such standard vocal repertoire pieces as *Yesterday, I'm Beginning to See the Light,* and *I Heard It Through the Grapevine.*
50449438 Book/CD $24.95

ESSENTIAL EAR TRAINING ▸ by Steve Prosser
Step-by-step introduction to the basics of ear training and sight singing, as taught at Berklee College of Music. Develop your inner ear and musical vocabulary, learn to hear the music you see, understand the music you hear, and notate the music you have composed or arranged. Complete course with rhythmic and melodic studies using conducting patterns.
50449421 Book $14.95

THE NEW MUSIC THERAPIST'S HANDBOOK, SECOND EDITION ▸ by Suzanne B. Hanser
Dr. Hanser's well-respected Music Therapist's Handbook has been thoroughly updated and revised to reflect the latest developments in the field of music therapy. Features an introduction to music therapy, new clinical applications and techniques, case studies, designing, implementing, and evaluating individualized treatment programs, and guidelines for beginning music therapists.
50449424 Book $29.95

HOW TO GET A JOB IN THE MUSIC AND RECORDING INDUSTRY
▸ by Keith Hatschek
The bible for anyone who has ever dreamed of landing a job in the music business, from producing or engineering the next Top 10 hit to running a record company. Featuring advice and secrets to educate and empower the serious music and recording industry job seeker, including: details on booming job prospects in new media, a resource directory of key publications and top industry trade organizations, interviews with pros revealing how they got their start, and networking tips.
50449505 Book $24.95

THE SELF-PROMOTING MUSICIAN
▸ by Peter Spellman
Take charge of your career with crucial do-it-yourself strategies. If you are an independent musician, producer, studio owner, or label, you should own this book! Features tips for writing business plans, creating press kits, using the Internet for promotion, customizing demos and getting music played on college radio, along with a comprehensive musician's resource list.
50449423 Book $24.95

THE MUSICIAN'S INTERNET ▸ by Peter Spellman
Promote your music online! Learn to reach new audiences, expand your online presence, and attract thousands of new fans. A must for any self-managed musician.
50449527 Book..............................$24.95

For more information about Berklee Press or Berklee College of Music, contact us:
1140 Boylston Street ▸ Boston, MA 02215-3693
617-747-2146
www.berkleepress.com

Visit your local music dealer or bookstore, or go to www.berkleepress.com

DISTRIBUTED BY